never chop your rope

Jim Shillito—born September 24, 1940

Jim is presently a woods foreman for MacMillan Bloedel on Vancouver Island. He is one of the few men left who can do splicing and highrigging. At 16 Jim was over six feet tall and hooking on the portable slackline steel tower, where his Dad was our woods foreman and rigger at Port Alberni.

Jim was backrigging and notching stumps with an axe before his 20th birthday. About this time he commenced competing in loggers' sports. He won the intermediate hand bucking competition at Sooke, and the springboard chopping at the Pacific National Exhibition. In 1973 he was on the Canadian team that travelled to Australia to take part in world competition. In his Duncan home Jim is proud to show you his many trophies. There he also displays several matched pairs of marlinespikes, his throwing axe, bucking saw, and a pair of climbing spurs complete with belt and rope.

never chop
your rope

A story of
British Columbia logging and
the people who logged

joe garner

Cinnabar Press Ltd.
Nanaimo, British Columbia
1988

Copyright © 1988 by Joe Garner

ISBN 09691343-4-7 Soft bound
ISBN 09691343-3-9 Hard bound

All rights reserved. No part of this book may be reproduced in any form or by any means, electronic or mechanical, without permission in writing from the publisher, except by a reviewer who may quote brief passages in a review to be printed in a newspaper or magazine or broadcast on radio or television.

Available at most book outlets
or order direct from:
CINNABAR PRESS LTD.
P.O. Box 392
Nanaimo, B.C., Canada V9R 5L3

FIRST PRINTING NOVEMBER 1988
SECOND PRINTING DECEMBER 1988
THIRD PRINTING MARCH 1989
FOURTH PRINTING MAY 1989
FIFTH PRINTING FEBRUARY 1992
SIXTH PRINTING FEBRUARY 1993

Cover photograph by Ken Flett

Published by
CINNABAR PRESS LTD.
P.O. Box 392
Nanaimo, B.C., Canada V9R 5L3

Designed in Canada by
MORRISS PRINTING COMPANY LTD.
Printed in Canada by Friesen Printers

Dedicated to my children

Contents

Preface

Never Chop Your Rope is a book of reminiscences about logging and some of the people who logged. It tells of oxen, horses, and even dogs used to haul logs out of the woods and of present day experiments and practices with balloons and helicopters.

It tells of the almost forgotten hand loggers, their skills and hardships, who struggled with hand saws, Gilcrest jacks, and with pike pole and rowboat boomed their logs in the inlets. I did this, and knew the old-timers.

A chat with Bob Swanson, with his great knowledge of steam engines and steam whistles of all sizes, shapes, and sounds recalls the steam era. There are the highriggers already becoming a legend in their own time. Jim Shillito and his son Jim speak for this breed. I knew young Jim from the day he was born in 1940 and gave him his first job as a rigging slinger when he was 16.

I was 11 years old and watching Ed Lumley trimming the limbs off a spar tree as he climbed with belt and spurs. He was about 40 feet up when his axe cut through a limb and chopped his climbing rope. He fell backwards making several somersaults before landing on some brush. Ed got to his feet, found he could walk, then took a new rope from the tool house and climbed back up to finish the job. This was before steel core climbing ropes were available on Saltspring Island.

At Vasey's logging camp at Pitt Lake in 1926 the high rigger was killed when he tumbled 120 feet and landed on some logs.

There are many other old-timers who rigged on the big steam skidders: Mauno Pelto, Grant Hawthorne, Ken Hallberg, Monty Mosher, the Nummi twins—Bill hooked and rigged and Tom operated the big steam donkeys.

Thelma Godkin was one of the first women to work in the woods during the Second World War. She had the courage to try it, and eventually became the only woman ever to be the whistle punk on a big Ledgerwood skidder.

Management and engineering types in the lumber and logging industry I dealt with include Percy Sills, John Hemmingsen, Walter Laidlaw, Gerry Wellburn, the Ordano family, John Humbird and H.R. MacMillan. Those still alive gave interviews and searched their albums for pictures and information to help preserve British Columbia's logging history. It is my hope this book will encourage present and future generations to treasure our logging heritage.

I would like to thank all the people who gave so willingly of their time and knowledge to help with this production.

A special thank you to Joan Davis for her patience in setting up the manuscript, and my daughter Joanne for tackling the arrangement and many other challenging deeds, then to Bill Davis for advice and final reading.

I extend my sincere thanks to: Ken Flett and his staff for photography and pictures; Jim Shillito for climbing the spar and "not chopping his rope"; and Dick Morriss and his capable publishing staff.

J.G.

Tom Garner in his heyday.

CHAPTER 1

Tom and Joe Garner

Tom and I started logging the summer of 1918. We had a falling and bucking contract on Saltspring Island for our nearest neighbour Captain Justice whose two sons were overseas in the First World War. Although my brother and I were young, we had been taught by Dad to use saws and axes. We would work after school and all day Saturdays and Sundays to keep their mill going. Tom was husky, 12 years old. I was a small wiry 10-year-old, quick as a cat. When the sawmill was cutting the bigger logs, Tom would work in the mill and I worked alone, bucking the felled trees. By trial and error I learned to keep the bucking saw from getting pinched and jammed in the cut.

On a Saturday in the fall that first year we learned about "widow-makers". We had felled a tall fir, which had lodged against the tree we would cut down next. The back cut was halfway through when gusts of wind began swinging the tree enough to pinch the saw. Tom looked first at me, then at the cut, and said,

"Better I put in a couple of wedges."

"Wind's getting pretty wild."

"Yeah, better we get this one down and call it a day," and he drove the wedges in with the heavy sledge. I was told to watch for any sign of the broken branches coming down. Two small ones shook loose, but the wind carried them off to the side. We worked on the back cut until there was three inches of wood holding on each side.

"I'll wedge her over from here. You pull the saw as far your way as you can, hold it, then take it out as she starts to fall," Tom ordered. We'd done this dozens of times. With the saw pulled toward me until the handle on the other side was tight against the bark, I stepped back, holding on with both hands. I kept looking up in case another broken limb let loose. Every blow of the sledge would made the tree quiver and move forward a couple of inches at the top. She was about ready to go on her own, so I looked to the backcut.

Then it happened.

In a flash, I was standing there with the broken end of the saw in my hands and looking at the four-foot chunk of a big fir limb quivering in the ground a few inches from my right foot. Without a sound, this limb had speared from 130 feet up, struck the saw dead centre about six inches out from the trunk, and snapped it off with a loud "ping". The next gust took the tree over, and Tom was able to see me standing there stunned, holding the handle with a short piece of saw attached. It must have looked funny because he started laughing! I had to laugh with him.

Tom laid the broken saw on the stump and together we tried to pull that widow-maker out of the ground, but couldn't. I was shaking now, probably in shock, when Captain Justice walked out to see what had happened. I showed him exactly where I'd been standing. He shook his head in disbelief. He tried to remove the limb but couldn't budge it.

"Now you boys know why loggers call them widow-makers," he said. "If you Joe, had a wife, and you had been a few inches

12

nearer that tree, she'd be a widow now. Too much wind out here to be safe, so how about coming up to the house for some tea?" The Justice family were English. Every afternoon they brought tea out to Tom and me.

Next year, Dad bought some cedar pole timber near where the Beddis road branches east off the Old Divide Trail. Tom and I rode our bicycles four miles to the farm, while we were making some 200 poles. This meant falling and peeling the tree, chopping all the knots off close and smooth so the wood didn't sliver off leaving a rough job. This took practice and a sharp axe. If worm holes were in the knots, or the tops, the pole was culled so we carried a knife to dig out the holes, then plug them with wedges. A couple of good wallops with the sledge-hammer would fix things so the worm holes didn't show.

We also had to feed and stable the horses in a woodshed. It was much too far to take them back and forth from the farm every day, and sometimes we batched right there in the abandoned Casperson house. We covered one corner with hay, threw a grey blanket over it and used our coats for pillows. An old patchwork quilt was our cover. Cooking was done with a cast-iron frying pan, a porridge pot, and we had tin plates and cups.

All that summer we cut the poles and yarded them into the clearing. Our skidding equipment consisted of one walleyed cayuse and a big old Clydesdale. We had to borrow a snatch block and about 100 feet of 3/8 inch galvanized cable to get some poles out of steep gullies. When we finished yarding the block and cable were returned to our blacksmith friend, Bill McAfee. He was a bachelor, so Mother sent a wild blackberry pie along with a "thank you" note. The smile on his face let us know there were some things much more important than "cold cash".

During the Christmas holidays, there was a foot of snow, and we learned a good lesson about taking advantage of the weather. Dad, Tom and I, with our lopsided team, coupled bunches of these poles together, dragged them down the main road and put them in the saltchuck near the blacksmith's shop. McAfee had put steel shoes with sharp cleats on the Clydesdale so he wouldn't slide and fall on the ice.

"That cayuse is just too ornery for shoeing," he said.

It took less than a week to get the 200 poles to the beach, and the day we finished it turned warm and rained. The gravel roads were bare the next morning and skidding would have been impossible.

Dan Lumley towed those poles with his fish boat to Montague Harbour on the southwest side of Galiano Island and they were loaded with thousands of others aboard a Japanese freighter. Tom, now 13, worked on the booms sorting and hooking up the poles. Dad was hired to help with the tallying. Tom made $5 for a ten-hour day and Dad earned $4.50.

Apart from the four longshore gangs, a dozen loggers from the various pole camps helped break up the cribs and get the cargo alongside the ship. There were six boats towing bag booms, but it took almost two weeks to get those poles hoisted aboard.

The longshoremen were fed and housed on two small scows. There was a bunkhouse on one and a cookhouse on the other.

Dad, Tom, and I slept on the beach, just south of where the old Montague Harbour ferry dock is now. We cooked on an open fire. I cut the wood, washed the pots and pans, then hunted crows for the 15-cent bounty. On the two Sundays we were camped there, Dad took us out to the floating cookhouse for three good meals. This was 1921, and the Baxter Pole Company was doing the exporting.

Tom finished grade eight that June and quit school. Dad had located a good stand of fir timber just over a mile from Vesuvius Bay, on the west side of Saltspring Island. This timber was too far from the beach to be logged profitably by horses so he bought a one-ton Model-T Ford. This little truck had solid rubber rear tires and pneumatics on the front. The wheels had wooden spokes and squeaked so much in dry weather we'd pour water on them every night to keep them tight. Dad had taken an order to supply 13 and 26-foot logs for another Japanese ship which would be loading in Vancouver. After cruising the timber, Dad asked, "What do you boys think?"

"Timber's good, but we can't haul a 26-foot log on this truck. Truck's too short. Even a big 13-foot log would lift the front end right up off the road," Tom replied.

"Maybe we shouldn't buy this timber," Dad said, looking up at the tall trees.

Tom came up with a great idea, a set of wheels hooked up behind the truck, with an adjustable reach. There and then, we began planning a logging trailer.

"There's an axle with two good solid rubber-tired wheels in a shed at the old Connery dairy farm. We could look it over on our way home," Dad suggested, and after inspecting it we agreed the axle was strong enough to carry all the logs our truck could handle.

"Buy the timber, Dad. Joe and I, we'll get those wheels and start building a trailer."

At the blacksmith shop Bill gave us a list of lumber we would need, including a piece of clear fir for the reach. At the Justice mill we loaded the lumber, but there was no 16 foot long 3 x 8 inch stuff, so we went with Clive Justice to pick out a suitable tree. We dropped the tree and in an hour it was on the sawmill carriage. It made two identical reaches in case one should break. At the blacksmith's shop next morning, Bill McAfee had the bolts and other iron work he'd made the previous afternoon. Two long days of threading bolts, boring holes, and fitting the lumber, and we were ready to haul logs.

McAfee had shaped and forged four steel cheese blocks from some flat iron, with heavy chains to keep the logs solid on the steel I-beam on top of the wooden bunks. He hammered out special grab-hooks, which could be released with a sledge hammer under pressure, for unloading. Tom and I were two very proud youngsters when we drove up to our new logging show near Vesuvius Bay.

This was 1922, and the start of truck logging on Saltspring Island.

Dad, Mother and our sisters, Ethel and Pearl, had taken the team and wagon over the day before, loaded with horse feed, a stove, blankets, pots, pans, dishes, and groceries. A table and fly tent were already set up when Tom and I drove in. By six o'clock supper was ready—and guess what? Dad had shot four young grouse. Ethel and our young sister, Pearl, had picked wild blackberries. Mother had brought loaves of fresh bread and homemade butter. We feasted on crisp fried grouse with deep blackberry pie.

Our camp was across the road from the timber and near a spring of good water. Pearl was eight years old and had already made friends with a big spotted-brown toad. When she was sent for a fresh pail of water for washing up, and didn't come back, I went to find her. She was sitting near the spring, on the empty water pail, staring into the clear water.

"Quiet, stay back," she whispered, pointing toward the brown toad which sat half submerged and staring at her from the opposite side of the little pool.

"That's going to be my pet."

"Mother is waiting for the water."

"Oh, okay, I'll get it."

She quietly filled the pail with a long handled dipper. The toad never moved, just blinked its eyes and stared. She asked me to carry the pail, then turned back to the spring. "I want to stay with my new pet," Her toad stayed around the spring all summer.

In September there were racoon tracks in the mud, and the toad was never seen again. Pearl was so upset she asked me to show her how to use the .22 rifle. After hunting for the racoon until late in the afternoon, she stuffed her belongings in a small flour sack, saying "I can't live here anymore with Brownie gone." In tears she swung the flour sack over her shoulder and walked the three miles home to Mother. Ethel now had to get the water, pick the berries, collect wood, and do a dozen other of Pearl's small jobs.

On Sunday mornings after the team was fed, Tom, Ethel, and I usually drove the truck home to exchange our dirty clothes for clean ones. Mother would have a special lunch ready, then fill a big box with fresh bread, eggs, jam, and a roast of pork or venison. In those days, game regulations were ignored when wild meat was needed for food and Ethel kept the camp well supplied with venison. It was a great experience. Tom and I slept on a bed of hay under a big bushy cedar tree, and Ethel had the tent all to herself after Pearl lost her pet.

It took two months to fill the log orders. We cut all but the very largest trees 26 feet long. Jim Ryan and Chester Martin did the falling and bucking on contract. Tom kept busy hauling the logs and replacing the worn-out brake and low gear bands. By the time we had all those logs in the water, Tom could unbolt the transmission case and install a new set of bands in complete darkness. That takes experience and know-how.

I was the teamster, doing the yarding and helping with the loading. The smaller logs were rolled onto the truck with peavies. The big logs had to be rolled up using a cable and the horses. More than once I'd have to drive the team to the beach and drag the truck and trailer up to camp so we could make repairs and be ready for hauling next morning. Tom always tried to be loaded and headed for the log dump by seven. I would have to be up by five to feed and harness the team, have breakfast, and be at the landing by no later than six-thirty.

Tom, Ethel and I were to share $1.50 per thousand feet for yarding, loading, hauling and booming. An awful lot of hard work. More than 200,000 board feet of logs were towed to Vancouver to a Japanese ship that fall. The ship was anchored in the bay east of where the Second Narrows Bridge would be on the south side. The logging slash from Renfrew Street to the east had been burned that year (1922), and was still smoking when we walked through from the end of the streetcar tracks at Hastings and Renfrew Street. When the logs were loaded and scaled, Dad was paid more than $4,000 cold cash.

A week later, we started logging a stand of fir and cedar along the Cranberry Road, a mile from Ganges. I learned a lot more about logging from Ira Becker who had the falling contract and hired me. On weekends and after school, we could cut down enough trees to keep everyone going. Becker was over 40 years old, and had been saw filing and contracting in the Cowichan Lake area since he was a teenager. He called his six foot and seven foot falling and bucking saws Swede fiddles. My pay was 40 cents an hour, which Dad deducted from his contract. Although I never did get any money from this job for myself, I learned from an expert the many tricks of the trade, including filing, underbucking over an axe handle, side-notching, cutting springboard holes, and chopping and sawing right and left handed.

Mrs. Becker, an excellent cook, would always ask me to stay for supper so I could help her husband sharpen the saws and axes. His eyes were starting to fail, but he was too proud to get glasses.

In his filing shed, a good bark fire in the heater and lights hung from a rafter, he taught me to sharpen the axes on his grind stone which was hooked up and turned by a bicycle chain and pedals. Next came the crosscut saws. I'd start sharpening. He just watched and corrected me if I was going at it the hard way or making mistakes. He would check the saw with a raker gauge, then feel the teeth with his thumb. Before saying a word, he would take a box of Copenhagen Snoose out of his left-hand shirt pocket, lay the box flat on the palm of his left hand, tap the lid a couple of times with a finger, then take the lid off with a neat twist. He'd put a good pinch under his bottom lip, then give me a pat on the shoulder, grin, and say, "Gad, boy, you sure as hell have sharp eyes and learn in a hurry. Those tools are as perfect as I could ever get them when my eyes were good."

I'd beam with pride and we'd go in for a mug-up. His wife always had cocoa and cookies ready. It was usually after 10 before I'd get home.

I also learned from Becker how to cut logs for better scale and grades. He was paid $1.25 per thousand water scale, with a bonus of 25 cents for all the #1 and #2 logs. He paid me a five-cent bonus for the better grades. I was now 14 and could help him decipher the government scale sheets and figure out how much money we had coming.

The Beckers moved to Victoria with their two young sons the next year and started a successful family business which has lasted three generations. The name "Ira Becker" is still known throughout the forest industry, but the product has changed from hand tools to power saws.

That winter, Tom and I kept busy clearing up the logging site. We yarded out all the long butts and cull logs, cut them into 4 foot cordwood, and sold it for boiler fuel to the creamery which made the famous Saltspring Island butter.

In 1924, Dad bought timber from Captain Cotsford at the north end of Saltspring. He also bought an old single-drum winch without an engine or sleigh. Again, with Bill McAfee's help, Tom and I built our first donkey sleigh. For power, Dad bought a "White" 10-horsepower one-cylinder engine that would run on gasoline or coal oil. The drum could handle a mile of one inch cable and was driven by belt and pulleys through a series of gears. We used a line horse to pull this heavy cable and chokers back to the felled and bucked timber. This gas donkey was tailholted to a stump just above the bay where we made up the flat booms. We placed a shear skid on the beach side of the donkey so the yarded logs would roll over the bank and float in the bull pen. Tom and I, with one of the Swiss loggers, would go out every evening to push the logs over into the water while the tide was high. We would then sort and stow them.

The first time the mainline broke, we had to get Atchison from the shipyard in Victoria. An expert at splicing, he explained each phase to Tom and me, as the crossing and rolling of the strands with the steel core cable had been our main problem. Thanks to Clark Atchison, we could now join a broken mainline by either a short or long splice. And practice makes perfect, as we found out during the next year.

Most of the shoreline of the Cotsford property was rocky and steep and for half a mile at the north end there were big old-growth fir trees along the bluff, not far from the beach. It was much too steep to yard these big trees up the hill, so Dad suggested Tom and I try hand-logging the timber into the water.

"I helped Dick Maxwell and his brother do some of this at Burgoyne Bay before you boys were born. The Gilcrest jacks and the big peavies, along with all the other tools, are stored in their barn."

That evening we paid the Maxwells a visit, and they gladly loaned us all their hand-logging tools. We loaded three big Gilcrest jacks, two huge peavies, a geared hand winch, a couple of snatch blocks, and some half inch cable. There was even a short piece of 3 inch round steel shafting.

"Put that in the undercut when the tree is about ready to fall, and it will jump off the stump," Dick said as he tossed the shafting onto the Ford.

That summer, with Dad supervising, Tom and I put more than 100 big trees in the water. We had a couple hang up behind some big boulders, and just couldn't get the logs started again. After a frustrating morning's work Tom said, "I'm going to drive down and ask the Maxwells what to do." Within the hour he was back with Dick Maxwell. They had brought some blasting powder. With the jacks up to their limit and a couple of well placed blasts, both trees were soon floating in the chuck.

Maxwell also showed us how to put the steel shafting in the

undercut, "Now take your backcut up to within half an inch of the undercut." When we had this done he stepped around to the back and began tapping the two wedges with the sledge-hammer.

"Now stand to the side and watch."

When the top of the tree had moved forward about 10 feet, the shaft was tight in the undercut and the tree was lifting up off the stump. At just what stage the tree started to move forward is hard to say. Everything happened in a hurry, but as I watched that particular tree it just seemed to leap forward and rocket out and over the rocks until it landed with a great splash.

"That's what we used to call a 'stumper', Dick laughed.

The Maxwells had logged masts and spars with oxen for export during the 1870's. Then they bought a wood-fired steam donkey and eight big horses to swing the logs and piling down a skid road to Burgoyne Bay.

By the fall of 1925, we had finished logging the Cotsford's timber. Tom was 18 and had tended hook. I was 16 and had run the donkey. Dad had sold more than a million board feet by the time we'd finished, and neither Tom nor I ever got a cent. Mother had cooked and looked after our family of nine, plus another four boarding loggers. After two years of 15-hour days, Mother returned to the big house in Ganges on October 28, 1925. She was exhausted and three months pregnant with her tenth and last child. Tom refused to work with Dad. Two years of hard work with no pay other than board and clothing was no good.

Charlie Parman was operating a tie mill for the F.M. Singer Lumber Company back of Price's Lake and he offered Tom $5 a day as head sawyer. He got a ten cent bonus for every tie over 150. He usually cut 200 or more a day, so his bonus equalled or exceeded his wages. Tom always shared half of his bonus with the mill crew.

On Saturdays, I would work in the tie mill, trimming and stacking the lumber and then cutting the slabs into stove wood lengths. Parman sold the wood and sawdust at $1 per truckload to anyone willing to load and haul it home. On Sundays, 10 or more trucks would come in. I helped load and collected the money. There was no income tax and few records were kept. In June of 1926, after finishing grade 10, I worked full time as head faller at Parman's mill for $4.40 a day.

F.M. Singer went broke in September of that year, and MacMillan Export took over the mills. This was also the year Mother, with eight of her children, including the new baby, Dorothy, left Dad and moved to Vancouver. We bought a lot and built Mother a house at 2nd Avenue and Windermere Street in East Vancouver.

Tom and I moved to Chemainus in 1927 to cut ties on contract for MacMillan Export, using one of their updated portable mills. I handled the logging end, while Tom was the sawyer and ran the mill. We were cutting mostly fir ties for export to England. Ed and Tom Woods came from Saltspring with their good team to do the yarding. Red Howard was my falling partner. That spring he fought Andy Wilson from The Mainland for the light heavyweight boxing crown of British Columbia. Chopping and swinging those 'Swede fiddles' built the muscle and conditioning needed to be a champion. Tom and I were his sparring partners and we knew Red could knock a guy down with one jab from either hand. After winning, Red was back falling the next morning with a thick lip and a swollen eye.

By 1928, Tom was 21 and I had turned 19. We could handle about any job in logging or lumber. We had also learned to hire good men. From Chemainus we went on to own and operate more than a dozen logging camps elsewhere on Vancouver Island and up the mainland coast as far north as Knight Inlet. We moved an outfit to Quesnel in the Cariboo district to contract log for Western Plywood's sawmill and plywood plants in the 1950's. We became one of the first companies to go into salvage and pre-logging for Bloedel, Stewart & Welsh, just prior to its amalgamation with the huge MacMillan complex.

Yes, we had our own private aircraft to locate roads, cruise timber, carry in repair parts, and transport mechanics and special crews when it was urgent. Yes, we did plan and prepare for helicopter logging of inaccessible timber in the rugged coastal area, and cruised 100 million board feet ready to log. We divided our equipment and other business assets a short time before Tom was killed attempting a glassy water landing near Desolation Sound on September 6, 1958. He was 52 years old, and his death was a great shock. With Tom gone, I began the winding down of Garner Bros. Ltd. and all the subsidiary companies, but not the innovative helicopter logging.

Through interviews and first-hand knowledge, the following chapters tell of the men and women we worked with over the years in what is still British Columbia's largest industry.

Tom Garner and the first logging truck on Saltspring Island, Vesuvius, 1922.

Typical Locomotive.

CHAPTER 2
The Dunsmuirs

In 1883, more than two million acres of timberland were granted as part payment toward the construction of the Esquimalt-Nanaimo Railway. This grant had a major impact on the development of the British Columbia forest industry and greatly added to the wealth of the Dunsmuirs.

In 1882, Robert Dunsmuir was elected to the Provincial Legislature, representing the constituency of Nanaimo. He wasted no time in advising government he was capable of building a railroad from Esquimalt at the southern tip of Vancouver Island to Nanaimo, sixty miles north. The Dunsmuirs were one of the wealthiest families in Western Canada, having made fortunes in coal.

The schedule and contract, reproduced in this chapter, was initiated by the British government on August 20, 1883, and

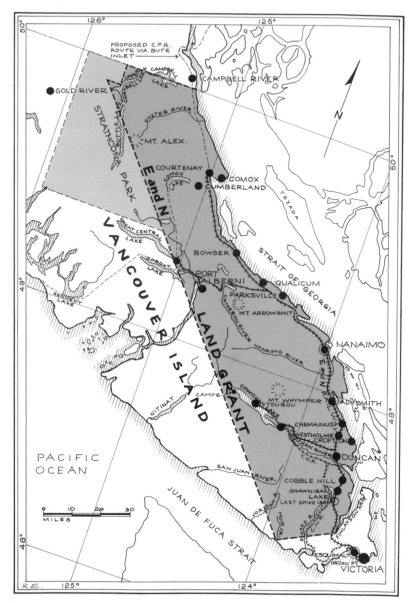

E. & N. Land Grant.
Thanks to Tom Scott, with his vast timber cruising
knowledge, for his help in producing this map.

24

was ratified by the provincial government on December 19, 1883.

For the Minister of Railways and Canals.
(Signed),   A. CAMPBELL,
                           Minister of Justice.

(Signed),   ROBERT DUNSMUIR,
   "   JOHN BRYDEN,
   "   JAMES DUNSMUIR,
   "   CHARLES CROCKER,
   "   CHARLES F. CROCKER,
   "   LELAND STANFORD,
             by Chas. Crocker his Attorney in fact.
   "   COLLIS P. HUNTINGTON.
             by Chas. Crocker his Attorney in fact.

Signed, sealed and delivered by the within named Robert Dunsmuir, James Dunsmuir, John Bryden, Chas. Crocker, Chas. F. Crocker, Leland Stanford and Collis P. Huntington, and by Sir Alexander Campbell for the Minister of Railways and Canals, as an escrow, and placed in the hands of the Honorable Joseph William Trutch, until the sanction of Parliament shall have been obtained to the payment of the subsidy and to the other stipulations on the part of the Dominion herein contained requiring its sanction, and until the Act passed by the Legislature of the Province of British Columbia, in the year one thousand eight hundred and eighty-three, entitled "*An Act relating to the Island Railway, the Graving Dock and Railway Lands of the Province,*" shall have been amended by the Legislature of the said Province in accordance with a draft bill now prepared and which has been identified by Sir Alexander Campbell and the Honorable Mr. Smithe and signed by them and deposited in the hands of the said Joseph William Trutch, in the presence of

(Signed),   H. G. HOPKIRK.

——

A.

(THIS IS THE SPECIFICATION MARKED A REFERRED TO IN THE CONTRACT HERETO ANNEXED, DATED THIS 20TH AUGUST, 1883.)

SPECIFICATION for a line of railway from Esquimalt to Nanaimo, in Vancouver Island in British Columbia.

1. The railway shall be a single line, with gauge four feet, eight and a-half inches, with necessary sidings.

2. The alignments, gradients and curvatures shall be the best that the physical features of the country will admit of, the maximum grade not to exceed eighty feet to the mile, and

25

and the minimum curvature not to be of less radius than eight hundred feet.

2. In all wooded sections the land must be cleared to the width of fifty feet on each side of the centre of line.

All brush and logs must be completely burnt up and none thrown on to the adjacent lands.

4. All stumps must be grubbed out within the limits of cuttings under three feet in depth or embankments less than two feet in depth.

5. All stumps must be close-cut where embankments are less than four feet and more than two feet in height.

6. Through settlements, the railway must be enclosed with substantially built legal fences.

7. Road crossings, with cattle guards and sign boards, shall be provided wherever required.

8. The width of cuttings at formations shall be twenty feet, embankments sixteen feet.

9. Efficient drainage must be provided either by open ditches or under drains

10. All bridges, culverts and other structures must be of ample size and strength for the purpose intended. Piers and abutments of bridges must bo either of substantial massive stone masonry, iron or wood, and in every essential particular, equal to the best description of like works employed in the construction of the Canadian Pacific Railway in British Columbia. Arched culverts must be of good solid masonry, equal in every respect to similar structures designed for the Canadian Pacific Railway in British Columbia. Box culverts must be of either masonry, iron or wood.

11. The passenger station houses, freight sheds, workshops, engine houses, other buildings and wharves, shall be sufficient in number and size to efficiently accommodate the business of the road, and they shall be either stone, brick or timber, of neat design, substantially and strongly built.

12. The rails shall be of steel, weighing not less than fifty pounds per lineal yard of approved section, and with the most approved fish-plate joints.

13. The roadway must be well ballasted with clean gravel or other suitable material.

14.

14. Sufficient siding accommodation shall be provided by the contractors, as may be necessary to meet the requirements of the traffic.

15. Sufficient rolling stock, necessary to accommodate the business of the line, shall be provided by the contractors, with stations and terminal accommodations, including engine sheds, turn-tables, shops, water-tanks, machinery, wharves, &c.

A. CAMPBELL.
Minister of Justice,
for the Minister of Railways and Canals.

ROBERT DUNSMUIR.

Some of the highlights of the act governing the Dunsmuir railway construction were: A subsidy of $750,000 to aid construction, to be paid by the government in instalments on completion of each ten miles of railway and telegraph line; the E & N was granted a 20-mile strip of land up the east coast of Vancouver Island from Goldstream near Victoria north to Seymour Narrows, to include the foreshore rights, all timber, coal, oil, ores, stones, clay, marble and slate on or under the surface of the land and water (the water included most of Georgia Strait and contiguous waters, including the lakes and rivers within the E & N land grant).

It was rumored Robert Dunsmuir, while in England in 1882, not only discussed the railroad but actually advised how best to set up the land grant and the $750,000 subsidy to aid in construction. He must also be given credit for contacting and making arrangements with L. Stafford, P. Huntington, Charlie P. and Charles F. Crocker, all Americans and known as The Big Four when it came to building railroads. Dunsmuir had planned the construction of the rail line from Esquimalt to Nanaimo very well indeed. As an M.L.A. representing the Nanaimo district, he certainly could have masterminded the grants of both money and lands to his own best advantage.

The E & N land grant was actually a crown grant which made the timber exportable around the world. The Douglas fir, cedar, hemlock, and pine were of the highest quality. Work on the railway commenced in early May of 1884 and was completed in the late summer of 1886. At one minute past nine on the morning of August 13, the last spike was driven near Shawnigan Lake. Present was a large crowd which included John A. McDonald, Robert and James Dunsmuir, Bell & Larkin Contractors and General Pooley.

In the spring of 1889, Dunsmuir bought the Chemainus sawmill for $100,000 from his son-in-law, Henry Croft, and his partner R. B. Angus, who were having financial problems. This purchase included the mill and all the town property, plus the timber on Block One. Croft then became involved with the neighboring Mount Sicker copper mines, and he built a smelter at Crofton. The town of Crofton, located on Osborne Bay, was named after this young family, and soon a railroad connected the new town with the main line of the Esquimalt & Nanaimo Railway near Westholme.

Many substantial American lumber companies were rapidly depleting their own forests east of the Rocky Mountains and were buying large tracts of timber in Washington and Oregon. Many of the larger firms began acquiring timber along the coast of British Columbia.

Dunsmuir was a mining man. He had no intention of being permanently involved with the timber industry, although he certainly realized the potential profit by selling the land and standing timber. He was soon contacted by several lumbermen from the United States. Two of the largest were Fredrick Weyerhauser Sr. and J.A. Humbird Sr. who had built up a massive lumber empire in the pine forests of the central states in the 1850's. They had also bought timber from railway grants throughout the Pacific Northwest. When they learned of the E & N timber, Humbird and Weyerhauser made a deal to purchase 100,000 acres of E & N Railway land and timber to be selected at random anywhere in the Cowichan, Chemainus, or Nanaimo River valleys, and north of the Malahat to Campbell River, a vast area. Their cruisers could select blocks of timber of any size or shape. The price would be $5.00 per acre.

Part of the agreement between Dunsmuir and the Americans was that The Victoria Lumber & Manufacturing Co. Ltd. (V.L.& M.) would be incorporated to construct a mill at Chemainus. Humbird, related to Weyerhauser by marriage, was president of the new company.

28

It was decided the Chemainus mill should be capable of producing 200,000 feet a day. The main building was 75 feet wide and 475 feet long. The equipment included the latest in band saws, gang edgers, plus a planing mill and dry kilns. At that time, this sawmill was one of the largest on the Pacific Coast.

The V.L.& M. brought in their own experts to select their timber lands. When they found good quality timber they just blazed a compass line around it. One block at the head of Ladysmith harbour resembled a four-leaf clover when it was put on their maps. This type of selection created great problems when land surveyors began to record the various blocks for registration. The rough maps and field notes made by the American cruisers left a lot to be desired.

After Robert Dunsmuir's death, his son James became general manager of the E & N and immediately started a lawsuit against John Humbird and the V.L.& M. James argued the timber blocks should be laid out in a more professional manner. The case wound up in the Supreme court of Canada, and the judgment went in favor of the Americans. The original agreement clearly stated, "The timber blocks may be selected at the purchaser's discretion, and can be located anywhere within the prescribed area. Size and shape are also to be at the discretion of the purchaser." Oddly enough the blocks are, to this day, exactly as originally blazed. The boundaries wander in all directions and the blocks are of every size and shape. It's a land surveyor's nightmare.

Although the Dunsmuirs were miners, they certainly left their mark on the British Columbia timber industry. Before his death in 1889, Robert had sold enough timber and land to make him a millionaire many times over.

When his son James took over the E & N in 1890, things began to change. In May of 1905, the E & N railway was sold to the Canadian Pacific Railway for just over $2.3 million, which included the land grant. In 1910, he sold all their coal interests to the Canadian Northern Railway Company for over $7 million.

In his earlier years James Dunsmuir was elected to the legislature and was later Premier of British Columbia. He also served as Lieutenant Governor.

Gerry Wellburn and his wife Ethel standing with
H.R. MacMillan at opening of the B.C. Forest
Museum just north of Duncan, 1967.

CHAPTER 3

Gerry Wellburn

Gerry Wellburn came to Canada in 1911 from England at age
11 to become a logger, mill operator, businessman, and a good
Canadian.

When he first worked in the logging camps, horses were used
everywhere. The 'bull punchers'—men like Frank Verdue of
Brentwood, the Halkin brothers and the Dubbin families of
Cobble Hill had just changed to horses, but they liked to talk
about their days of logging with oxen.

Gerry left school in 1916 to work for the *Victoria Times*
newspaper. Their advertising manager was planning a trip to
Toronto to drum up business, and he wanted a booklet of
photographs promoting Victoria and Vancouver Island. Gerry
was good at drawing and photography so the editor asked him
to put together something eye-catching to lure business west.

"Get some pictures and write a short story beneath each one," his boss ordered.

A recent front page picture in the *Times* of a big sawmill and a strange steam locomotive, with Victoria Lumber & Manufacturing Company painted boldly on the engineer's cab, caught Gerry's eye. This locomotive had vertical cylinders and a tender loaded with coal and four foot cordwood. Gerry was pretty excited about the picture, so he asked, "There's no such mill here. Where is it?"

"In Chemainus, about 50 miles up Island."

Gerry asked permission to go to Chemainus to get some pictures and a good story, saying, "I've a new bike and could ride up there in a day if I leave early."

"Maybe two days," his boss corrected, and handed him five bucks for expenses.

Gerry persuaded a friend to go with him. It was gravel all the way, except for a short stretch of paving by the Colwood golf course, the only bit of paved highway on Vancouver Island. Gerry took the time to get some good pictures of this strip of road for the promotion booklet.

The first night the boys camped at Shawnigan Lake, got an early start, and had breakfast in Duncan. It poured rain from there to Chemainus. They arrived after dark, soaked and cold. After some inquiries, they found the cookhouse down near the sawmill.

"Too late to get a meal?"

'No, come on in and I'll get something for you," the cook said. "Just stand over by the stove there and dry those wet clothes a bit." She handed each of them a mug of steaming cocoa and a doughnut, then served them warmed-up roast beef with gravy and potatoes, and followed by logger-sized pieces of lemon pie.

When they told the cook they were going to camp out in their little fly tent, she said, "It's too wet for tenting. There's no night shift tonight, so go on down to the mill and ask for Harry Ganlin, the night engineer". Harry thought it was a great joke—two boys riding bikes all the way from Victoria just to see their steam locie. He showed them the boiler room and pointed to a short handled scoop shovel.

"Take that shovel," he told Gerry, "and flatten out the sawdust for your blankets and sleep right there near the boiler where it's warm."

The boys told Ganlin about their project, and asked if they could see the locie and get some pictures of the logging. They'd have to get permission from the woods foreman.

"Tell him you're friends of mine and he'll probably let you ride out to where the logging's going on."

The woods boss was intrigued to hear they had cycled from Victoria to go for a ride on a logging train.

"If you promise to behave yourselves and stay in the cab with the engineer, you can go. I'll tell him you're coming."

The youngsters were at the roundhouse an hour early to watch the fireman get steam up. Gerry remembers taking many pictures of the huge trees as they puffed along their way, pulled by Number 9.

They watched the men working with the steam donkey and saw the big logs crash in on the landing. After the crew loaded the 15 cars, the locie pulled them out onto the mainline and headed for tidewater. They weren't allowed to go to the log dump because it was considered too dangerous, so they scrambled up on the bluffs to take more pictures and watch the huge splash as each load of logs thundered into the water. Gerry's pictures turned out fine and the brochure was excellent.

That was Wellburn's introduction to logging, and instinctively he knew this was what he wanted to do.

He was almost 19 when the First World War ended. The shipyards and factories were shutting down, and many of the soldiers coming home to take up the jobs they had left were to be disappointed. There had been eight sawmills operating in and around Victoria before and during the war. Now there was one. Most of the big machine shops had shut down. The breweries had closed. The shipyards were laying off hundreds of men. This was how it was for the next two years. The city was in such a slump that Gerry and his wife decided to move 120 miles north to Courtenay.

He was immediately offered a job with the Gwilt Lumber Company. The firm was logging with horses and hauling to its mill on a narrow-gauge railway. There was a haywire, single-tank steam locie on a five mile bush track. Three loaded log cars were about all it could handle at one time.

Built in 1915, the old #9 Climax was donated to the B.C. Forest Museum by
the Stone family to commemorate their father, Carlton Stone, who was the
founder of Hilcrest Lumber Company. Phil LeMare of Duncan stands by.

A full view showing the size of the engines and drives.

Pat Hind and Phil LeMare who help keep the machinery in mint condition.

The huge pinion gear driving the wheels of Lima Shay.

Gears on the driving wheels of Lima Shay.

Walter Pafford and George Williamson, who presently take passengers for the ride through the Forest Museum. When George was asked to tip his cap back for a better photo, he replied "I'm a locie engineer not a movie star."

Concaved wheeled skeleton logging car used by Shawnigan Lake Lumber Company in the early teens

This Dolber Spool steam donkey was built in San Francisco and delivered to Chemainus in 1894. It helped to replace the bull and horse teams yarding the logs out to the skid roads.

An old Heyster arch and big fir log in the B.C. Forest Museum.

3-drum RD-8 Caterpillar tractor yarder manufactured in the mid 1930's, now at the B.C. Forest Museum

Standard 3-drum steam yarder used in the 1920's is presently in the B.C. Forest Museum.

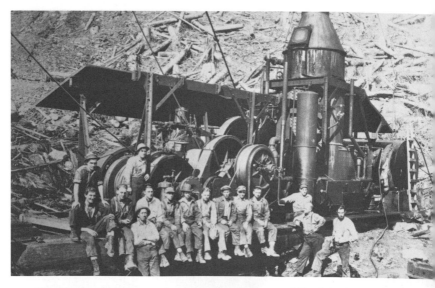

Washington Skidder used at Lake Logging west of Cowichan Lake in 1936. Because of its great speed the machine was known as the Flyer. This and the two photos following are from the Wilmer Gold Collection at the B.C. Forest Museum, with permission and thanks to Local 1-80 of the I.W.A.

Leyland Truck and trailer with a load of logs in May of 1937. This type of wreck was common when trucks became 'bunk bound' because of the lack of a compensating hitch to the trailer.

Nitinat Camp fallers October 16, 1948, with one of the early 2-man power saws. Power saws and hard hats were pretty new to fallers of the day.

A replica of the Chemainus over-shot waterwheel that drove the first up-and-down saw in Elliot's original mill.

Early pulp grinding stones from one of the first paper mills in British Columbia.

Gwilt bought a chain drive White truck with wide solid rubber tires in 1922. The company also bought a small steam donkey, then built a mile of plank road from the donkey location out to the government road. The trucks, unlike the railway, could go up and down hills with grades up to six per cent. That was the start of truck logging in the Courtenay area.

When Tom Gwilt learned that Gerry had some experience in bookkeeping and office work, he promoted him to assistant manager. The lumber tallies, cost accounting, and other paper work was all done after supper or on Sundays. Being the assistant manager did not relieve him of his regular work in the mill.

Following the disastrous earthquake of 1923 in Japan, Gwilt Lumber was flooded with orders for baby squares to help rebuild Tokyo and Yokohama. (A baby-square was a log that had been partially squared on four sides before it was shipped.) These rough logs would be re-manufactured in Japan. Loading this extra lumber caused many problems. There were no phones, so urgent communications were done by telegraph, which involved using the Canadian Collieries' line to Duncan, and having messages sent across to Vancouver. Gwilt and Gerry also had to make many trips to Vancouver.

Young Wellburn remembers going to the Metropolitan Building on Hastings Street where the H.R. MacMillan Export Company had its offices. There was only one girl handling the typing and making up the shipping documents. In this office he met H.R. MacMillan, Van Dusen and Percy Sills. He got his first lessons from Van Dusen on how important the dates of delivery and the paper documents were to their export business. Van Dusen was a kind and patient person and they became lifetime friends.

"To get to Vancouver in those days, we'd go to Comox and catch the night boat to Powell River. We'd sleep on the boat and arrive in Vancouver the next morning. To get back, we usually took the boat from Vancouver to Nanaimo, then caught a stage. We'd get into Courtenay about midnight, then have to walk the last three miles on a gravel road to get to camp. Twenty-hour days were common on those trips."

The Gwilt Lumber mill burned in 1927. Rather than rebuild, Gwilt and Gerry took over a portable tie mill at Deerholme, near Duncan. The timber was good, and about the right size for a tie mill. The mill was powered by an old Fairbanks Morse one-cylinder, 20-horse kerosene engine. The mill could be moved to the timber, and the logs skidded in with horses. It was a good operation. Tom Gwilt soon realized that it didn't need two men to manage one tiemill, so he went back up Island and started his own retail lumber yard.

Wellburn heard that Dave Madill, a logger at Cowichan Lake, had bought a gasoline powered Caterpillar 60, and was looking for winter work. He drove to the lake, watched the machine for half an hour. This, he decided, was much better than horses. Dave soon tired of travelling the 20 miles of rough gravel road from Cowichan Lake to Deerholme daily, so he rented the Cat to Gerry with an option to buy, which Gerry did.

From the beginning, Gerry shipped his lumber through the MacMillan Export Company. Since E & N timber was exportable, the ties were shipped to England, South America, South Africa, India and Australia. The whole world needed top quality ties.

In the late 1930's, the Cameron Lumber Company had a fire near Cowichan Lake and lost their mill. Felled and bucked timber was on the ground, some scorched, and Cameron was anxious to have these logs cut into ties and lumber. Gerry made a deal with Jamie Cameron—they had been friends at school in Victoria. Gerry's portable mill was hauled in, and they renamed the outfit Wellburn Cameron Lumber Company. Wellburn also agreed to do the logging and formed the Wellburn Tractor Logging Company. The Cat now had an arch and could really produce logs. Their lumber was loaded at the Canadian National siding at Mile 62, and the area was known in those days as The River Bottom. By the time the Wellburn Cameron Company had finished cutting the Cowichan River timber, and moved back to Deerholme, the depression and the Dirty Thirties were all but over.

Gerry next decided to build a rail siding at Deerholme with a stationary steam mill much larger than his portable tie mill. Using Cats and a gas donkey to yard and load the trucks he could deliver logs to the mill at much lower cost than most big companies. Because of this larger new mill, he was able to purchase a very substantial block of timber.

He had to finance the timber purchase, build the steam mill and buy up-to-date logging equipment. The advance money came from the MacMillan Export Company. H.R. liked people he could depend on, and Gerry was a favorite of the tycoon. They had been friends since 1912 when H.R., as British Columbia's chief forester, had an office in a small wooden building at Superior and Government Streets in Victoria. Gerry was a paper boy for the *Times* and had delivered to H.R.'s office. A long friendship began.

Gerry recalls, "Our lumber was all loaded directly onto CNR rail cars. These cars were delivered in a matter of hours from Deerholme to shipside at Victoria's Ogden Point docks. The lumber was lifted directly onto the ships from the rail cars. It was a top-notch arrangement because the stevedores did everything once the loaded cars were at the docks.

"I remember watching a ship being loaded with some of our lumber, and a few weeks later seeing the same ship unloading at the London docks."

"Was that the time you went over to exhibit your stamp collection?" I asked him.

"Yes. The autumn of 1947."

Gerry had been collecting stamps for years and his collection had been rated among the best in North America. At a New York exhibition in 1936, he did well enough to be invited to show in London. Gerry's showing in London was not only a credit to B.C, but to all of Canada. His was among the top 10 collections in the world.

Gerry has won five international philatelic awards. His book, 'The Stamps and Postal History of Vancouver Island and British Columbia' is a 164-page, full color limited edition of 1,000 copies, and represents an invaluable postal history of B.C. He continues to upgrade his collection, which is kept in an undisclosed location. A wonderful way to preserve the postal history of the province.

Gerry is also a logging historian. Proof is the B.C. Forest Museum, just north of Duncan on the Island Highway, and he says, "It all started in 1938 shortly after I joined the Chamber of Commerce in Duncan. In 1939, the president moved to Nanaimo, and I suddenly found myself in the president's chair."

When war was declared a few months later, he became involved in the war effort so his dream of a forest museum was put on the back burner for six years.

In the early 1950's, the Canadian Chamber of Commerce held its annual general meeting in Victoria. H.R. MacMillan was on the entertainment committee and he phoned Gerry for ideas. Gerry suggested inviting the delegates to Duncan for a tour of the Deerholme logging operations.

"We could show them some of the biggest timber in the world and let them watch the most modern ways of logging. I can arrange a demonstration of the newest chainsaws because we have one of the very first gas-driven power saws ever used. We could fall a couple of big firs to let them see the improvement of the new saws over that old one. We could bus them to the Copper Canyon operation and have a loggers' lunch in the big new cookhouse."

"Great idea," H.R. replied.

When the delegates arrived, there were three bus loads from all parts of Canada. They watched the falling, and photographed a high rigger as he topped a spar tree. The visitors watched in awe at close range, as huge logs crashed into the landing and were loaded on trucks. Down at the sawmill they watched logs turned into lumber. A train came in to switch out a loaded car and chug away down the track. Everything went marvellously well and H.R. was pleased. That evening, at the wind-up banquet in the Empress Hotel, Gerry Wellburn was guest speaker.

"I remember them cheering me when I came in. The cheers, of course, were for the effort and success of the day's logging show. That was the first time in my life that anyone had ever cheered me. It was really something, to find out how interested they were,"

Even before construction of the Forest Museum had begun, Gerry always had the Museum's interests at heart. He had half an hour to speak to the delegates, and he used it to push home his dream of a logging museum. There was a standing ovation when he finished.

H.R. thanked Gerry. The big man was at his eloquent best, and concluded, "This day has done more to explain our lumber and logging industries to Canada than anything up to this date.

36

Your logging museum is an excellent idea. I'm sure you have the backing of every person in this room (everyone stood again). It must go ahead. Please accept our thanks."

When the railroads were torn up in favor of truck logging at Chemainus, Gerry made a special trip to the yard where all the old locies and steel rails were stored. He remembers seeing workers cutting up those old steam locies. He'd come to look for Number 9, the old Climax engine he and his bicycle partner had ridden on in 1919. He actually watched as they moved the cutting torches in and prepared to start hacking that beautiful old machine into scrap.

"I told the men to hold off because I wanted to buy the locie as it was. I rushed straight to the office and explained my wish to purchase the '9 Spot' for the logging museum.

The manager argued that all the scrap had been sold to Japan.

"Well, I would like to get the '9 Spot'. I'll write you a cheque for it here and now, but get a message to those men to stop the cutting." He paid the scrap price of $1,730, and the locie was his.

Gerry wanted it brought to Deerholme where it could be repaired and painted. It was too heavy and too high to be moved over the highway bridges from Chemainus. So it was put on a scow, towed to Vancouver, transferred onto the CNR line at the mouth of the Fraser River, and then barged to Cowichan Bay. The '9 Spot' was then shunted up the track, into the siding at Deerholme, and then winched onto an old donkey sleigh using a D-8 Cat. There was about two feet of snow, and two big Cats gave the 42-ton locie a sleigh ride over to the shop.

In the meantime, a 100-acre block of land was purchased just north of Duncan. Most of this acreage was a growing forest with some of the Douglas firs six feet in diameter and 150 feet tall. The land was on the west side of Somenos Lake and along the east side of the Island Highway. Donations of all sizes and sorts were received from the forest people and most business enterprises in the Cowichan Valley. B.C. Forest Products and the MacMillan companies came through handsomely. Gerry remembers they also donated antique logging equipment. H.R. MacMillan was an enthusiastic booster and adviser, and personally gave generously, and the Hillcrest Lumber Company and the Stone family did their part. Today, '9 Spot' rests in the Forest Museum and is probably the oldest steam locie in the province.

Gerry Wellburn put in countless long days and thousands of dollars from his own pocket. David Williams, a Duncan lawyer, donated the legal work and became the museum's first president, with Hall Mackenzie as secretary. It later became necessary to get financial aid from the Provincial government. After five years, the Duncan district ended up with one of the finest tourist attractions in Canada. The museum and park is run by the British Columbia government, and provides true living history of the old days.

Gerry, 87 in 1987, is still on the board of directors and attends many of the policy meetings. More than 20 years ago Wellburn was acclaimed Citizen of the Year for the Cowichan district. This made him very proud. The honor went a long way in repaying him for his tireless efforts.

Lima Shay built in 1924 for Mayo Lumber. Courtesy of the B.C. Forest Museum.

H.R. MacMillan shown at the Loggers' Festival, Vancouver, B.C. Courtesy of the *Timber Journal*, 1969.

CHAPTER 4

H.R. MacMillan

Harvey Reginald MacMillan was born on September 9, 1885. In his statesman years he would be addressed as "H.R." or "Mac". His father, John Alfred MacMillan, died of consumption in Ontario when his only son was just three years old. H.R.'s mother, Joana, went home to live on the MacMillan family farm, and later took a job as housekeeper for a neighbor family at $4 a month. As a school kid, Harvey worked long hours helping his uncles and grandfather with the chores.

Sunday was the only day he had time for himself. He had collected all his mother's books which were neatly arranged on a shelf below the one small window in his crowded attic room. He gradually withdrew from his uncles and aunts, and his grandfather rarely spoke to him. Grandma was the one who told him what he was expected to do, "I want those jobs done neatly or I'll take a stick to you." The stick was a short bit of broom handle about two feet long.

Many an evening H.R. would read and study until he dropped off to sleep with the book in his hand. He passed into high school with top marks at age 11. He sailed through Aurora High School and graduated with honors. He and his mother decided he should enter the Ontario Agricultural College (O.A.C.) at Guelph, mainly because it was the cheapest higher education available.

L.S. Klinck, who was Dean of Forestry, took a special interest in the young man, and got him a job in the school's forestry experimental plot producing seedlings. His pay was nine cents an hour. To earn more, H.R. edited the college magazine and did some reporting for the local Guelph Mercury. Next year, Klinck was invited to be dean of the University of British Columbia.

H.R. was not yet 20 when he graduated with honors from O.A.C. with a Bachelor of Science degree in biology. With earnings from his summer job with a survey party, he was able to pay the tuition fee for a term at Yale University.

The following summer, in 1904, H.R. was employed at Canada's first forestry nursery station at Indian Head, Saskatchewan. Even with the money he earned, it took frugal management to buy clothing that did not cause him embarrassment at prestigious Yale. He was offered work during the Christmas break at a logging camp in Maine and, although the pay was low, he had free board and lodging.

He arranged to visit his mother for a day on his way back to Yale for the spring term, and she told him how proud she was of his good marks.

Summer came with three offers of forestry-oriented positions. He chose to work in Manitoba for the Federal Department of the Interior. His title was Assistant Inspector of Forests, in charge of a group responsible for finding land suitable for growing trees. They laid out areas suitable for parks and ranching and the rest was reserved for forests.

That fall he was caught high in the Rocky mountains of Alberta, when an inexperienced young wrangler let their two pack horses get away. MacMillan had gone on ahead to mark a park boundary, when a sudden snowstorm forced him to turn back. His helper told him the pack animals had bolted down the back trail two hours earlier. In the packs were their supplies, including food, matches, blankets, and heavy clothing. The storm developed into a raging blizzard. They were above 4,000 feet in below freezing temperatures. They tried desperately to reach a trapper's cabin where they had camped the previous night. The snow was above their knees when they reached some timber, and it was dark and still snowing.

"We'll camp here," Mac ordered.

Huddled together on pine boughs, they shivered until first light. It was still snowing and had turned colder. They brushed the snow from their clothing and staggered off in the direction of the trapper's cabin. It had been more than 30 hours since they had eaten. When they finally stumbled into the warm cabin, they were exhausted. The trapper had a venison stew simmering on his tin campstove.

"I saw your pack horses in the meadow about a mile below here," he told them. "One pack saddle has slid around and was under the belly of the big one."

After hot coffee and grub, H.R. thought they should be moving on. The trapper had caught the pack horses and salvaged what he could from the packs. They headed down the mountain and returned the horses to the rancher from whom H.R. had hired them three days earlier.

On his way to Ottawa by train, a heavy chest cold set in. After spending a month completing his maps and reports, he consulted a doctor who found advanced tuberculosis in both lungs. He was sent to a sanatorium in the mountains of New York State to take the cure. Six months later, a second examination found his condition to be worsening. A year later his mother insisted he be transferred to the new sanatorium at Ste. Agathe, Quebec. She came to help him make the train trip and get settled in.

He was relieved to learn the costs of care in Canada were less than half of what he had been paying in the U.S., so he could afford a lengthy treatment. When his new doctor had finished a week of examinations, he informed MacMillan his condition was serious.

"Young man you're very ill. You must start today to do

everything in your power to try and improve your lungs. Otherwise you'll not be with us."

A telegram was sent to his mother. She quit her job and moved to Ste. Agathe, determined to do all she could to save her son. H.R. had sent for a post-graduate paper on the treatment of his dreaded disease. He kept daily records of his first cough, and of every cough during the day. He explained to me years later, while we were fishing at St. Mary's Lake on Saltspring Island.

"I almost smothered myself trying to cut down on my coughing. I'm positive that it was my mother's care and encouragement, each and every day, that started a change for the better and saved my life. It was over a year before we knew which way things were going. In all, I spent over two years at the sanatorium. I read about three books a week and was constantly making plans for the time when I would be well enough to get back to my forestry. I thought and planned only for the future. In the spring of 1911 my doctor told me I was cured. He also told me I was his thirteenth patient at Ste. Agathe, and the only one still alive."

For the first year of his sickness Mac received his full federal government salary and half of it during his stay in Ste. Agathe. He wrote many papers outlining his forestry plans for Canada. During his recovery he was furnished with forestry books from all parts of the world. On his return to Ottawa he was promoted to Assistant Director of Forestry, in charge of Statistics and Planning.

In August, 1911, he married Edna Mulloy, whose father had taught him in high school. They had corresponded during his illness, and had planned their wedding for the earliest possible date.

A few months later, M.A.Grainger of the B.C. Forest Service offered Mac the position of first Chief Forester of British Columbia at $2,400 a year. This was a dream come true. He discussed the offer with his superiors. They encouraged him to accept, but made it clear he was welcome to return.

The newlyweds and H.R.'s mother travelled west in a style befitting the importance of his new position. A private coach had been arranged, and Joana was so proud of her son she just had to let some of the other passengers know how important he was.

42

When Grainger introduced MacMillan to W.R. Ross, then Minister of Forestry, there was an awkward silence. Mac was only 26 years old. He was pale and skinny. He looked too young for the job ahead. When he chaired his first meeting a few days later, with the minister and all the senior forestry personnel present, it was a different story. H.R. had studied a recent Royal Commission report and discussed it with Grainger. He had already met and knew most of his top staff by their first names. He told them he intended to have the province divided into districts with a qualified forester in charge of each and that a start would be made on an inventory of all government timber. There would be no further timber leases granted at two cents per acre for 21 years because "this method is not getting a fair and reasonable return for our timber resources."

Grainger was the first to stand and applaud the new boss. The others did too, including the minister. Ross was first to step forward, shake his hand, and offer congratulations.

"There will be reports and suggestions one week from today, same place, same time," H.R. announced. He had established himself as a man of action.

For the next two years, he had the forestry department in a whirl. Legislation was passed to help prevent forest fires and have funds set aside for fire fighting. In less than a year, at a convention in Ottawa, his former boss stated: "B.C. now has the best forestry legislation in Canada. Our thanks for this must go to H.R. MacMillan for his foresight and energy."

The First World War was declared in the summer of 1914. With most of his young men enlisting, surveys and inventories came to an abrupt halt. Mac volunteered for military service but was turned down because of his health. In the spring of 1915 he was appointed Special Trade Commissioner to represent both the Dominion and Provincial governments, expediting lumber sales throughout the British Empire to satisfy the needs of war. It was arranged that H.R. should meet Sir Richard McBride, a former B.C. Premier and then Agent General for British Columbia with headquarters in London.

McBride immediately began introducing H.R. to people responsible for purchasing timber for the British government's war needs. The most important was Montague Meyer, a well established timber importer who had recently been appointed timber buyer for Britain. When MacMillan explained to Meyer how British Columbia had to ship through agents in the U.S. to get their lumber to markets in Europe, Meyer realized for the first time how costly that system was to the province and to Britain. They immediately implemented a new system whereby Britain, through M.L. Meyer Limited, could deal and import directly through the B.C. and Canadian governments. They arranged to supply Sitka spruce for aircraft manufacturing and Douglas fir timbers for the shipyards and railways. Orders were immediately placed for some 30 million board feet of Douglas fir, and all the Sitka spruce that could be shipped to Britain. H.R. and Meyer discussed shipping and arrangements were made to use the Panama Canal which had been opened for business earlier in 1915. This enabled the west coast to ship war supplies to Europe more cheaply and efficiently.

With letters of introduction to all the important timber buyers among the Allies, Mac booked many orders. He continued through Europe, then went on to India and Australia. His order files were now so extensive that he had doubts the lumber industry in Canada could fill the contracts. He had orders for over 200 million board feet by the time he returned to the West Coast. Almost single handed, in just over a year, H.R. had established British Columbia as a world exporter of timber. His greatest satisfaction was that Canadian lumber no longer had to go through American agents.

On a personal level, the luckiest incident of this world trade tour was a missed sailing to England. H.R. had been booked to sail in April, 1915, on the *Lusitania*. A last-minute conference with E.P. Taylor caused him to miss a connection and when his cab arrived at the dock the fated ship was several miles out to sea. When he arrived in London via another ship, newspaper headlines told how German torpedoes had sunk the *Lusitania* off the Irish coast.

In the autumn of 1916, his federal government duties at an end, H.R. decided to find work in the coastal timber industry. E.J. Palmer was manager of the big lumber mill at Chemainus. He persuaded H.R. to become assistant manager at a salary better than he was getting as Chief Forester. Palmer was nearing retirement age, and he hinted he was looking for someone to take his place. Before leaving the government, H.R. recom-

44

mended to his minister that Grainger would be the best man to fill the position he was vacating. Grainger got the job in the fall of 1916.

Chemainus was a different show. Palmer was not the type of boss to give his assistant the authority to make company decisions. H.R. was not the type who could work without the power to make changes. In the spring of 1917, a logging contractor was putting logs into Cowichan Lake at $4 per thousand. The contractor was Matt Hemmingsen, and he told MacMillan: "We need at least $1 per thousand more for all timberstick logs over 60 feet long if we are to keep logging." H.R. agreed the increase would be made. The next day, when he told Palmer, there was hell to pay, adding, "I thought I was going to be fired on the spot. It was a week before he agreed to back me and pay the extra dollar".

The story around Chemainus to this day is that Palmer fired MacMillan in July, 1917, and as H.R. walked out of the company office he turned and said, "The next time I walk through this door, by God, I'll own this outfit, lock, stock and barrel." Another story says his doctor advised him to slow down, or he would be sick again, so he handed in his resignation. Whatever, that old office door, now at the main entrance of the new office in Chemainus is a legend.

The old office building was torn down in January, 1985. The legendary old door which was hand made in 1898 was hauled away as junk to be burned. Ernie Shorter told me he was able to have that old door salvaged only hours before the trash pile was burned. An exact replica of the old door was made and is used as the main entrance for the office. The new door is in daily use, the old one right beside the new, fast in the old frame, is not opened. On July 30, 1985, to commemorate 123 years of lumber manufacturing at Chemainus, and the 100th anniversary of H.R. MacMillan's birth, a suitable brass plaque was placed on the panel between the new and original door of the first mill office.

H.R. took a position with Austin C. Taylor, as Assistant Director of Aeronautical Supplies for the Imperial Munitions Board. He was responsible for all Sitka spruce production in the province. The Queen Charlotte Islands became the main source of supply. There were trees on these northern islands as

45

high as 300 feet, with diameters at the butt of 12 feet. Van-Dusen was hired as general manager of both logging and saw mill operations for spruce, and together these two arranged for some 200 contracts which produced more than 300 million board feet the first year. The tug boats on the coast were towing spruce logs lashed together in huge cable-tied rafts. It was a long and treacherous haul from the Charlottes to mills in the Lower Mainland and Victoria.

In November, 1918, the war was over. The need for aeroplane spruce was no longer a priority. By year's end, settlements had been made with the contractors, business details were tidied up, and H.R. was out of work. He refused offers from two universities to head their forestry departments. He was anxious to start his own business. He sent a wire to Meyer, his friend and lumber dealer in London. Meyer made the long sea/train journey to Vancouver and he and H.R. agreed to form an export shipping company. Each put in $10,000. Meyer offered to put up all the capital, but the business-wise MacMillan, though not wealthy, wanted a fifty-fifty deal. He mortgaged his home. On June 12, 1919, the documents forming the H.R. MacMillan Export Company Limited were signed. Meyer handled the lumber imports for Europe and the British Empire and MacMillan expedited the buying and shipping of West Coast lumber. It was an ideal partnership.

Following the end of the war, there was a rebuilding program far greater than anything before. Growth was so rapid in the new shipping business they were hard pressed to keep up with the hundreds of orders that poured in. MacMillan Export owned no mills or timber. Its function was to obtain orders, arrange letters of credit, contract with mills, and arrange for space on ships for deliveries. The system was F.A.S. (free alongside ship). The export company was paid after the ship's captain signed the completed document of insurance and inspection. Under VanDusen's supervision, every one was kept happy. "We try not to make the same mistake twice" was his favorite saying.

In 1922, the MacMillan Export Company bought the Blue Bird Lumber Company which owned some standing timber and a small outdated little mill just west of Qualicum on the E & N Railway, on Vancouver Island. This acquisition was the

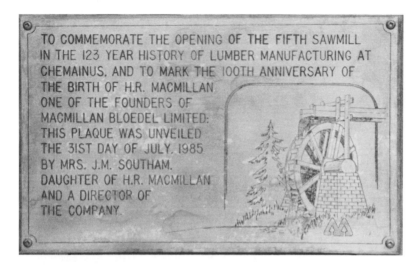

Plaque between the legendary door that was hung on the first office building of the Victoria Lumber Company and the replica now being used on the new MacMillan Bloedel Office building at Chemainus.

The small plaque high on the old door reads, "This door was hung originally on the first office building of the Victoria Lumber Company. It was made by hand about 1892."

first for H.R. in timber and sawmilling. Percy Sills, a shareholder in the mill and export company, was sent from Vancouver to manage and produced lumber and railway ties.

Things were going great until September 5, 1923. At 5:00 that morning the phone rang. Half asleep, Percy crawled out of bed to hear H.R. shouting, "That you Percy?"

"Yes, it's me. Still dark over here."

"Well, I need you to go to Japan. There's been a terrible earthquake over there. Thousands killed, cities burned, and to help out we'll reroute two shiploads of lumber over there."

"Fine, but I have this sawmill to run."

"To hell with the mill. It's five o'clock. There's a boat leaving Nanaimo at seven. Be on that boat! *The Empress of Russia*, she's leaving Vancouver for Japan at noon today. I'll meet you at the dock with some Japanese money and the tickets. Be on that boat for Japan!" There was a click in Percy's ear.

Sills packed, called Ed Stewart and put him in charge of the mill, and was on his way to Japan with a briefcase full of lumber documents on the noon sailing.

This was typical. H.R. MacMillan sometimes dominated the men he worked with throughout his career. There was only one boss. From this little Blue Bird sawmill operation, he went on to head one of the largest timber empires in the world.

H.R. lived on to be 91 years of age.

Percy Sills and son Pip, summer of 1915,
in Vancouver.

CHAPTER 5

Percy Sills

Excerpts from Percy Sills' diary of his trip to the disaster areas of Japan:

September 6th, 1923.

Aboard the *S.S. Empress of Russia* bound for Japan.

I wish this old Pacific Ocean would leave me alone and stop knocking me about like a shuttlecock. I'm not a sailor. I, who for two years have sworn that the ghastly doings of the *Exporter* shipwreck was the last slap she'd get at me—yet here I am, driving forward through the night across the world to be an atom in the greatest catastrophe of history, and one in which this same Ocean was the prime devil of the piece. I owe her no allegiance. I'm a lumberjack, a plain, roughneck sawduster, and yet every couple of years or so she drags me out and pounds and buffets me, freezes and frightens me, and jeopardizes my soul from the cursing of her, and my body by the might of her.

There was no resisting the demand of her call this time, disguised as it was by the necessity and stress of a friend—but it is all her irresistible manipulating nevertheless, and the luxuriousness of this floating palace and all the other reasons do not blind me to the fact that I am embarked on a real job for sure, and dangerous withal, and glad I'll be when it's over, but between that and now I fully realize comes the overwhelming need for every faculty, mental and physical, that I possess.

September 7th

Today is practically uneventful. I found Sid Abbott aboard as 4th Engineer, also have succeeded in interesting the wireless operator in my behalf. There is little merriment on the ship. I take it that as in Danny Deever, they're " 'Dreadin' what they got to watch," and the shadows of coming events are being cast before.

September 8th

This day I've worked all day bringing order from the chaos of documents I carry, and of which I have as many as a Soviet delegate at an International loot division.

September 10th

Rough today. The old boat lurches and pitches, takes water over the bow and kicks up her heels, but she's most remarkably steady, and to me the lack of throb and vibration due to these turbine engines is wonderful.

I am daily getting and sending wireless from and to Mac, but tonight we pass beyond shore communication. Today Sid Abbott took me through the engine room and stokehold—four turbines. The outstanding feature to me is the lack of "moving evidence" of the terrific power. These turbines sit like dynamos and work quite as silently, and only the steam gauges indicated to me the enormous controlled power everywhere round about.

The stoke-hold is to me a place of uncanny and tremendous interest — ten boilers, they were enormously big and dwarfed the human all about. It is an inferno, dirty, black, the roar of the drafts, the clank of the doors and shovels, the shouts of the coal passers, the shrill almost continuous whistles of the head-boys, and the stokers— they might be denizens from the bowels of the earth, stripped to the waist, sweaty, dirty, like pigmies scuttling below these towering masses of iron, and yet I was firmly gripped, held and fascinated by the whole scene. I can still see one face in the glare of the furnace when he opened the fire door, the face of a Red Indian against a back-

50

ground of black velvet, a long thin face of low intelligence, almost animalistic, but a face kindly and intensely interested in the work at hand, and a most evident expression of the joy of doing a hard job well.

September 17th

And now we are off the Japanese Coast, with land plainly in sight, and in the morning will be in Kobe.

September 18th to October 11th

In the ruins of Yokohama and in the remnants left of Tokyo, under conditions abnormal, tragic and chaotic beyond words, I travelled on their trains back and forth through the hundred or so miles of indescribable desolation between these two cities, usually the only "foreigner" in a great multitude. I was at the Honjo district in Tokyo where 32,000 burned to death, and the iron was still warm from the cremating of some 80,000 of them, and although the air was filled with the chanting of strange rituals of religions unknown to me, and the open spaces with orderly funeral processions in ghastly frequency, I heard not one whimper, not a complaint did I hear.

For one class I will claim kinship with the immortals, for their deeds of that "love" of which Christ said, "greater than which there is not", and I refer now to the Japanese servants and children's nurses, and their devotion, bravery and sacrifice. Strong men, fathers of families, officials, younger men not usually interested in this sort of thing, every one and all of them told me these tales of rescue, protection and care of the helpless little ones, and in most cases the pressure of emotion made difficult the speech with which to finish the telling, and although I'm pretty "hard-boiled" I'm willing to admit I breathed with difficulty, and from both my eyes the tears ran out. I see one big fellow crumple as he tells me how he found his baby alive, but only so from the over covering fire-killed remnant of what had been its nurse. And another discovered his servants doing absolutely without that the family might divide the pittance of rice, and so on and so on.

But now to attempt a description of the actual catastrophe is a task so far beyond the powers of my poor efforts, that it is but a waste of time to mention my incapabilities, and I think that even to one accustomed to transmitting word pictures it would be a stupendous task to wrap suitable and sufficient words around this Japanese disaster.

So picture Yokohama, a crowded half-European, half-Oriental city of 450,000 people, at one minute before noon, on a sunny,

51

September morning, a Saturday noon, business just ending for the week, streets filled with people, hotels and clubs just filling, a Cabinet meeting in session, the *Empress of Australia* leaving for Canada in one minute,—a picture of peace, prosperity and contentment.

In one minute the entire city practically was a shapeless heap of masonry, iron and wood. In ten minutes fires had started which continued with increasing ferocity until the entire city was absolutely, completely destroyed, Tokyo three-quarters likewise, an area one hundred and forty miles long completely desolated, and the greatest loss of human life in history in a like time had taken place.

There were two outstanding quakes, thirty minutes apart. The earth swayed from side to side and violently up and down in great sharp shocks, understand, not gradual swayings, but violent up-heavals. People were thrown down, rolled around, got up again and again and were again thrown flat-horses and animals the same. The great, grinding roaring and crushing of falling buildings was deaf-ening, the flying dust and dirt blackened everything and everybody, causing instant temporary darkness. A great brown, yellowy cloud arose from the city, whether from fissures or dust I've not been able to determine, and the whole city heaved and rolled like a blanket does when shaken from each corner horizontally.

Ghastly silence for an instant—then shrieks and sounds increasing in ghastly volume as surely before had cursed no ear. Fires increased with rapidity appalling beyond words, and only understood by remembering that the loose state of the bone-dry interiors of the modern buildings furnished perfect draft to fan the flames. The Japanese houses are nearly all constructed of 1/4 inch cedar with grass mat carpets and oil paper windows and have very flimsy inflam-mable partitions.

The quakes during all this time were so frequent as to be almost continuous, there being just under 4,000 quakes the first seven days of September.

In Tokyo, a city of two million people, it was practically a repetition of Yokohama, except that the fire loss was greater, and the quake loss less, there having been preliminary warning shocks there, while in Yokohama the first great shock came instantly and without warning.

In and around Yokohama great oil reserve tanks, broken by the quake, allowed great quantities of crude and refined oil to cover the harbour in sheets or lakes and on the Sunday this took fire, igniting barges and boats, and greatly endangering the liners and large steamers in the harbour, now loaded with refugees and wounded. This oil was in places seven or eight feet deep, and oil in this condition

52

burns in a very spectacular way, throwing up great spouts of flame two hundred and three hundred feet in the air.

Then the younger Japanese hot-bloods, claiming the excuse of protecting their families and the remnant of their belongings, also banded together, and bloody war was on, in which ghastly killings took place in ghastlier ways. No foreigners of any kind were safe. Japanese martial law soon got this phase pretty well under control.

Just one thing more, an expression from me of what I heard from every side, without exception and in terms of great appreciation and thankfulness and admiration, viz., the great charity and the great kindness, the great skill and ability, the great demonstration of all the very best of humanity and civilization shown during this time by Captain Robinson and the entire staff of the *Empress of Australia*. I own no C.P.R. stock, I owe the C.P.R. no money, but it is the veriest truth that what I heard from all sides about this ship and her complement made me proud again to be Canadian.

Percy Garrett Sills was born August 11, 1884 in Ontario and came west when young to live a very active life in its development. He was one of the prominent pioneers in the coastal lumber industry.

Percy's wife, Sophie Laidley Deane, was born March 11, 1890, and was always known to her friends and family as just plain "Tote".

She and Percy were married in Vancouver. It was a posh 1911 wedding, both families very much in the social whirl. A son, Percival Dean, known as Pip, born July 8, 1912; then much later twins, Margaret Joan (Peggy) and Jack Loring, born March 21, 1921. Peggy was secretary to her father during the war years, then married Charles Heisterman. Jack, a pilot in the R.C.A.F., was stationed in North Africa during the Second World War and was killed over Italy.

Mrs. Percy Sills was living in her lovely apartment overlooking the harbor and downtown Victoria when her son Pip and I visited her. She was then in her 96th year, and could remember vividly her wedding and winning the Julian Trophy as skipper of the sloop *Wideawake* the same year. An excerpt from the Royal Vancouver Yacht Club records:

E.B. JIMMY DEANE, owner and skipper of *Alexandra* in the Alexandra Cup races, was one of the most active of the racing skippers in the early days of the club. He held the Graveley Cup for two years with the sloop *Tillicum* in the 21 foot class, and he challenged for the international Mackie Trophy with his sloop *Wideawake*. He also owned the B Class sloop *Titania* and the 73 foot power cruiser *Davey Jones*. His two daughters, Mrs. Harold A. Jones and Mrs. Percy Sills, were for many years among the most active of lady yachting enthusiasts; both won the Julian Trophy for lady skippers, Mrs. Jones née Miss Louise Deane in 1913 and again in 1935 and 1946, and Mrs. Sills nèe Miss Sophie Deane in 1911 and later in 1930.

(The *Wideawake* was built by Captain Beddis of Saltspring Island. The author's parents, when they first came to Saltspring to look for a homestead, were guests of Grannie Beddis and travelled aboard the *Wideawake* from Victoria to the Beddis Beach in March 1905).

One of Percy's first business ventures was a Vancouver wholesale lumber complex known as The Premier Lumber Company His two small offices were in the Metropolitan Building on the seventh floor at 837 West Hastings Street. Percy had excellent business connections and was doing well. Shortly before the First World War ended, MacMillan approached him regarding a partnership, and H.R. bought some shares in Percy's lumber company. It was in these two small offices, in July of 1919, that the H.R. MacMillan Export Company had its beginning. At first this new export company operated with only H.R., Percy, and Miss Edna Irwin as their secretary.

Business and sales increased, and soon Harold Wallace was brought in to do the book work for the ever increasing letters of credit coming in from around the world. Sales continued to grow, MacMillan offered his college friend, W.J. VanDusen, 17 per cent of the company with a salary of $350 per month, plus 10 per cent of the net profits. Van's position was director and general manager.

H.R. and Van pushed their two desks together and worked facing each other. Miss Irwin and Wallace shared space in the small adjoining room in among the filing cabinets, stationery boxes, and other gear. Percy, having lost his desk to Van, worked from a table near the door. As customers and salesmen would come in, Percy greeted them with a cheery "Sorry boys, standing room only today". Within a very short time this export business had grown from five to more than 80 people and had taken over the entire seventh floor of the Met Building.

In 1921, H.R. learned that a ship carrying a cargo of lumber had been wrecked near Aberdeen, Washington. The *Canadian Exporter* had run up on a sand bar just outside Grays Harbour. H.R. and Percy decided to see if there might be a quick profit in salvaging the lumber. They sped south to inspect the wreck.

"What's she worth?" H.R. asked.

"Not more than $2000, on a quiet day."

"Think you can get the lumber unloaded onto a scow?"

"If the weather stays calm, then yes. But it's a gamble!"

They contacted the insurance company and the offer was accepted. It was Percy who stayed to look after the hazardous operation. There was enough coal aboard to get steam up in the boilers and operate the winches. $20,000 and two months later, when the September winds set in, Percy called a halt. He persuaded the U.S. Coast Guard to tow the scow into the harbour, where he sold the lumber and equipment for $18,000. Except for several near drownings, Percy felt it had been worth the gamble. From that time on, he had a healthy respect for the power of Pacific storms.

According to his son, Pip, the last thing Percy did before leaving the battered ship was to build a platform of heavy timbers, then bolt the two winches and one of the boilers to it. He winched this gerry built platform to the very edge of the port side, then threaded both winch lines up through the cargo boom blocks and back down, to be shackled to cables bridling the platform. With a full head of steam they quickly "pulled the fire", then lowered this contraption down onto the scow. Only 20 pounds of steam pressure showed on the gauges when the platform landed smoothly. Without that last bit of steam pressure, the platform and engines would have crashed and split the scow.

"This was another of Dad's calculated gambles," Pip said, with a grin. Percy Sills must surely have had a canny knowledge of steam to handle the winches and be able to pull off a feat requiring such precision and timing. He salvaged the winches and boiler and sold them at a good price.

Percy and H.R. travelled to Qualicum in 1922 to buy a small mill with considerable timber on a rail siding about a mile

55

southeast of the village. The Blue Bird Lumber Company was steam powered, and could produce up to 35,000 feet of lumber in a 10-hour shift. This mill was MacMillan Export's first step into standing timber and manufacturing. The timber was of excellent quality and on level ground. Percy was appointed manager, and stayed over to complete the takeover and run 'the show'. Ed Stewart, who had three good logging teams, was hired to keep the mill supplied with logs. When Percy returned from Japan in the late fall of 1923, he went to Qualicum to finish cutting the timber and close down the Blue Bird sawmill.

By 1927, MacMillan Export was producing ties with about a dozen portable mills, and was also contracting with other private mills for ties and lumber. Eight mills were cutting the Hemmingsen timber on the Malahat near Shawnigan Lake. Another five were cutting ties on Mount Provost to the west of Duncan. Percy was looking after the Mount Provost operation. There was a substantial amount of good white pine timber. Ed Stewart was doing the logging, and he and Percy made an agreement to log the pine timber and haul it to the Chemainus wharf.

At Chemainus, the logs were roughly squared by broadaxe and chalkline, a method devised to give a straight timber from end to end. To get the line onto the logs, chalk or blueing was rubbed onto a strong fishing line. The line would be attached to each end of the log with nails, then stretched tight and tied. The axeman would then go to the centre of the log, press the line down straight and tight. With his free hand he would lift the chalk line straight up then let it snap back down. The result was a perfectly straight blue line. Sounds a bit complicated, but an experienced broad-axe man could do this on a 40 foot long log in less than five minutes.

These pine timbers exported from Chemainus were a very lucrative venture, and the business carried on for several years using nothing more than a couple of good men with broad axes. Pip tells me he spent more than one of his summer holidays there, cleaning up chips and fishing through some holes in the wharf for cod and shiners.

MacMillan and John Humbird of Chemainus were rivals in the export business, so Percy made all the arrangements at Chemainus. He and John became good friends and many

56

favours were extended. Humbird arranged for Sills to have a large section of the Victoria Lumber & Manufacturing wharf for his hewing and storage, and always made lumber carriers available when it came time to take the pine squares to shipside for loading. It could have been because of the success of this Chemainus operation that the MacMillan Export Co. decided to buy the Pacific Cedar Co. mill on the North Arm of the Fraser River. They later renamed it The Canadian White Pine Co. During these years VanDusen was president and MacMillan was vice-president. Percy was general manager of the mill, and recognized as a specialist in the pine export business. It was because of Percy's friends in the British Admiralty that all the pine they could produce was sold to the British Navy.

Jack Sexton started working on the boom at the Canadian White Pine Mill, June 7, 1931. The mill was located on the North Arm of the Fraser River and was being modernized to cut Douglas fir as well as white pine. With the changes Percy made, production almost doubled. It was Sills who brought Sexton in and persuaded him to get a B.C. scaling certificate. Jack remembers it was Percy and H.R. that put him in charge of the log sorting and buying. When this upgraded mill started cutting fir timbers in addition to the pine squares, Sexton was hard pressed to find enough good logs to keep both the plywood and pine mills going. Percy had connections with some loggers in the U.S.A. around the Oakville, Washington district. He and Jack would go down a couple of times each year to select and purchase all their high grade pine and fir logs. They would sort the best logs, then have them boomed and towed out to Olympia. It was here that Jack scaled the logs as they were loaded on the scows. His Canadian scaling certificate was accepted by both the American producers and the Canadian buyers. This is probably one of the reasons Percy encouraged Jack to get his certificate. Through other sources Percy somehow obtained export permits, so the pine could be shipped anywhere in the world. These huge timbers were usually remanufactured then used for pattern stock.

Then followed the building of the British Columbia Plywood plant, near the White Pine Mill. That was the start of major plywood manufacturing in British Columbia. The trade name for their new product was "Sylvaply".

From the very beginning, with good peeler logs, the Plywood Mill produced a high quality product, and found it difficult to keep up with the orders that poured in. When war was declared in 1939, B.C. Plywood became a three-shift operation because buildings could be constructed much faster, and with less men, using plywood in place of shiplap or other conventional sheathing. Their profits were tremendous.

In 1941, and, for reasons best known only to himself, Percy Sills moved to Victoria on Vancouver Island. No one seems to know what actually happened. He had been one of the original partners, and his withdrawal was the end of the original partnership and friendship of Sills and MacMillan. Years later, Jack Sexton and I were chatting, and he admitted "I'm not sure whether Percy was squeezed out or bought out. He was quite bitter, and every time we had drinks together in Victoria he'd want to talk about it."

Once relocated in Victoria, Percy and his son Pip started their own business. They had an agreement with the MacMillan Export Co. to cut and market spruce that was needed in the manufacture of aircraft. The Sills built a huge splitting saw to cut the biggest logs into halves or quarters if need be, so the Victoria mills could get them onto the carriage and through the head saws. Pip worked with his Dad at their Victoria assembly lumber yards at the Ogden Point docks. He more or less inherited the business with all the responsibilities when his Dad's health failed and Percy passed away in 1953.

The early 1950's were a boom or bust period in the lumber industry. The new Social Credit government had just been elected under the leadership of W.A.C. Bennett. Forest management licences were new, forcing some hectic and very competitive bidding at government timber sales. This was the beginning of the end for the small, independent loggers and sawmill people. Pip bid at several timber sales but lost most of them when desperate "Gyppo" loggers bid more for stumpage than he could get for the manufactured lumber.

In 1960, Pip sold out in Victoria and decided to try sawmilling at Quesnel in the Cariboo forest district. He formed a partnership with Bernie Peal, who had some land just north of town, and they built a gang mill there. Things went along fairly well for the first couple of years, but the time came when the

Percy walking to his office in Victoria shortly after the dinner given by Austin Taylor at the Hotel Vancouver, where Percy and others active in Aeronautical Supplies reminisced over spruce logging during World War One.

AUSTIN C. TAYLOR
555 BURRARD STREET
VANCOUVER
CANADA

October 30, 1947.

Dear Percy,

        I am having a few friends who were associated with the Department of Aeronautical Supplies (I.M.B.) in World War I, to dinner on November sixth, when we can discuss and mellow over old times of thirty years ago. Since you had such an active part in the spruce activities, I hope to have the pleasure of your company at dinner.

        Date - November sixth
        Place - Hotel Vancouver, Social Suite
        Time - 6:30 p.m.
        Dress - Informal

        Sincerely,

        Austin

Mr. Percy G. Sills,
   2595 Lansdowne Road,
      Victoria, B. C.

Invitation to the gathering of World War One aero spruce producers from Austin Taylor to Percy.

60

bigger and more established mills didn't want to share the annual allowable timber cut with any newcomers. When Sills and Peal would bid at a timber sale needed to keep their mill going, there would be up to five others there to bid against them.

"Usually it was Pachet, Brown-Miller, Western Plywood, Beaver Lumber and Gardners at the sale," Pip remembers. "They would bid up the price of stumpage so high it was financial suicide to carry on. This forced us to buy logs from the local loggers and farmers. We carried on until 1965, when the lumber prices went down below the price we had paid for our logs. We had to close the mill because we were losing money on every log we cut. Things were desperate," Pip remembers.

"John Ernst had acquired a large acreage with good pine timber on it in the early 1950's. That was before the pulp mills were built in the northern part of the province and pine was not considered merchantable timber. His mill and timber were on the west side of the Fraser River and about 15 miles south on the Garner logging road. John Ernst offered to buy us out for cash and really treated us well. We had almost enough money to pay off our debts. I worked for Ernst for almost a year as office manager, shipper and tallyman. The cold weather got to my lungs and put me in the Quesnel hospital with pneumonia. It stayed 40 degrees below zero that winter for weeks on end. When I was well again, the Twin Harbours Lumber Company hired me as tallyman and shipper for their Buck Ridge mill.

"It was January of 1966. It took me until after 10 in the morning to get our car started so I could drive out to the office. It was so cold they couldn't start the big diesel engines. Only half of the mill crew showed up. Mr. Anderson, an American and the owner, arrived about noon in a closed-in Jeep. 'Let's leave her sit till the weather warms up,' he shouted and headed back towards Quesnel.

"My wife and I were having a few hot rums that afternoon, when Joy checked our thermometer. 'My God! It's 45 below', she exclaimed. We had another rum in silence then went to have another look. It had dropped to 47 degrees below zero. Joy turned to me, looking very serious."

"'Let's pack up and go to Mexico,' she said."

Within two days, the Sills were in Seattle heading south. Though they had never been in Mexico before, it was 10 years before Pip and Joy came home to B.C. and retired on Vancouver Island.

One of the good times—in style. Percy and Sophie "Tote" leaving for Hawaii to celebrate 25 years of marriage.

Born 1912. John Hemmingsen in the early 1970's as
Executive Vice-President, Natural Resources,
MacMillan Bloedel Limited.

CHAPTER 6
John Hemmingsen

As we sat in John Hemmingsen's Vancouver home chatting
about his years in logging, he talked about his father, Matt.

"As a young man, Dad started keeping diaries, and had
detailed descriptions of decking and driving logs on the rivers
in Wisconsin. At 15 he started working for the Humbird family
in 1890. In 1906, he was called out to British Columbia to try
and clear the logs they had dumped in a river near Courtenay.
Even when the rains came in the fall, he found the river much
too shallow to float the bigger logs that were jammed along the
banks. It took a lot of blasting and team work to clear the river
and get these logs down into Comox Harbour for booming.
Because the rivers were small and the logs big, he told them no
more river drives should ever be attempted.

"Dad must have brought the highlead idea west with him,

because that was how they had decked the logs along the rivers in Wisconsin. He was one of the very first to rig a spar tree at Cowichan Lake when he started contract logging for the Victoria Lumber & Manufacturing Co."

H.R. MacMillan was also busy in 1907. Timber licences then were readily available from the B.C. government. It was only necessary to set one corner-post with a written description of the boundaries to identify a square mile block of timber. Those licences usually started at or near the beach and extended back in any desired direction to take in the best timber. H.R. and Aird Flavell cruised and identified timber blocks from Howe Sound up past Powell River as far north as Bute Inlet, then worked their way back along the east coast of Vancouver Island.

"Dad was supervising the logging camps at Cowichan Lake in 1912 when he got word of my birth, and he immediately left for Chemainus. He was relieved to find his wife doing well with the midwife and his two daughters fussing over me.

"When Dad went to the office to report before going back to camp, there were some heated words. E. J. Palmer, known as Old Hickory for his toughness, was then general manager for V.L.& M., and he didn't appreciate his logging superintendent not being on the job.

" 'Why are you not in camp?'

" 'Come to Chemainus to see my new son and heir.'

" 'That's not reason enough to leave the job,' Old Hickory told Dad.

" 'If that's the way you see it, you can find someone to take my place,' my Dad said, and he walked out of the office. When Youbou management heard about this, they offered him a superintendent's job at double the salary he had been making."

Matt Hemmingsen logged at Cowichan Lake from 1912 until 1929. He could have been called a gyppo, but he was a very substantial gyppo. He logged blocks 106, 107, 113, and most of the North Arm on Cowichan Lake. He put in more than a billion feet of timber during that time.

Though Matt and his brother Ed were partners, they didn't always see eye to eye. Following several heated arguments, Ed left to do some farming in the state of Washington. However, he must have become homesick because he came back a few years later to buy and operate the Riverside Hotel at the south end of Cowichan Lake.

In the meantime, Matt had negotiated directly with the E & N Railway Company for a block of timber on the Malahat which E & N cruisers had estimated at 32 million board feet. This was block 205, and, after Matt had walked through it, he estimated the quantity to be more than 60 million feet of mostly good fir. That was in 1928, and it was his first major timber purchase.

It was common knowledge that the MacMillan Export Co. needed all the timber it could get to fill tie orders. H.R. heard about this Malahat timber deal and had driven most of the night, then slept in his car, blocking the logging road he knew Matt would have to pass. It was barely daylight when H.R. was shaken awake.

"What on earth are you doing here at this time of the morning?" Matt asked.

"I'm here to buy your block of timber."

"I'm not sure I want to sell it. I've only owned it for a few days."

"I'm willing to give you double what you paid. I'll write you a cheque for $15,000 right now, pay six per cent on the balance, and $15,000 a year for the next three years."

Matt looked down the road at the wall of trees for several minutes, then nodded his agreement. Using his briefcase for a desk, H.R. wrote the cheque, handed it to Matt, shook hands, and drove off toward Victoria. Though things were getting rough financially by 1932, H.R.'s last payment was handed over almost on time.

The Malahat block had excellent tic timber, and was very beneficial to MacMillan Export which immediately put in portable mills cutting ties. The operation continued right on through the Great Depression. After that Malahat deal, Matt Hemmingsen never looked back.

John was nine when his father gave him a job as spark watcher and said he could have his meals in the camp cook-house with the men. Predictably, young John grew up to believe that logging was the only worthwhile employment in the world. Those huge plates full of eggs, hotcakes smothered with butter and maple syrup probably helped. In 1937, John

65

graduated from the University of British Columbia with a Bachelor of Applied Science and a Forestry degree. His father offered him a job with the Hemmingsen Cameron Logging Company Ltd., at Port Renfrew, on the southwest coast of Vancouver Island.

Earlier, in 1926, E.P. Butchart of Butchart Gardens, near Victoria had bought thousands of acres of timberland in the Port Renfrew area and hired contractors to start logging. After several years, these contractors left Butchart in debt for well over a million dollars, but they had put in 15 miles of railroad, bought 17 steam donkeys, three locomotives, two tugboats, and built two booming grounds with camps. More than 400 million feet of standing timber existed at the Port Renfrew operation. It had been idle for 10 years when Matt Hemmingsen and the Camerons of Victoria bought everything on an "as-is where-is" basis, and began logging.

John arrived in the Renfrew camp from UBC and had good reason to wonder why he had ever bothered with higher education. He worked for $5 a day slashing brush along the telephone lines. He was even more dismayed to find room and board at $30 a month was being deducted from his wages. The board expense was serious and he told his dad he intended to look for a better-paying job. He was promoted to assistant surveyor working under Walter Laidlaw, with a healthy increase in pay, and free board to boot.

Laidlaw was a very experienced engineer who had worked for the V.L.& M. for many years. It didn't take long for John to realize his real education was just beginning. When the railroad locations and logging plans were laid out and well ahead, Laidlaw decided to take a job closer to home. John inherited the chief engineer's position. A few months later he was put in charge of the entire logging operation.

"You can bet Dad kept a watchful eye on me," John said.

Ron McEachern had been a superintendent for the Hemmingsens for more than 20 years, and he and young John worked well together. John soon learned there is no substitute for experience. He was absolutely amazed that McEachern could judge distances and lay out a grade just by looking at it, almost as accurately as he could with a transit.

By 1945 Matt Hemmingsen at 70 was showing his age. Labor

unions were becoming awkward, and oldtimers like him just couldn't cope. E.P. Taylor, owner of B.C. Forest Products, made an offer to purchase the timber and equipment. It was a good offer, so the partners agreed to sell. John agreed to stay on for a month to show their engineers what had been planned for future logging before he left British Columbia. He was now able to take up an offer made the previous year by the Newfoundland Pulp & Paper, a subsidiary of the huge Bowater operations. The company wanted him to reorganize their total logging operation. Bert Dudley, their woodlands manager, arranged to meet John in Montreal to explain exactly what they wanted done in Newfoundland.

Their pulp plants were the largest in the world at that time and it took a great amount of wood to keep them operating. They had 120 logging camps, 7,000 loggers, and 400 horses scattered all over Newfoundland. Logging was done during the winter. Dudley wanted John to explore the possibilities of developing some kind of mechanical logging system that would eventually retire the horses and some of the men. They also had about 400 sleigh dogs, for use when the terrain got too steep for the horses. Each dog pulled a little sled on which a few pieces of four-foot pulp wood were tied with rope.

"That was how they got the wood down to where it could be loaded on the horse sleds. In the summertime, those 400 dogs were left to run wild in the woods and fend for themselves," John recalled. "Those wild critters were just like wolves, and far more dangerous because they had no fear of humans."

John set up his headquarters in Cornerbrook. The next day, Dudley left for the Philippines to buy war-surplus tractors, expecting to return in about three weeks. It was three months before he returned. By that time, John's family had come east and he and his wife lived in a hotel with their two young children. It took almost two years to find a suitable house to move into.

John's toughest job was training the men to work with the new tractors. Next, he designed some portable spars for yarding the cordwood from areas too steep for the tractors or horses. John was pressing to have all the yarding done on a tree-length basis, but Dudley was stubborn.

"John," he said, "I don't give a damn what system you

develop here as long as the pulpwood arrives at the mill in four-foot lengths.''

"That's ridiculously expensive and a very poor way of logging," John told him disgustedly.

Even with the portable spars, they were cutting the logs into four-foot lengths. They would stack the wood into piles four feet high and eight feet long, put two straps around each pile, then hook the straps to the butt rigging and try to yard this through the brush and stumps down to flatter ground. There the wood could be loaded on sleighs and hauled to the river with the new tractors. It was an expensive mess.

The average tree in Newfoundland is only eight inches in diameter and 30 to 40 feet tall. Because of the very cold climate, the trees grow slowly. A tree 10 inches in diameter could well be over 100 years old, and one would need a good magnifying glass to count the annual growth rings.

John spent four years in Newfoundland before he admitted it was a waste of time trying to change these old ways.

"Newfoundland is not a wealthy province, but it's sure filled with beautiful people," he remembered with a smile.

John made a presentation of his proposed logging systems to the Pulp and Paper Association of Canada at a convention in Montreal. The report was awarded first prize for being the most advanced concept of logging ever produced. His major change recommended that producers stop cutting their timber into four-foot lengths in the woods. He declared that the timber should be logged 'tree length' and do all of the four-foot cutting at the manufacturing plants. That method would reduce logging costs by 50 per cent or more, his report stated.

When the family returned to the Pacific coast, John's father suggested he should take a position somewhere in the MacMillan logging organization, saying, "That group is expanding so rapidly, and with the change in logging equipment they desperately need experienced young men. The potential for advancement is unlimited."

John was offered another job. Since the late 30's, Frank Ferries had been Vancouver Island sales manager for Caterpillar Tractors, and he had sold Matt several big D-8s. Frank was so impressed by John's descriptions of logging in Newfoundland that before the social visit was over he had phoned his boss, Earl Finning, and arranged for John to have a company car so he could start promoting and selling equipment for the Finning Tractor Company.

One of the first people John met on his new job was Sid Smith, manager of logging for Bloedel, Stewart and Welsh at Port Alberni. Sid showed John around the various camps and then astonished him by saying, "John, I want you to come and work for me."

"I can't do that. Earl Finning was kind enough to take me on. He's given me a new car, and wants me to just travel around."

"We'll see about that," Sid said as he showed him to the guest house.

Sid must have sent some kind of message to Finning, because Earl phoned John that same night and said, "You'd better go to work for Sid. He's one of our best customers and a very big wheel in the logging business."

Sid put him on the payroll as Assistant Chief Forester under Charlie Dunham. A few months later the company became MacMillan & Bloedel Limited so John ended up doing exactly as his Dad had suggested—working for H.R. MacMillan.

M & B was a huge new company with plenty of opportunity for advancement. Sid Smith was soon transferred to head office in Vancouver, and John Hemmingsen went to Great Central Lake to take over as regional manager. Within months, John had brought in Madill portable steel spars to replace the old trees of high rigger fame.

He also separated engineering and road construction from the actual logging. This was new, but everyone liked it. The engineers did what they did best: layout, road building, and bridge construction. The loggers were happy because they were doing what they liked best: yarding and loading the logs onto the big trucks.

By 1955, John had reduced logging costs in those two divisions by more than 30 per cent. Bill Loukes was the general foreman and was responsible for logging to the plans the engineers laid out. In winter they would log the low area and in the spring follow the melting snow to the higher hills. For the first time, the Sproat Lake division was ahead with their road building because John insisted they just keep on building until

69

John and May at their elder son's 25th wedding
anniversary, Spring of 1988.

they had several years of settled logging roads ahead.

When H.R. noticed the costs—the lowest anywhere—he
made a special trip out and spent several days at the camp. He
asked the questions; John gave the answers.

"Simple, but good organization," H.R. concluded.

In 1956, John was promoted again, taking over Jack Chal-
mers' job as general manager of logging in the Alberni area,
which included Sproat Lake, Alberni Pacific, Franklin River,
Serrita River and Kennedy Lake. A couple of years later he was
transferred to the Nanaimo office as regional manager of
logging.

When the Powell River Company amalgamated and became part of MacMillan Bloedel in 1959, John was transferred to head office in Vancouver to be responsible for all logging. More than 1.5-billion feet of logs were needed annually to keep the mills supplied. When he was promoted again to vice-president, the company split the logging into three districts. Never again was one person in charge of such a huge complex.

In 1961, through John's insistence, the company implemented a new forestry program under the able supervision of Angus McBean. Angus had the courage to try new things, such as planting hybrid seedlings and thinning to promote faster growth. He also hired many young foresters to experiment with various fertilizers to create a healthier new forest. McBean was the man who started what we know today as intensive forestry and most of his theories have produced excellent results.

"If we get the new forests ready sooner, then we can log our mature timber faster," John maintained.

Angus McBean died in the early 1970's, but the people in the industry will always owe him a debt of gratitude for the many good ideas he so ably initiated.

John Hemmingsen was later put in charge of lumber marketing, and this job took him to all parts of the world.

John and May are proud of their four children.

"Strange as it may seem, neither of our two sons went into logging," John remarked. "John, the elder, is vice-president of a big steel company in Ontario, yet, he has kept some ties with the logging world by marrying Cherie, Ian Mahood's daughter. Shawn travelled and worked around the world before going to university to become a cell biologist. He and his wife, also a biologist, are presently in research. Our elder daughter is married and lives in New York and our younger daughter is here in Vancouver."

John and his wife are enjoying retirement in Vancouver, where John has much more time now to spend polishing and monkey wrenching his vintage cars.

Shorter family. *Back row*: Harry, Marguerite,
Lawrence's wife and Ernie. *Sitting*: Mother, father and
Lawrence.

CHAPTER 7

Ernie Shorter

Ernie Shorter was born in 1904 while his father was a superintendent at the old Hastings sawmill in Vancouver. The family lived near the corner of Gore Avenue and Main Street and his father could walk to work.

"When I reached school age, we moved out to the Grandview district where I attended Lord Nelson School," Ernie recalls.

The summer Ernie turned 12, his father gave him a job in the mill yard learning to tally and grade lumber. His pay was 10 cents an hour and he worked 12-hour days. The soldiers in the First World War were earning $1.20 a day, and most sawmills paid the same.

Each evening at nine his Dad would call him and they'd get into their big Maxwell touring car and drive home.

"We had a "Model T" before that, but the Maxwell was much more prestigious, the latest thing in style. Most of the foremen at the mill were real car buffs and were always trying to outdo each other. They were quite the guys, with bowler hats, colorful scarves, leather gloves, and driving goggles.

"Jack Reid, the head shipper, had a big two-toned McLaughlin with shiny wire wheels. Joe Vickers, the mill foreman, owned a jet black Stutz sedan, while Testy, my boss in the yard, drove a flashy Oakland Roadster. Vickers was a real character. He'd come to work in a black suit complete with bowler hat and bow tie. He strutted much like a bantam rooster, I thought, as he made his rounds of inspection."

The following summer—just a kid of 13—Ernie was put in charge of loading the scows and rail cars, and his daily pay was increased by 15 cents ($1.50 a day). His crew were mostly Chinese, but there were also Japanese, East Indians, and a few remittance men from England. This created an almost impossible language problem for young Ernie so he went to his Dad for advice.

"Why don't you just pick out a couple of your smartest young men and use them for interpreters?" his father suggested. When he did, things became a lot easier.

"I gave the orders and they passed them on to the Oriental crews. These two young Chinese fellows were with me until the last day I worked there. I never saw either of them again until I went to work at Chemainus some 30 years later."

Some of the sailing ships coming to load at the Hastings mill had such small hatches the longshoremen would have to make other openings. The longshore boss would say, "Ernie, go and get the saws and chisels." Then he would mark out a sizable square in the stern and proceed to cut that piece out. The longshoremen would put up a sloping ramp and use the winches to slide the big timbers through the opening, to be stowed below deck. When the ship finished loading, the crew would patch the opening, raise the sails, and head off across the Pacific. Some of the larger ships carried deck loads lashed down with heavy chains.

"One day I was busy taking inventory of the lumber stacked out in the mill yard when Dad came up and suggested a new and different system. He said, 'Before you start, head up each page with the different sizes of lumber. Then when you've finished your tally, everything will be segregated, and you'll be able to tell at a glance exactly what we have'." His Dad stayed to show him how. Ernie later used this system in a grading competition and won the B.C. championship.

The historic Hastings sawmill closed in 1928, the property was taken over by the Vancouver Harbour Board, and for the next eight years he worked for several sawmills. In 1936, Ernie was hired by the MacMillan Export Company, as yard foreman and shipper for their huge Alberni Pacific division at Port Alberni. He was promoted to superintendent four years later and updated the loading dock and put some new equipment in the sawmill.

"I used that same inventory system in all the different mills, and it was the secret of my success. If you know what you have in the yard, you can sell it."

Ernie had first met H.R. MacMillan at the Hastings sawmill, and each developed a great respect for the other. H.R. was placing orders with him as early as 1919 for his then new export company. H.R. would place the orders, but from then on, Ernie and VanDusen would straighten out the many details.

The Lumber Workers Industrial Union (L.W.I.U.) was becoming established in the big Chemainus mill. Shorter was concerned about the Alberni mills. John Humbird was the major shareholder of Victoria Lumber & Manufacturing, and he fought the unions tooth and nail. Tom Young, who was office manager recalls Humbird's reply when Joe Morris, spokesman for the union, asked for permission to hold a meeting at the recreation hall:

"No bloody way is any labor union ever going to hold a meeting in a company building as long as I'm here. Tom, you give him his pay cheque and tell him he's fired," Humbird shouted.

When John Humbird's grandfather came from California for V.L.& M.'s annual meeting, held in John's private office. As office manager, Tom Young was to record the minutes.

"The older Humbird was getting hard of hearing and it was almost like a shouting match. They weren't angry or anything; they just spoke loudly so that grandfather Humbird could hear and understand.

74

"Son," the old man cautioned, "the unions are here to stay so you must learn to work with them."

"There's no way anyone is going to tell me how to run this bloody sawmill," young John shouted. He stood up, and walked over to stare out the window toward the mill and the ship loading lumber.

"Well, son, the only alternative is to sell the whole damn outfit," his grandfather said.

Tom remembers John standing there, with his back toward them, for almost five long minutes. When he turned, his face was grim.

"Rather than put up with unions, I'd be agreeable to selling out," John said. It was an emotional moment.

"It wasn't long after this meeting that E.P. Taylor heard about the intended sale of Chemainus, and he offered Humbird $8 million cash for the V.L.& M. shares which included 100,000 acres of timberland. A long standing personal grudge existed between MacMillan and John Humbird because H.R. had once beaten him in getting a juicy timber contract in London.

"Though this deal was finally closed, I'm almost certain Humbird never suspected MacMillan had asked Taylor to deal for him," Tom Young said. "As far as the Humbirds were concerned, it was E.P. Taylor & Associates that bought Victoria Lumber & Manufacturing."

Tom chuckled, remembering: "When I carried that $8 million into the little bank up at the top of the hill, escorted by two burly policemen, I thought the bank manager might have a heart attack."

Joe Johannson was sent over by MacMillan Export to run the mill supposedly on a management basis for E.P. Taylor and his associates. Harry Berryman became manager after Johannson was promoted to head office in Vancouver as personnel manager.

Tom remembers that John Humbird stayed on in the manager's old house only for a couple of weeks. When Johannson took over, a gale blew up and rain poured down. He had to move his bed out into an upstairs hallway because the old roof was leaking so badly.

Garner Bros. Ltd. were building some new bunkhouses for the Copper Canyon camp at the time. I got a call at six on

Monday morning. Johannson wanted to see me before seven.

"Joe," he said, "you're going to start the roof this morning, I take it?"

"Well, don't you think we need some sort of a contract?" I asked.

"It's cost plus 10 per cent," Johannson declared, and we shook on the deal. "If we need a better contract, don't come to work," he said with a smile.

"That's dandy with me!"

Johannson kept Garner Bros. busy for months on that handshake. We had 12 men on the job by eight, and the new roof was completed before dark that same evening. Our crew even slid Johannson's bed back into the room where it belonged.

Some time after the takeover MacMillan showed up at the Chemainus mill office. The operation was not showing a decent profit and it was arranged to bring Ernie Shorter in as general manager of the whole operation, including logging.

The night Ernie arrived at Chemainus, the old Chinese bunkhouse burned to the ground. Next morning, when he went to inspect the damage, Ernie noticed one of the Chinese crew staring at him. It was Abu, his friend and interpreter from the old Hastings mill.

"I invited him to come and visit that evening. We chatted about old times, and I gave him a box of special candies. The strange thing is that I never saw him again, even though I went to Chinatown several times looking for him. 'Abu gone some place, no sabe where,' the old Chinese would say when I asked."

Ernie had been at Chemainus for only a couple of months when H.R. arrived and said, "Ernie, if you can't make this mill go, nobody can. I'm not at all happy with past results."

"I don't see anything wrong with this mill that can't be cured," Ernie assured him.

"Well, it's been losing money."

"We're just not getting the right type of logs to fill the lumber orders on hand," Ernie explained and the next day he and Tom Coates, the logging manager, made a trip through their operations at the Copper Canyon camp. After driving over the show, Ernie pointed out several stands of good fir timber suitable for the sawmill.

76

"The new pulp mill at Harmac in Nanaimo is almost finished, so all this small timber you are now logging can go there," he told Coates. Ernie also called Jack Sexton, head of log supply, and advised him not to take any more of their logs from Chemainus to the mainland. Not long after that, Ernie received a letter saying how very pleased MacMillan was that the mill was now showing a profit. To further reduce costs at Chemainus, they put in a new high-speed planer near the main sawmill with capacity enough to handle the biggest part of the sawmill's production. This was near the loading docks and eliminated a great deal of unnecessary and costly handling.

Ernie has another little claim to fame. He told me, "When those locomotives from Copper Canyon were being dismantled and sold for scrap, the brass bells came to me. The ladies of the church wanted the bells so they could ring them on Sundays. I was pleased to see them stay in Chemainus. If you go up in that church you'll see my name on a brass plaque. It just says, 'Thank you to E. G. Shorter'."

During Ernie's stay in Chemainus, the merger between MacMillan and Bloedel took place and made headlines in most of the major newspapers across Canada. The media declared the amalgamation created one of the largest lumber consortia in the world. At the beginning of 1952, Ernie was again promoted and moved back to Port Alberni to manage that huge, new complex. Charlie Dunham was the engineer in charge of the woods operation, and John Hemmingsen had just recently joined the company, and under Hemmingsen's supervision a start was made on better utilization of M & B timber.

On November 19, 1954 the Franklin River in flood washed out a bridge foundation. The locie, hauling loaded log cars onto the bridge, broke through and plunged into the river. Fireman Stan Malachowski was thrown into the frigid waters. In spite of heavy clothing he struggled to the nearest shore and scrambled to safety. Brakeman Ernie Erickson drowned in the locie, his heavy overalls jammed in a door. Engineer Ed Crosbie was later found dead on the beach in the Alberni Inlet.

Ernie told Hemmingsen, "John, take your suitcase and get down there. Don't bother coming back until you can show me how to get rid of the railroad and all those bridges, and put in a truck road."

"John was back several weeks later with a plan that short-ened the haul distance by 20 per cent and eliminated most of the trestles and bridges," Ernie remembers. "The storm that caused the train wreck actually triggered the end of all our logging railroads. This turned out to be one of the most profit-able and progressive moves ever undertaken by any of the MacMillan Bloedel logging divisions. Costs were reduced as much as 50 percent on the Franklin River log hauling.

For all these improvements, MacMillan always wanted more from his men. During this period, both Ernie and H.R. were at their summer homes at Qualicum Beach. They would visit almost every evening to chat and discuss business in general. Ernie had been doing some home repairs when H.R. strongly suggested that he should put in more time on his job and hire someone to work on his house. Ernie just shrugged and sug-gested that maybe someone else could produce better costs.

"H.R. put in some ungodly hours and expected his top men to do likewise, yet, he was one of the best fellows I ever worked for."

While Ernie was general manager of the Port Alberni div-ision, Wally Emmerson and Dan McIvor were the pilots of the aircraft which Shorter and MacMillan used on company busi-ness. It was a Grumman Goose. One day, Wally came to Ernie and Dan with a clipping from an American newspaper about five big Mars aircraft that were going to be sold for junk.

"You know, those would make great water bombers for fire protection," Emmerson suggested.

"I'll have a talk with our directors, and if they're interested we'll go down there and get a price on them," Ernie replied. They did, and after negotiating, they had the five Mars ferried to Patricia Bay Airport near Victoria.

Shortly after, Ernie received a call to say that a hurricane-force wind at Pat Bay had torn one of the aircraft loose from its moorage and smashed it beyond repair, but all the usable parts were salvaged.

Fairey Aviation was hired to outfit these aircraft for fire fighting. Ernie insisted they convert them one at a time, so that after testing they could benefit from any mistakes. A very wise decision. These fire fighters justified their cost. They proved to be the best in the world.

Because of his successful innovations and the good men he had working for him, Ernie Shorter worked his way to top management. When H. S. Berryman, president of MacMillan Bloedel, had a heart attack in 1956, Ernie was called to head office to take his place.

After retirement, Ernie and his wife, Irma, bought a home in White Rock, where they now live. They happily pursue their favorite hobby—gardening.

Ernie at the amalgamation dinner of MacMillan Bloedel and Powell River held in 1963 at the Hotel Vancouver.

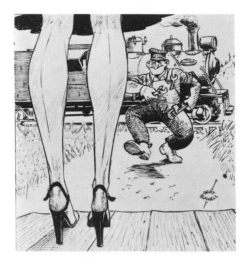

Pictures in this chapter shown by the kind permission
of Bob Swanson from his *Bunkhouse Ballads*.
Illustrations by Bert Bushell.

CHAPTER 8
Bob Swanson

STEAM ENGINES, TO WHISTLES, TO THE ROYAL HUDSON

Bob Swanson should be classed as a common sense genius.

His work with steam engines and whistles is world renowned. He's reputed to have been able to repair and keep running any steam engine he ever came across.

I first met Bob when he came to Chemainus in 1937. He asked me to do the fireplace and other brick work in his new home, and when I finished, he asked, "Joe, how would you like to take on the brickwork for the steam boilers down at the mill?"

"If the pay's good, I'll take it."

More than 50 years later we are still good friends and keep in touch. Bob is, and always has been, a man of his word.

During a visit in 1987, Bob reminisced about his early years.

CLIMAX COURAGEOUS
by Bob Swanson

It was out on a haywire, homeguard show
Where the ground was rough and the crew was slow;
Where a rusty, crooked railroad track
Wound out of camp past the rigger's shack.
Within that shack, in wedded bond,
Resided the rigger's wife—a blond
Who was wont to wave with a glint in her eye
At the engineer as he thundered by.
His ancient Climax, worn with years,
Would clash and clang its hypoid gears,
Shiver and shake and hump its back
As it wheeled those cars up the crooked track.

Now Dusty Dan, the engineer,
Was fond of women, wine, and beer,
But a fondness, still, excelled all these:
He'd tinker and toy on his bended knees
Down underneath, in the filth and stench,
And tighten up nuts with a monkey-wrench.
The Climax coughed like a horse with the heaves
Shedding its nuts like autumn leaves,
Till scattered along that right-o-way
Full many a bolt and pinion lay.
But at last one day, with her valve-stem slack,
She stalled in front of the rigger's shack.

Out piles Dan, as the Old Girl stalls,
Doffs his cap and his overalls,
And in he goes, as large as life,
To monkey-wrench for the rigger's wife.
The panting Climax, standing by,
Was shedding grease on the railroad tie.
And every day when the line was clear
Her air pump churned the atmosphere:
Till the ties in front of the rigger's shack
Were covered and coated with gear-grease black.
(And the Super learned from the office clerks
That the chief was fixing her water works.)

81

But out in the woods where the cables hum
The main-line had bust right close to the drum,
An empty landing, bleak and bare,
Greeted the train crew's dismal stare.
The loaders slept beside the grade,
While empty tongs in circles swayed
Above the empty cars, below,
Where loaded logs had ought to go.
The weary engineer leaned out
And harkened to the brakeman's shout:
"We'll wait for loads—so spot yer fire
And monkey wrench to yer heart's desire."

The breathing pulse of the air pump dies,
While Dusty Dan his art applies
Deep in the guts of her vital points,
A-wrenching the nuts of her flexible joints.
Like a monster wakes from a fitful dream
Her pistons throbbed the pulse of steam!
And Dusty Dan rolled down the bank
As he missed the grabs on her water tank.
Away she rolls, down the crooked track,
Shedding her nuts with her brake-shoes slack,
And gathering speed, with the switches lined,
She left the gaping crew behind.

As thunder rolls on a mountain ridge
The Climax crossed the Bear Creek bridge,
Her flanges screaming upon the rail
As she steered her course down the mountain trail.
While far to the rear in hot pursuit
Galloped the crew—with the Super to boot.
The brakeman said, as he cursed his luck,
"She'll pile in the weeds or she'll plunge in the chuck."
But an awful silence strains their ears,
No more is heard the clash of gears.
With her smoking wheels still on the track
She was stalled in front of the rigger's shack.

A natural story teller, he kept me entertained and laughing all evening.

"My family came out from England, with a short stay in South Africa, before arriving in British Columbia. We settled in East Wellington, near Nanaimo. Danny, my older brother, was born in South Africa and my family gave him the middle name of Africanus. Danny became a well known logger, mostly because he could write poetry. He could cuss for 15 minutes non stop without using the same word twice."

A little locomotive ran out past the Swanson family home in North Wellington, on a narrow gauge track. Young Bob was fascinated with this railroad from the time he could walk. Its locie was a little dinky thing that came from a New York elevated railway. Bob was three years old when the engineer took him on his first train ride.

"My old man gave me a walloping for it, but by God, it was worth it. Some people won't believe I rode that train at such a young age, but I'll swear an oath to it."

Bob was venturesome, crawling inside barrels and pretending they were steam boilers. He got into a beer barrel once and couldn't get out. His Dad tried to lift the hoops off but couldn't, so he had to cut them off. When the barrel spread open, Bob popped out and his old man picked him up and gave him a good shaking.

"Look at what you've done, you've spoiled a perfectly good barrel, you little so-and-so," and he grabbed a broken stave and paddled his backside.

When he was twelve, he spent his summer holidays helping his Dad build chimneys in Nanaimo and also helped clean and repair the boilers at the Jingle Pot coal mines. Bob's father had a contract to do the brickwork and boilers for Strait's Lumber Company at Nanoose Bay, so growing up to love trains and steam engines was only natural.

As a teenager his first job was firing a steam donkey in East Wellington, and then helping repair engines in the shop. Soon he had put in enough extra firing time to get his 'Donkey Special'. At night he looked after the mill boiler to get the time needed for his fourth class steam papers. Steam whistles always fascinated him. In 1926, while working at the Boulder Creek mill near Nanaimo Lakes, Pete Inkster, the boss, needed a whistle for the mill and asked Bob to build it. This was like handing a penniless kid a double decker ice cream cone on a hot summer day. There happened to be a young machinist at the mill who was making up blower pipes for the planer mill.

"These pipes were pretty heavy, and I thought, by God, these would be strong enough to build a mill whistle out of. So we riveted them together and about ten o'clock that night I climbed up onto the boiler room roof and connected this invention to a steam pipe. When I had climbed back down to the ground with the whistle wire in my hand, the machinist wanted to try it. He gave the wire several pulls—clouds of steam belched into the air. Anyone within five miles must have heard the roar," and Bob Swanson laughed.

Jack Miller, one of the owners, arrived quickly with 40 Chinese with axes, shovels, and buckets of water, ready to do fire battle.

"If we ever do have a fire the crew will sure know about it," Bob said and jerked the wire for a couple of extra blasts which were so loud they echoed from one mountain to another.

Bob stayed on as engineer when Nanaimo Lumber took over Number Three Mill at Boulder Creek. This mill was originally owned by John Coburn who sold it to investors from Chicago. Lassiter and Shelby Saunders came out to run it. Bob was away from the steam plant on donkey repairs when they had a major blowout. The mill and woods crews were laid off until the new parts arrived to repair the boiler and broken pipes. He knew it would take a month to get things going again so he quit and was off to Vancouver to find a new job. They did things that way in those days.

He spent a couple of days hanging around the loggers' hiring halls on Water and Carrall and read on the job board on the third morning that they were advertising for a man to run 'duplex on a boom'. "When I inquired, the guy said, 'You ever run duplex on a boom'?"

"No, but I can soon learn." Wrong answer. An experienced fellow got that job, but took Bob aside and gave him some advice he would always remember.

"If you're worried about a job," he said, "just tell them you've been working at Cowichan Lake Camp Six. The foreman, his name is Peck, Bert Peck."

That afternoon another job for a duplex operator was listed. Bob went to the desk, and he was asked, "Yuh ever run duplex?"

"Yup".

"Where?"

"Camp Six Cow Lake."

"Who's the foreman?"

"Bert Peck."

"That's all I need to know. Sign here."

He handed Bob an envelope, then stamped "FARE ADVANCED" on the back of his hand. The next boat for Nanaimo had Bob aboard, on the way to Port Alberni to run duplex on a boom.

"I met this big bruiser that was the foreman. He showed me the bunkhouse and where to find the machine. Just before dark I went out and turned on the steam to try everything out. 'I can handle this,' I said to myself."

On this type of log loader, the operator has one lever in each hand and a third strapped to his leg to swing the boom. It was probably one of the most cantankerous and dangerous pieces of equipment for a steam engineer to operate. Next morning they started loading a rail car. Two small logs were placed one on each side of the bunks. Then the tong men put two cable straps around a 40 foot log about seven feet in diameter. As Swanson picked it clear it swung too far over the car. He started to lower the monster and it tipped one side of the rail car up off the steel. Everyone was hollering and giving hand signals but Bob ignored them, turned off the steam, and let the engine just ker-chug, ker-chug, ker-chug back, until the car settled down on the track again. The boss ran over, tapped him on the shoulder and grinned, "Jesus, you sure have run a duplex before."

"That's why I'm here," Swanson replied calmly.

The loading crew had tested him. That size log should never have been picked up until the new operator had four or five hours to get the feel of the machine. A man needed nerves of steel to run a duplex. Both engines have to go forward or reverse at the same speed, and if they don't an inch cable can snap like a piece of thread and someone could be killed. One wrong move could mean death to the tong men.

They loaded 14 cars that first day, but from then on they put out 24 to 26 carloads. These China Creek logs went by rail to the sawmill in Port Alberni. About two weeks later, the superintendent told Bob the mill at Nanaimo was fixed and they wanted him back.

"You're a pretty good man. I hate to lose you. Before you go I'd like you to work with our donkey puncher Eddie Hodges. He needs help to put in some boiler tubes."

They finished the job the next day by noon and Eddie said, "You should get your first-class donkey ticket. You sure know what you're doing."

"You think a better ticket would do me some good?" Bob asked.

"Sure won't do you any harm."

They shook hands and Bob left for the Nanaimo Lumber Company. He did some donkey-doctoring for a week, then headed south to Mile 35 on the Canadian National line to be the mill engineer for Kapoor. Bob worked for three different outfits that week, putting in seven ten-hour days. That's how they got experience in those days and there was no need to be out of work. When Kapoor closed for snow that winter, Swanson went over to Vancouver and worked for the McNair Shingle Mill looking after their steam boilers. He went back to work for Kapoor in the spring, but didn't stay long.

"When I was trying to get in enough time for my first-class steam ticket, brother Danny would get me out of bed at four, make breakfast, and send me off to work. It was a four-mile walk, but all three donkeys would be steamed up when the crews came at 7:30 a.m."

When the shift finished and the weather was hot, Bob would stay to cool the boilers and act as fire watchman. It would be after 10 o'clock when he got home those nights, but his steam time was building.

One machine was a Washington skidder. Its boiler was built in 1918 and carried 170 pounds of steam. Some forty years later, Bob salvaged this old boiler and moved it to Fort Steele where it's still carrying 170 pounds and operating a steam locie as a tourist attraction.

Swanson, in 1936, was the youngest First Class Steam Engineer to operate. Ken Alexander was younger but never did anything with his ticket. He went to the machine shop at Chemainus and stayed there as foreman.

Bob was chief engineer for the Port Mellon pulp mill on Howe Sound when they had a 400-pound steam boiler. He then moved on to the Consolidated Mining Company at Princeton. From there he applied for the position of Chief Engineer for Chemainus. John Humbird told him the job was his. It became Bob's responsibility to check the hog fuel barges.

"Humbird had me measuring the barges that were going to Port Angeles. A complaint came in about the units of hog fuel being less than the billings. Humbird called me and said, 'You get down there and check those barges immediately, and do it right.' I was so confident I answered,

"Mr Humbird, you know that my measure will have to stand."

"'Well, get down there and check it again. You know it shakes down a bit, so make allowances for that. I want to win this one.'"

"I drove like mad to Victoria and arrived in time to see the Canadian Pacific Railway boat pulling away from the wharf. That was some predicament! I called Harold Elworthy of Island Tug and Barge and he arranged for a seaplane to take me to Vancouver. There I chartered a wheel plane to Seattle and took the bus from there to Port Angeles. I arrived about the same time as the hog fuel barges, and started to re-measure, using a 100-foot steel tape. Four university boys came aboard and began measuring (checking) with a piece of brown hay bailing cord with markers tied on it every 10 feet. I watched a while, had a good look at their figures, and told them what they were doing wrong. They were not allowing for the crown of the load from the edges to the centre. I told them to take the averages, not the stanchion height. They had to agree I was right. That made my quantity dead on. I also suggested their measuring string might stretch longer in dry weather.

"When I told Humbird this he just growled, 'Damn good thing you were right.'

"Later he called me into his office, 'Heard you missed the boat in Victoria'.

"Yeh, just by a few minutes, Mr Humbird."

"'Well, just what would you have done if you hadn't been able to get a plane to Vancouver?'"

"Had it all figured out. I was gonna hire a rowboat and row the 21 miles."

"'You're the kind of man I like.'

"Humbird smiled and patted me on the back. I believe he was the toughest egg I've ever worked for."

While he was at Chemainus, Swanson designed and built a huge mill whistle. Wally Emblem did the welding at his home at Saltair. Most mill whistles have two-inch steam pipes, but the one at Chemainus needed a four-incher and it was the biggest whistle in Canada. It weighed more than a ton. Bob's brother Dan helped hoist the giant whistle onto the roof of the boiler room. This was on May 10, 1940. At first it didn't sound so loud because they kept the valve way down. But each day Bob opened it up just a little so people gradually got used to it. Humbird never did mention the whistle, but 47 years later it is still in Chemainus and blowing the starting and stopping whistles every day in the new mill.

Bob said, "It's a wonder Humbird let me get away with it. Guess the only reason he didn't fire me was because he was kinda tone deaf. Dan really liked that big whistle so he proceeded to dedicate a poem to it."

DEDICATION POEM

Oh, you three-belled chime a'nestling in the shadow
   of yon smokestack
You have boomed the hour of twelve again to-day
To a microscopic fraction, I have chorded all
   your vocals,
You're a work of art, I'd say
You're the nonpareil from Mexico to Nome
And when Gabriel blows his trumpet and the world's
   last shadows fade,
May your almighty volume blast down Heaven's dome.

Bob Swanson had the poem and Danny's name cast on a brass plate mounted on the whistle.

"Education was never very important to me; I thought the

only thing was to be a good mechanic. When a government job as boiler inspector was offered, I found a university degree was required. The chief inspector came over from Vancouver to Chemainus to offer me this position. He let me know I could go to university and get my degree. Enough spare time would be arranged for me to do this, so with some help from our MLA, George Pearson, the final papers were signed.

"The inspector's salary was $240 a month, $35 less than I had been earning. Humbird heard I was leaving and offered me $290 a month. I decided to turn down his offer and go for my degree. Then I was told that the government had a substantial travel expense account which was available to me. For the next two years I attended UBC, and in 1942 I became a professional engineer.

"In my day you seldom heard of people from the mining or milling communities getting a higher education. A good logger didn't need that because they usually started to work young. By the time I was 18 years old I could tend hook, head load, top trees or run a steam donkey.

"With my new engineer's degree and all the practical experience behind me, I found if you had a flair for teaching, it wasn't difficult. When I lectured to engineering students at UBC it was mainly on the advantages of the new diesel over the old steam engines."

As well as his steam engineering, Bob has a whistle farm near Nanaimo.

"When we first started designing whistles up there, some big orders came in from England. One company wanted their whistles tested before they were dismantled for shipment. To do this we needed a steam boiler, so I borrowed an old steam threshing machine from a farmer and headed up the Nanaimo Lakes road. The sparks and flames were coming out of the stack and were making quite a show in the dusk."

Crown Zellerbach boss Joe Cliff saw this show and parked his pickup truck crosswise in the narrow road.

"You're not going any further with that! We're not having one of those goddam things on this claim. You'll set the whole bloody woods on fire," Cliff shouted.

"What am I going to do? I have tests to do that require steam."

Joe would have done anything to get that contraption off the road, and said, "Hell, we'll give you a boiler. There's one at the top end of Second Lake. Danny will show it to you."

With the thresher parked in a gravel pit, they went off in Joe's pickup to look at the boiler. It looked okay but it took a couple of days to get steam up using wood.

"At the whistle farm we have living quarters, and my daughter likes to come over to do the cooking. We often have visitors from all parts of the world. For instance, Captain Brown of the U.S. Coast Guard once spent a week here testing foghorns. He said there was nowhere he knew that could compare with this place. The U.S. Navy wanted their whistles crated as parts so they could assemble them on the site.

"We made special foghorns for those big oil drilling platforms. All the tests were done here. We calibrated the sounds and the amount of steam or compressed air they required. We have all this data on file here at our whistle farm. The Amtrack people from Washington, D.C. came to test and adjust for different chords. We ended up making all their train whistles.

"This idea of a whistle farm just grew from nothing into a world wide business. I designed and made hundreds of whistles. The Canadian and British railways use our designs. We manufacture in Vancouver, England, and New York, and test the tones and volumes between the two high mountains on opposite sides of the Nanaimo River valley.

"One special and interesting assignment was the whistle for Engine 374. Engine 374 was the first transcontinental engine to arrive in Vancouver, way back when, and the committee wanted the whistle to sound the same as it had 100 years earlier. The old engine for '374' was being rebuilt at the Burrard Shipyards in North Vancouver. This is where we also overhauled the whistles. Its steam boiler was more than 100 years old and not capable of carrying steam enough even with extensive repairs. We had a meeting with the committee.

"They were unanimous the steam had to be seen coming out of the whistle. We located a small automatic electric boiler which would make enough steam to blow the whistle and we put this device in the tender and hooked it up to an automatic switch with a timer. Using this arrangement the whistle could blow every ten minutes, every half hour, or whenever they wanted just by adjusting the timer. We had fixed the original whistle so it sounded and looked exactly as it did a century ago."

Bob did a test to find how much steam the various whistles used, and which sounded the best. He and his associates used flow meters and various instruments on all the steam pipes. They blew all the whistles they could get their hands on.

The old whistle from the Number One Mine at Nanaimo was chosen by the committee as having the best sound. The next best whistle was one from the Western Fuel Mine in Nanaimo, also more than a century old.

The whistle farm, located among mountains, is perfect for giving echoes they can measure. The farm, encircled by young Douglas fir trees, is a fitting resting place for the old donkey sleigh and boiler. Few would recognize the old shed, with whistle horns stuck up on frames, as a site for testing and designing whistles and foghorns used worldwide.

During the Second World War, Bob Filberg, manager of Sitka Spruce Logging, drafted Bob Swanson from his job as boiler inspector. Spruce logging had the highest priority because the wood was perfect to build Mosquito high speed bombers. Filberg chartered a float plane and Bob left for the Queen Charlotte Islands to inspect and repair the steam engines. He made a list and phoned Filberg in Vancouver for the parts. Most of the parts were sent up on the next boat, and the boilermakers worked double shifts. They had most of the equipment working when Filberg arrived a week later.

"We need you to stay up here."

"I'd like to do that, but what are you going to pay?" Swanson asked.

"Don't worry about that. I told you once, I'll see you are properly looked after."

"Okay, I'll leave that to you, but remember, we'll have to work practically day and night to keep these haywire machines running."

"I know damn well you will," Filberg agreed.

Five locomotives, 43 boats and 38 steam donkeys all needed repairs, some major. Filberg set Swanson up with a salary of $750 a month, plus board and travel expenses. That was a phenomenal wage in 1943. No one had ever been paid that much, but Filberg, as president of Aero Timber and a dollar-a-year man during most of the war knew a top man's value.

Swanson stayed in the Charlottes until just before the war ended then went back to work as the government's boiler inspector, starting in April. A political argument arose about the man who had replaced Bob. Bob suggested the government keep both of them on until the end of the year, then make the decision as to which would be senior.

Herbert Anscomb, then finance minister, approved both salaries and asked Bob why he was asking for competition.

"Competition? I didn't know I had any," Bob replied with a smile. At year's end, Swanson was chosen senior inspector.

Shortly after the war ended, Gerry Wellburn was again working on his logging museum at Duncan. Bob knew where all the old logging donkeys and locomotives were and what shape they were in. Gerry asked Bob if he would help. Swanson's brother, Blondie, ran the camp for Wellburn, so it was easy for Bob to visit to do the inspecting and keep the old machines coming in.

In the late 1940's, Bob was put in charge of the Vancouver wharves. The Harbour Commission was in trouble with the longshoremen's union and couldn't get trained men. Bob's office was used to train longshoremen to become railroad people. These union men were told that if they passed the exams they would get operator certificates to run the yard locies. At first they didn't believe this, but when a couple of them passed, the atmosphere changed and he got the cooperation he needed. Bob operated on the belief that if you lived up to your word, and were a bit tough, you could usually get along with most union men.

His ingenuity was further demonstrated in 1956 when the old Pacific Great Eastern, renamed B.C. Rail, was extending its tracks north of Quesnel. It was 30 degrees below zero and the railway wanted to lay a mile of track a day. This wasn't being done because there was no way to get rid of the empty cars after the rails had been unloaded.

"They put me in charge. We rented a shipyard in North Vancouver and hired an old 'car-knocker' from Chemainus. His name was Klaus Willing and he had built disconnecting rail cars for logging. We built 39 disconnecting cars for this job.

Two sets of wheels were spaced about 30 feet apart on the tracks, then loaded with the rails, which were cinched tightly to both sets of wheels. As the steel rails were laid down and the cars emptied, the boom on the locie could lift one set of wheels at a time and set them off on the side of the track. Then another load was moved up to the locie. We loaded at night and started each day with 10 to 12 carloads of rails. I gave the orders from the front end of the train and we laid a mile of track the first day. The ties were placed first, then the rails, spikes, and track bolts with plates came next. We completed a mile of track every day even though the weather stayed at 30 below or worse. Goddam cold it was, and the road master, section foreman, and I always ate our frozen lunch by a fire out on the job. These men could tell by just looking if the track was out of line."

Bob reminisced about other good men he'd known. Some he worked with, some worked under him, and some were just friends:

"Len Harding did a good job in the Charlottes. On Vancouver Island there was Dave Miles, who bossed the woods for Mayo Lumber for years. Died of cancer in Ladysmith. Lem Traer, a good high rigger, was super for Hillcrest Lumber at Cowichan Lake. Lem is living in Vancouver and must be about 90 years now. Another is Bruce King, an engineer. I knew his old Dad when I was a little kid. He surveyed our farm for us.

"Joe Cliff, he bossed for Comox Logging and made me park the old threshing machine on the side of the Nanaimo Lakes Road. He built the first banjo-head portable steel spar at Nanaimo Lakes for Comox Logging.

"Mauno Pelto was high rigging when he was only 16. Later he worked for Comox Logging and started some of the first salvage logging. Walter Laidlaw, an engineer, was a pretty good location man. He worked for me. Lived down along the beach in Chemainus.

"That's only a few of them. Mostly all good fellows. They'd give you the shirt off their back."

Bob Swanson is well known for his logging poetry, *Rhymes of a Western Logger*, but his real love is steam trains and whistles. It's only fitting we complete the Swanson story as we started it, with one of Bob's poems.

THE CAT-SKINNER'S PRAYER

I've shivered and shook on a Dozer
  I've ranted, and raved, and I've cu'sed.
My kidneys are dislocated
  And I've swallowed ten bushels of dust;
My fingers are broken and bleeding
  From wielding the tools of repair.
O God of Internal Combustion,
  Please answer a cat-skinner's prayer!

Now, I've studied your parts-book Bible
   And here are the things I require:
A pair of unstretchable cat-tracks
   That will never "come off" in the mire;
But the thing that would tickle my fancy,
   When I'm miles from the fuel supply,
Is a tank, for both gas and for diesel,
   Of the type that will never run dry.

Oh, send your toil-worn disciple,
   Who has gobbled and swallowed your smoke,
A heaven-invented fuel pump
   That will fire on every stroke,
A set of perfected injectors
   With guts that will never wear.
O God of Internal Combustion,
   Please answer a cat-skinner's prayer!

Please send me the grease of perfection
   And a change of eternal oil,
Some diamond bearinged cat-rolls
   That will run in abrasive soil,
A final-driving assembly
   With everlasting gears,
And a set of sleeves and pistons
   That will run for a million years.

Oh send me the lining, immortal,
   For my steering-clutch mechanism,
And a cranking-motor magneto
   With permanent magnetism;
A set of valves and tappets
   At which I will never swear.
Oh God of Internal Combustion,
   Please answer a cat-skinner's prayer!

Great God of the Red-Hot Piston,
I have worshipped and served you well,
Forsaking the Gods of my fathers,
'Till my soul has been slated for Hell!
If you'll send me the things that I ask for
I will never work Sundays again;
But I'll worship Internal Combustion
Forever and ever. Amen.

Bob's whistle farm in 1988, located just west of Second Lake, off Crown Zellerbach's logging road southwest of Nanaimo. The whistle horns are facing the mountains to the north where the echoes bounce back to check tone and clarity.

John Ulinder was born in 1907. Picture taken
in the 1950's.

CHAPTER 9

John Ulinder

A BULLBUCKER'S OPINION

John Ulinder was born in Sweden and was brought to B.C.
when he was two. The family settled on a small farm at Mission
in the Fraser Valley, near an uncle. John's father, a carpenter,
died when a scaffolding collapsed while he was working in
Vancouver.

"Mother was left in the city with three small children. She
took in washing and did housework to keep food on the table,"
John remembers.

During the Spanish Flu epidemic of 1918-1919, the family
came down with the dreaded disease and his mother died. The
orphans went to live with an uncle in Vancouver and attended
John Oliver School.

At age 14, John was eager to be independent. His uncle in the Fraser Valley took on a falling contract for Keystone Logging, and this was young John's first try at falling and bucking. The following year, he and his uncle cut shingle bolts on the mountain east of Port Coquitlam on contract. They used hand tools: axes, spring boards, eight-foot falling saws, a seven-foot bucking saw, steel wedges and two heavy sledge hammers.

Pounding the wedges to topple the huge trees was tiring work. In their blacksmith's shop there was a 20-ton jack he and his father had used to lift and level an old two-storey building. John got an idea to try lifting the tree with this jack instead of pounding those wedges. They cut into the stump below the back cut, split out the slab of wood, set the jack in place, then used a three-foot bar to turn the jack and lift the back side of the tree. With all that pressure, the cut opened and the tree fell exactly where they wanted it. They would put two steel wedges in the back cut on either side of the jack, and keep them tapped in tightly to be safe and help guide the tree as it fell.

The big cedars were bucked into 52-inch lengths, then split into bolts that averaged about 30 pieces to the cord. The bolts were hauled to the shingle mill on a skid road using long narrow sleighs pulled by horses. John stayed with the shingle bolt cutting for several months, 10 hours a day, seven days a week, but became so exhausted he looked around for an easier way to make a living.

In Vancouver he applied for a banking job and was told he had to take a special course. When he completed it, the manager offered him $8 a week for the first year, with a possible raise in the second year. He tried it for two months and found it was impossible to live on such low wages, so he quit.

He signed on with the Canadian Government Merchant Marine, making his first trip on a lumber freighter bound for Australia, wages were $30 a month with board. The first stop was in North Queensland, where they put off a big part of the lumber, then to Sydney to finish the unloading. There they took on a cargo of wool, mutton and other goods, and were back in Vancouver five months later.

The early 1920's were bad times. Few jobs were around, so John signed on a lumber freighter for a trip to Japan. Some miles outside Yokohama they encountered a typhoon with winds of more than 100 miles an hour, on September 4, 1923. The engineers had to stand at the throttles and shut off the engines every time the ship heaved enough for the propeller to come out of the water. When they could see into the harbor it was a mass of smoke and flames—the big earthquake had happened the day before.

The ship was ordered to stand off the harbor and go on to Kobe for unloading. Except for the glare of burning buildings, Yokohama was in darkness. The smoke and dust hanging over the whole area was so dense the sun was obliterated for days.

"Before our return cargo was loaded, martial law was declared and we were confined to the ship. The wind, blowing down the coast from Tokyo and Yokohama, carried the sickening stench of burned bodies. It kept most of the crew vomiting over the side of the ship. This was a terrible experience. That quake caused the world's greatest loss of life ever in a single day.

"It had been one hell of a rough trip," he concluded, when he got home.

He went back to the woods, worked on the rigging for a while, and did many different jobs and soon was experienced enough to handle a rigging slinger's job at Rock Bay, just north of Campbell River.

John left Rock Bay the following spring with a buddy, intending to go to Alaska on a falling contract. They'd heard the wages were much higher in the north. They arrived at Prince Rupert on May 1, to be told that the next boat for Alaska would not leave until after May 15.

"My partner did some asking around and found that meals would cost a dollar or more apiece and that we had to have our own blankets. We talked it over and decided to go to the Queen Charlottes instead. At the last minute, my buddy heard it was going to be a real rough boat trip crossing Hecate Strait and he chickened out, so I went on alone."

The trip across was one of the roughest, as the old *Prince John* rolled all night and did everything but turn upside down. Most everyone was seasick. John helped the stewards lash down the tables and chairs in the dining room.

He bought his ticket to Kelly's Logging camp on Louise

Island where Gary Robbins was the superintendent. He put John bucking wood for a steam donkey, and asked if he would file saws on weekends and evenings. John was paid 75 cents for filing a saw and made up to $140 a month extra by doing a job he liked. He was a good filer, and is one of the few men left on the coast who has the tools and know-how to properly sharpen an old crosscut saw. John stayed in that camp until Christmas before going to Vancouver for a logger's wing ding.

The party over, he was recalled to the Queen Charlottes, and was offered free passage on the *Nora Jane* if he would serve as deckhand and take his turn at the wheel. She was a well built 65-footer and Kelly Logging used her for towing and as a camp tender. The skipper, hung over after partying all night, took her out of Vancouver Harbour, then called John to do the steering.

"Need some sleep. Keep her on course and wake me at Squirrel Cove up there north of Powell River," and headed for his bunk.

John looked in on the sleeping captain as they passed the north end of Texada Island, but he didn't stir when called. It was a moonlit night and the tide was half flood so John took her through the Eucletaw Rapids and into Labouchere Passage. It was breaking day before the skipper came into the wheelhouse.

"Where the hell are we?" he asked, rubbing his eyes.

"Just across from Kelsey Bay," John said, pointing to the spot on the chart.

"Why didn't you call me earlier?"

"Nobody could wake you up," John said, and left to have breakfast and get some sleep.

The captain took the ship out into heavy weather, past Pine Island and on into the Inside Passage. Just past the south end of Banks Island, he nosed the *Nora Jane* out into Hecate Strait. It was snowing heavily with a north wind and a big sea running. Half an hour out was enough of that. They were taking such a pounding that the skipper turned back to the shelter of Captain's Cove and anchored for the night. Next morning the snow had stopped but the seas were running 15 to 20 feet. It was too rough to even make coffee. The crew tried hardtack and couldn't keep it down, headed for the rail and 'fed the fishes'. It

100

took 12 hours to cross and reach shelter at Sandspit. John got off at the Louise Island camp, and stayed there for another 15 months without going to town. Back in Vancouver, economic conditions had worsened.

"You couldn't buy a job, but you could get a good meal for a quarter," John remembers.

"I had $2,000 in the bank, and decided to take a course in accounting at Pitman's Business College. I was 25 and I've never regretted the time or money spent. It has been useful, especially in scaling, timekeeping, and cost estimates."

John applied his newly acquired knowledge to his bank account, and decided he could afford a trip to the World Fair at Chicago. He returned to Vancouver in the fall with $12 and went straight to Black's hiring office where he was offered a job second loading at Elk Bay, north of Campbell River. Tom Coates was the side push there, and John worked for him. John would work for him again many years later at Copper Canyon, where Tom would give him his first bullbucking job.

John became a member of the L.W.I.U. (Lumber Workers Industrial Union) in 1934, and that same year was involved in the union's first strike. The union was asking for an increase in wages.

"Some camps on the coast were already paying the 10 cents-an-hour increase. I was working for B.C. Pulp and Paper at Quatsino Sound. We were considered a fair camp because we were already getting the raise, so we were allowed to work if we chipped in a day's pay now and then to keep the union going. It took almost four months for things to settle so everybody would get the 10 cents-an-hour raise. That was considered a substantial increase in those days.

"I still remember at Halfway River camp, on Quatsino Sound, when the organizers came there on a gas boat to sign up the crew. The manager wouldn't allow the boat to tie up. It was a floating camp so a couple of our men held the bow and stern lines while the union organizers spoke to the workers from a few feet out from the float and signed up most of the crew. The loggers just stretched out a hand toward the boat with money for dues and received their union cards. There was a lot of resentment towards the unions by management, yet they found ways of getting into the camps.

"I can see Reg Pringle, who later had a real estate and insurance business in Ladysmith, holding on to that stern rope even now. I still kid him about it.

"I remember my first hard hat when I was falling at Rock Bay in the spring of 1937. An eastern Canada salesman was in the camp showing the benefits and he gave me one. The compensation board made a ruling a few years later, and hard hats became mandatory as a safety precaution. There was no compensation coverage after that if you were hurt while not wearing one."

John remembers starting for Comox Logging at Ladysmith in 1940 as a head faller, about two years before the first power saws were used there. The first Stihl saw was brought in, in the fall of 1942. A company started manufacturing the Barnette power saw in the United States in 1943. Then came the Mercury, I.E.L., and the Homelite. The first power saws were heavy, two-man machines, and it took a while to get the old hand fallers to accept these noisy contraptions. Some very heated arguments arose about fallers' rates when power saws first came on the job. Those first saws came out with four, five and six-foot bars and chains to match. For the first couple of years they were used only for falling, and seven-foot hand crosscut saws were used to buck the trees into log lengths. It was all piece work and good crews made up to $12 a day, not much different from hand falling rates until the war ended in 1945. Once the power machines were improved for one man bucking, the cutting rates changed and $1 a thousand was considered high. Fallers in 1972 were put on a wage of $84 a day and the productivity per gang dropped by half. Contractors are again taking over and being paid on production.

When the Ladysmith camp closed for fire season early in the spring of 1944, Copper Canyon camp was ready to start logging. Tom Coates, the manager, asked John to bring his gang there.

"We're in virgin timber, and we'll probably fall right on through fire season," Coates explained. "We could use a dozen good gangs to get some timber ahead. How many can you bring with you?"

"I'll let you know tomorrow," and he rounded up 10 three-men sets. Most of these fallers went back to Comox after the fire season ended but John stayed with Copper Canyon for the next 27 years as a scaler, then bullbucker, in charge of all the timber cutters there from May 1945 to the spring of 1971.

"I was bossing 96 men and had six scalers, two saw filers, and a power saw mechanic. We hired Olaf Fedgie in 1944 to train the fallers at Copper Canyon. Then I was promoted to falling bucking superintendent for all MacMillan Bloedel camps. I spent two years at it. I enjoyed the travelling and seeing all the different logging methods, and especially when I helped Angus McBean with their tree planting."

MacMillan Bloedel had five Quonset huts 50 feet wide and 220 feet long for raising 2,400,000 seedlings in 1985. "Temperatures in the huts are controlled by computers. If the weather gets too hot, screens automatically come up on the sunny side. They have special cooling systems, and spraying machines that work the full length of the hut—all automatic and computer controlled. A special automatic machine puts each seedling tree into a fertilized container and they can package over four million per year."

Because of his years in the Charlottes, John Ulinder was asked to make a submission on the Lyell Island-Haida Indian controversy. The following are some excerpts from John's submission to the Wilderness Advisory Committee of British Columbia on January 14, 1986 regarding the park and tourist potential on Lyell Island versus timber harvesting:

"... My first trip to the Queen Charlottes was aboard the old *Prince John* in May of 1926. I worked for Kelly Logging at their Lockport camp, directly west of Lyell Island near the main Moresby Island, for five years as a head faller and timber cruiser.
... In 1971 and 1972 I inspected and cruised these same areas for MacMillan Bloedel. Most of the areas, where we had logged 40 years earlier, had either been relogged or were being harvested for the second crop of trees. Those islands are the fastest growing timber sites in British Columbia.
... During the summer it can be reasonably safe for pleasure boats to cross Hecate Strait. Unpredictable winter storms make it very hazardous for anything less than a 60-foot boat with an experienced captain and crew aboard for other seasons. Another hazard for tourists, during the spring and summer months, is the hordes of mosquitos, black flies and horse flies—not to mention the swarms of deer flies that actually take a piece out of you when they bite."

John working on a road with 1927 model Fordson tractor, using an old-fashioned hand-scraper. Picture taken on Vancouver Island in the early 1930's.

John closed his submission by simply stating he believed Lyell Island would be much more useful and pleasant if the old, decadent trees were harvested and replaced by planting a healthy new forest. However, the politicians, both federal and provincial, saw fit to stop the logging on Lyell Island and declare it a park.

John feels that the main loser was Frank Beban Logging Company and the men who worked for them. Even Jack Webster on his Vancouver television program agreed with John's concept. While young Frank Beban was supervising the shutdown and moving his heavy equipment off Lyell Island, he died from a massive heart attack. Whether the attack was caused by stress and frustration can only be surmised. In any event, British Columbia lost one of its most progressive and efficient loggers.

In direct conflict with the logging concept represented by John Ulinder is the Island Protection Society's Don Plum. He summed up the environmentalists' presentation by assuring the Wilderness Advisory Committee that during the Ice Ages on the North American continent no ice sheets had ever reached the Queen Charlotte Islands. That is what makes the South Moresby group so unique, and why it should be saved.

The conflicts between loggers and environmentalists will continue, and there will always be issues like Lyell Island.

John and Maisie were married in Vancouver and in 1939 moved to Ladysmith on Vancouver Island. They believed it would be a better place to bring up their two children. Their son and daughter finished highschool in Ladysmith and went on to college.

John is presently very involved with senior citizens, and is a past-president of their local chapter. He also takes an active part in politics. He and his wife live in a comfortable home overlooking the harbor and are enjoying their flowers and retirement. John can usually find time to play poker with his old logger friends.

Ken Hallberg in his working togs.

CHAPTER 10

Ken Hallberg

Ken Hallberg's family was of Swedish descent, his grandfather coming in 1883 to settle on a small cattle ranch near Springfield, Illinois. Ken's father, Frank, was born on February 9, 1890. His mother's ancestors farmed in Ontario before moving west to a homestead near Winnipeg where his mother Lily was born in 1894. Frank and Lily homesteaded in Alberta for several years.

Ken was born on July 4, 1914, on Vancouver Island, not far from the north end of Ladysmith Harbour in the Cedar district. There were three boys, Cliff, the eldest, then Ken and Archie.

Ken was an infant when his Dad took a job working for Matt Hemmingsen, who was logging on the west side of Cowichan Lake. The family moved to a float house at Wardroper Bay.

A short-handled pike pole was Ken's first contact with any kind of logging equipment. His mother stepped out onto the narrow porch of their float-house to get some stove wood, and saw her son, face down, bobbing in the water. She snatched the pike pole from its pegs on the wall, snagged the hook into Ken's diaper, and hauled him out onto the porch. Picking him up by his feet, she gave him some hefty shakes to get the water out of his lungs.

Ken's Dad was logging foreman in 1927 at the Hemmingsens' camp and when it closed down for fire season he stayed on as watchman and took a contract to build the new sleigh for their Empire skidder. There were no schools near the camp so Lily and the two younger boys lived in Vancouver, but during the summer holidays they came to stay with their Dad and help him build this huge sleigh. The two main skids were 56 feet long and 40 inches thick at the small ends. Their older brother Cliff was punking whistles at Camp Six and he joined them when that camp closed. On Sundays the boys and their Dad would pack a lunch and head off to hunt grouse, pick berries, or sometimes prospect for gold and fish along the Nitinat River.

When the new sleigh was finished they cut wood and gathered bark to get steam up in the donkey boiler. By using timbers and an assortment of cables and blocks they slid this monstrous machine, including the boiler, over and onto its new sleigh.

Frank was showing Ken how to splice a new eye in the passline, near the bottom of the spar tree. As they finished trimming the strands, he looked at his son and asked, "How'd you like to get in this chain and ride up to the top of the spar?"

"How high is it up there?"

"Oh, about 180 feet."

Sure it would be fun, Ken climbed into the chain and was shown how to hook it up and hang on. His father walked over to the machine, cracked the throttle, pulled on the strawline friction, and Ken was on his first trip up a spar tree. He was more than a little scared but didn't admit it. The strawline, from the machine up to the top of the tree, weighed slightly more than the boy. As he got up near the top, the weight of the cable was taking him up faster than the machine was pulling. By clutching at the bark with his free hand and using both feet against the tree, he slowed himself to a stop. But his weight was not enough to start him back toward the ground.

"Grab hold of the bark and pull down with your hands," his Dad shouted.

He did so, and was soon safe on the ground. He wiggled out of the chain, fastened it to the bottom of the spar, then turned and sauntered over to the machine where his Dad stood smiling.

"You sure did a fine job for your first time up."

"I'm going to be a high rigger," Ken told him, as they stood together looking up to where he had just been.

Later that fall, Clarence Whittingham rowed across the lake for a visit. He had brought his rifle, and they decided to go up the mountain for a deer hunt. A two-point buck was flushed out of a salal patch above camp and stopped to look back.

"Let young Archie have the shot," Frank Hallberg said quietly. The deer was 30 yards away and Archie didn't miss. They cleaned it out, hung it in a tree, then moved on up across the slash.

"We need a couple more about that size for our winter's meat," Hallberg said, and when they reached the standing timber, they rested to discuss the hunt.

"Ken, you and your buddy Clarence go north to climb the mountain. Archie and I will go south and hunt the ridges. Try and be back at the cabin no later than four. Don't get caught out in the dark."

A cold north wind was blowing, and it began to snow. Before long, it was snowing so hard the boys lost all sense of direction. The two young hunters walked for a couple of hours when they came to tracks in the snow. Their own. They had walked in a complete circle, and were totally confused.

"Better we find a creek and follow it down to the lake," Clarence figured.

They were soon dropping steeply down the side of the mountain, but had no idea in which direction they were travelling. Soaked and shivering, Ken begged Clarence to stop and build a fire.

"Better we keep going, or we'll have to spend the night out here," Clarence said grimly.

For more than an hour they fought their way through snow-bound thickets, then broke out in the clear in freshly bucked timber. They could see the railroad tracks. It was only a couple of miles to camp. At the cookhouse one of the bakers was still working. He sat them by the big wood stove and made some hot cocoa. The boys were so cold it took both hands to hold the mugs. It was still snowing hard and getting dark, so the baker insisted they spend the night there. Before daylight Archie and his Dad headed out to look for Ken and Clarence. They were relieved to find the boys safe and warm.

Archie told his brother and friend about the two big bucks he and his Dad had shot up near the bluffs. After a breakfast of hotcakes and all the bacon and eggs they could eat, the Hallbergs headed up the mountain to bring the three deer down to Clarence's boat. Frozen stiff, the deer slid down over the snow like toboggans. After the skinning and cutting up, the meat was wrapped in packages.

Ken and Archie each took a box filled with venison to their mother in Vancouver. After praising her boys as hunters, she suggested Ken should get started in school. He said, "No! I'm going to go logging." He had already missed the first two months of school, was now past 15, weighed 120 pounds and considered himself an experienced logger.

His Dad called a few weeks later to say there was a job for him at Shawnigan Lake cutting and splitting wood to fire the steam donkey being used to build some bridges. At first he couldn't cut wood fast enough to keep steam up. One of the bridgemen would give him a hand to keep things going until he learned a few tricks about splitting wood.

During his second week there Ken heard for the first time the seven long whistles that mean someone has been killed or seriously injured. The signals came from about a mile up the track. The crew stopped what they were doing and rushed to see if they could help.

Elvin Waldie, the high rigger, had been raising a spar tree. His second rigger had driven a wooden wedge into a guyline eye splice to open it for the shackle. When he fastened it to the spar, he neglected to knock the wedge out. As the tree went up and the guyline tightened, that wooden wedge flew out like a bullet and came down to strike Waldie just above his right temple. He was knocked to the ground unconscious.

Fifty-five years later, at Betty and Bill Brown's 50th wedding anniversary in Duncan, Waldie recalled looking up to make sure the tree was plumb and then, as he turned to signal the second rigger to spike the guyline, the wedge hit him.

"I was unconscious for 10 days. When I came to in the hospital, Dad was sitting by the bed," Waldie remembered.

It took five hours to get him to the Duncan hospital. First, the crew had to wait for the locie to come out and take him the four miles to the road, where an ambulance picked him up. The X-rays showed major skull fractures.

"Dr. Bissett told my father I would certainly die unless they operated. Even then, it was less than one chance in ten I would survive.

" 'One in ten is a lot better than none at all,' Dad said to the doctor,' so you must give it a try.'

"With a silver plate and other gadgets, Dr. Bissett must have done a good job. I've never worked in the woods since the accident, but I'm doing fine for an old logger who's getting near to his 85th birthday," Waldie said with a big smile.

Shortly after the Waldie accident, Hemmingsen had to close the Shawnigan camp because of the depression. Young Ken was lucky enough to land a job blowing whistles for Grosskleg and Trueman near Cowichan Lake. It was a jerkwire show and Ken didn't yet have the know-how to properly string the wire.

"Experience was needed to blow short, sharp signals. My whistles were long and mournful," Ken remembers. "They put up with it for three days and then fired me."

Next spring, Ken and his Dad took a yarding contract for Joe Kerrone, usually referred to as Gyppo Joe, who would tackle logging shows no one else would touch. This operation was on Blue Grouse Mountain above Cowichan Lake and over a mile from the beach. Albert McNeil, a cat logger from Duncan, was hired to swing the logs from the spar tree to the lake.

Albert's Gas 60 had no blade, but did have a winch mounted on the back end. He had built up a wheel-type arch he called a Bummer to keep the forward ends of the logs up off the ground. This was before track arches.

Kerrone was making a go of it until the Youbou sawmill had no more orders for hemlock, so he tried leaving the hemlock standing, and taking only the fir. It was ridiculous to even consider such a method because the standing trees were a death trap for the rigging crew. Joe was forced to shut down and Ken and his father were out of work again.

By October, 1930, most of the logging camps were closed. Thousands of men were travelling across Canada in box cars looking for work of any kind. On government relief single men could get $9 a month and married men $12, earned by working on government roads at 25 cents an hour. To earn the $12 a married man had to put in six eight-hour days.

Frank Hallberg, too proud to accept this government 'relief', went trapping for the winter. A Swedish friend nicknamed Snookum, one of the finest woodsmen on the Pacific Coast, joined Frank and his sons Ken and Cliff. They'd trap the high mountain ranges between Cowichan Lake and the headwaters of the Nanaimo and Chemainus Rivers.

They hired an old truck in Nanaimo, loaded it with flour, beans, rice, dried fruit, spuds, carrots, cabbage, tea, coffee, bacon, all their bedding and winter clothes, traps and other gear and drove up the winding road along the Nanaimo River. About 10 miles out they were stopped. A gate keeper came out with a loaded shotgun.

"Where are you planning to go with that outfit?" he asked. When he was told they were heading out for the winter to do some trapping, he opened the gate and let them through. All the supplies had to be backpacked several miles from the end of the road up to an old hunting cabin. Cliff then returned the truck and walked back the 20 odd miles from Nanaimo.

Near the headwaters of Jump Creek they found an ideal spot to build a log cabin. They felled cedar trees and cut them into lengths. "Better than sawn lumber," Snookum declared proudly after he had broadaxed the logs for the walls. The only nails used on that cabin were for the roof shakes which Cliff and Ken split with a maul and froe.

When all the supplies were in their new quarters it became apparent another room for bunk beds and storage was a must. It took another week to add the extra room.Then they set out the traps. One of the lines ran from Jump Creek high into the mountains. Another went up Green Mountain, down to the abandoned Silver Mine trail, then back into the headwaters of

111

the Chemainus River. They were catching several marten a week, which they hoped would sell for about $9 each.

Cliff and Ken, once checked a trap containing a big marten which they thought was dead. When Ken picked him off the ground by the trap chain the marten made no movement. Suddenly, the animal leaped forward and sank his razor sharp teeth into the joint of Ken's index finger. They had to pry its jaws apart with a stout stick to free Ken's finger.

One evening after a six-inch fall of fresh snow, Cliff and Ken went out to play. Without warning, a snowball hit Cliff on the back of his head. They heard a laugh, and when two big cougar hounds trotted towards them they knew it was Jimmy Dewar from Extension. Jim slept on the floor and before leaving next morning, he told them of a good trail over the mountains to Cowichan Lake he would travel. He drew a sketch on the lid of a cardboard box showing exactly where the trail started through a pass into the McKay Creek valley. The pass was mostly through huge old growth fir timber, so Jim added plenty of fresh blazes to make the trail easier to follow. The Hallbergs used the route to pack in their supplies for the rest of the winter.

Cliff and Ken went out checking their traps and were surprised to come on fresh tracks they thought had been made by a small bear. The animal was definitely following their trapline. Half a mile further along Ken had set a marten trap in a hollow cedar log. Approaching quietly, they could see that the snow had been trampled down around the end of this log. They knew some animal was inside. Cliff said excitedly, "Bears should be in hibernation at this time of year".

"Yeah, I know, and we don't have a gun, only a hatchet." Ken reminded him.

Ken handed his brother the hatchet, saying, "Cut a club about the size of a baseball bat". From his pack Ken took out a large No. 2 trap. They then cut a long slender pole, wired the big trap securely to the end of the pole then set it.

Cliff stood beside the hollow end, the club raised high. Ken shoved the trap in. There was a vicious growl and a smash that almost knocked the pole out of his hands. The mystery animal was caught fast in the bigger trap.

"We could hear his teeth snapping as he bit into the wood and the chain. I pulled back on the pole until the head came out into the open. That was all Cliff needed. Whap! and Ken dragged the animal out."

They realized they had killed a 40-pound wolverine. There is no more dangerous an animal in the world for its size. It stank, so they tied a rope around its neck and dragged it over the snow back to camp. At first they were heroes, but soon the stench almost drove everyone out of the cabin.

"Get that stinking critter out of here and hang it in a tree away down by the creek," their Dad ordered.

Perhaps it was a combination of spring fever and cabin fever, but Snookum left in mid-February with all his gear. He took the pack trail to Youbou, and borrowed a rowboat to get across the lake to Camp Six and home.

In mid-March the three Hallbergs broke camp, bundled their furs, and packed them out to Youbou. Ken Gillespie, a licensed trapper, shipped them on to his buyer in Vancouver. He estimated the winter catch would sell for more than $500.

"We closed the cabin, and headed out down the mountain. It was good to step on some green moss again after five months of nothing but snow," Ken remembered.

They forded the Nanaimo River and walked on out to one of MacMillan's old tie camps. It was deserted except for two watchmen, Eric and Magnason Pros, who gave them one of the empty houses rent free. They patched the roof, set up camp and lived there for the next several months. Blue grouse were plentiful. The males could be heard hooting from early morning till almost dark. Ken was able to hit them in the head with almost every .22 rifle shot. "Those hooters made mighty fine stew meat."

They made a summer trip down to the Nanaimo River for salmon. They worked carefully along a narrow ledge until they were practically under the falls. They could gaff salmon in mid air as they jumped to get over the rapids. Cliff would hold a gunny sack, Dad gave the orders, Ken handled the gaff. They landed enough spring salmon in a couple of hours to last them for a month. One of the biggest weighed more than 25 pounds. After several feeds of fresh salmon, they salted down the remainder in an old five gallon crock that had been left under the house.

Cliff and Ken walked down to the Gogo's farm every week to

buy milk and vegetables. Though he was reputed to be unfriendly, Gogo always welcomed them.

"Usually we'd take him some salted salmon and fresh wild blackberries, and we'd sit for hours listening to his stories about the wolves and cougars he'd shot when he was young. He'd rarely let us leave without an extra pail of fresh milk or some special vegetables.

"Dad had gone to the Buck & Turner Logging show and got a falling contract at 40 cents per thousand. This kept us busy that summer and gave us some cash."

This was one of the first truck logging operations of any size on Vancouver Island. Buck & Turner were able to log in spite of the depression and low prices for logs. Their trucks could handle steeper grades, get closer to the timber, and produce logs for substantially less money than the railroad operations.

When the falling contract finished, Cliff and Ken panned gold along the Nanaimo River. Back breaking work but they collected a small poke of dust and a few nuggets. This created great excitement when they walked into a jewelry store in Nanaimo to cash in, and it started a minor gold rush on the Nanaimo River.

Sam Craig had stopped in at the Hallberg shack with his three Blue Tick cougar hounds. One was a runt, not quite a year old, short legs and very long ears. Cliff and his fox hound, Duke, immediately fell in love with this young pup. Craig noticed, and gave Cliff the runt.

There was an early snowfall in October of 1932, and their Uncle Joe drove out in his truck. "Collect your gear and jump in. You're all coming down to the farm for the winter." The Hallbergs were more than willing to leave this old lumber shack to the mice. Aunt Hilda was an excellent cook and the boys appreciated her meals after batching for months in the back country.

The Hallberg men promptly set to work building a new barn. The boys dug a basement with their uncle's team and scraper while Joe and Frank built the big truss frames. After the concrete foundations were in place, it was a real learning experience for Cliff and Ken to help their Dad raise the heavy timbers with the team and tackle.

The barn was ready to have the roof put on by February, so they piled gear into their uncle's truck and headed for Cowichan Lake to cut shakes. For $2 a month the boys' father rented a cabin with a cook stove and a couple of old beds. There were big cedars near the road and in two weeks they had cut and split enough shakes to roof the new barn. Mr. Gordon owned the general store at the foot of the lake, and agreed to trade potatoes for groceries so Uncle Joe dropped two or three sacks of spuds off each time he came for a load of shakes. Things worked out well and the Hallbergs contracted to supply shakes for two other barns. Those same shakes have kept the hay dry for over 50 years.

One morning both hounds put their noses to the ground and started their mournful bellowing. It was a cold trail and old Duke, the fox hound, was having trouble. Buck, the pup, with his short legs kept right on the trail and in less than an hour they had three prime racoons. Before the depression ended those two dogs had treed 31 cougars and over 100 racoons.

With the cougar bounties and the sale of the 'coon skins they took in over $2,000, a large sum in those tough depression days.

Gold was worth $32 an ounce in 1933, so when spring came and there were no jobs, their father decided that rather than go on government relief they should all go north and try their luck at gold panning. He wanted all three of his sons with him. Guv Blake and young Bill Hemmingsen also wanted to go and they were accepted when Bill's father, Matt, agreed to grubstake the party for a share of the profits. Guv's brother had a Reo truck and a deal was made. He would take the mining party up to Summit Lake, north of Prince George, for $25 plus expenses, or a share of the profits, whichever was greater.

April 1, 1933, the excited crew piled gear on the Reo and left Victoria on the midnight boat. Beyond the Fraser Valley, they were on gravel roads for the next 450 miles, and it was into breakup time when they passed through Quesnel.

North of Prince George there was still about six inches of snow on the hill going up to Summit Lake. They had to hire a team to pull the Reo. Theirs was the first vehicle to get through that spring.

They bought lumber from a mill and built a flat-bottomed

115

boat eight feet wide and 16 feet long, to carry the gang and their gear across Summit Lake and down the Crooked River. They would be the first to attempt to cross the lake so Jorgenson, who freighted for the Hudson Bay Company on the Crooked River, advised them to wait until all the ice was out. Nope. Too impatient. The Hallberg party took off in their scow-type boat on May 24th. The river was running wild.

Ken had a close one when a big chunk of underwater ice knocked the pole out of his hands and he went head first into the surging muddy water. His head surfaced and was immediately pushed under again by a chunk of ice. Brother Cliff was just able to shove his pole out full length in the surging river. Ken grabbed it or he would have drowned.

Panning and sluicing all summer, tortured by black flies and mosquitos, the six washed out only $350 worth of nuggets and fine gold. Hardly a profitable venture.

When the fall rains started in earnest, a huge cottonwood tree washed out and came down the river crosswise to sweep their whole camp and sluice boxes off the beach and down the river. They had hired two dugout canoes, so they loaded up what little was left and started upriver towards Summit Lake.

Geese and duck were coming out of the north in flocks. The second day the weather turned cold and the temperature dropped well below freezing. Young Archie had heard the geese honking nearby and was out of his sleeping bag long before daylight. He loaded their .22 with a long rifle cartridge, then proceeded to sneak up on a flock of these honkers. He cocked the gun, quietly moved closer, took careful aim on a big gander and pulled the trigger. Nothing happened. The firing pin had been wet and had frozen solid. Disappointed, he trudged back to camp and stood by the fire. He held the gun in front of him with both hands over the muzzle. The flames warmed the firing pin, the gun went off. Archie slumped to the ground screaming "I'm shot, I'm shot!".

They tore off his shirt. The bullet had gone through one of his fingers without breaking the bone, travelled up through the fleshy part of his arm, and out just short of the shoulder.

"There was a lot of blood. Dad used our last bottle of iodine on the wound then bandaged it tightly with rags from the shirt. We laid Archie on some sleeping bags in the stern of the bigger canoe," Ken recalled. "When the bleeding had almost stopped we were away again."

The north end of Summit Lake was icing up along the shore. They paddled all day, through the night, and pulled into civilization about four next morning. Archie slept most of the way and almost froze. They hammered on the door of the only restaurant until the cook finally woke up and let them in. He had a huge pot of moose stew which he heated while the coffee came to the boil. When the stew was gone, the exhausted party collapsed on the floor—boots, clothes and all. By noon the next day they had unloaded the canoes and, when a local Indian drove up with a half ton truck, they swapped him the canoes for a ride to Prince George. Archie got his wound properly dressed at the hospital and soon was fine.

In Prince George their gold sold for $33 an ounce which gave them just over $200 profit for the entire summer's work. They bought an old Chevrolet car for $75 to get them to Vancouver. At 83 Mile House the night temperature fell below zero and the radiator froze solid. It leaked so badly that water had to be added every 10 miles. At Clinton, an old cowboy rode up while Ken was refilling the steaming radiator.

"I see youse got a bad leak thar. Best thing in the world for that is a dry horse turd. Just grind it up in your hands and poke it in," he said.

The Hallbergs tried it. It worked. Driving down Hastings Street in Vancouver was an unforgettable experience, Ken remembers. "People gazed at our overloaded vehicle in astonishment until they got a whiff of the boiling horse manure. Then they'd cough and were long gone.

"The car was sold to a junk dealer for $5, but there wasn't quite enough money to pay for our boat tickets to Nanaimo. Dad had to swallow his pride and go to the nearest government relief office for help. We sat on those hard benches for several hours. They wanted to send us out to a relief camp for single men. After a phone call assured them that once on Vancouver Island we could live at our Uncle Joe Trudell's farm, they advanced just enough money to make up what we needed to buy the tickets. Not one cent more.

"We arrived at the farm in time to help harvest the potatoes we had planted before going north.

"Dad did a stint on the roads to earn money enough to repay the advance for our boat ticket and sent them a money order for the exact amount. My Dad, Frank Hallberg, typifies the rugged independence of a logger who would do anything rather than accept a government handout."

February came and Ken left the farm to look for work at Camp Six. He was hired and batched with Andy Norstrom in his float house. He started working as a chokerman on March 10, 1934, and worked six days a week for $3 a day. The first month's wages went to pay for a rain test coat and hat, two pairs of tin pants, three pairs of socks and his first razor. A good pair of Paris logging boots cost him $9.50. Groceries cost Ken and Andy about $15 a month each while they batched. When they moved into the bunkhouse and ate at the cookhouse, they were charged 95 cents a day.

"This was a little more expensive, but it was much better than cooking your own meals after a hard day's work," Ken recalls.

The camp shut down for five days on December 24, 1934, and Ken spent that holiday with his mother and family in Vancouver. A school chum was selling insurance and he talked him into buying. It cost 25 cents a week and his Mother would get $500 if he died or was killed. If no payments were missed Ken would receive a monthly pension of $25 at age 55 for the rest of his life. This seemed like a pretty good investment at the time. During the depression a person could live nicely on such a pension.

In the fall of 1935 Ken was promoted to second hooker. Shortly after, big Jim Ferguson lost an arm when blood poisoning set in from a rusty jagger wound to his right hand. The foreman asked Ken if he would take Jim's place as head hooktender. A big promotion, a lot of responsibility for a 20-year-old kid. He also became responsible for all the crews working on the logging side, including the donkey engineer and the landing crew. Top man!

Industrial Timber Mills opened a new camp at Kissinger and Ken was transferred there as logging superintendent. The responsibility of being the big boss just fell into place without any major problems. He got along well with his men, and soon earned a reputation as a highball logger.

118

Camps and mills in 1936 were operating steadily and beginning to show profits. Wages had been raised several times. Chokermen were making $4.50 a day and a high rigger got $6.25. The IWA union was becoming very active, things got rough and the bosses had orders to ban all organizers from the camps. In spite of the pressure by the logging companies, enough members were signed up to support a major strike that year.

Ken remembers one operator near Cowichan Lake: "Jesse James was a contractor for Empire Timber Company at Cottonwood Creek during the early 1920's. This was about a mile west of the old Youbou mill. He employed about 120 men and provided them with a gambling hall, a bootlegging joint, and a couple of cathouses."

With a monopoly on such a lucrative business, it's hard to understand why Jesse went broke. Ken was only a kid, but remembers Jesse as a highroller, driving big cars at high speeds. It was said that he was his own best customer at his houses of ill repute. In most camps liquor was not allowed. Bosses would confiscate the bottles, tag them, and only give them back when the logger was leaving camp.

"There was one man who set chokers for me on some very rough shows. He had a wooden leg. He just put a leather sole on it and then drove caulks into the leather. He could set chokers with the best. Then there was Lew Edwards who had lost one arm at an early age. The first time I met Lew he was bucking wood with a Swede fiddle for a steam donkey. Later, he became our first fire chief. I knew another man who had a peg leg and operated a piledriver. Those loggers had physical handicaps, but they were very proud people and rarely complained and never asked for special favours.

"Loggers are tough, independent. Bill Lloyd operated a grade shovel, and told me about the time he quit the V.L.& M. Camp. The railroad they were working on was through a swampy area. He told the superintendent he needed some mats (timbers bolted together) so the shovel wouldn't get mired in the swamps. Highball Isbister, the superintendent, told him to keep going without the mats. Bill Lloyd argued that he'd get stuck in the mud, but, 'If that's the way you want it, that's the way you'll get it,' and stomped out of the office, back to the shovel. He worked until the thing was hopelessly mired up over the tracks and part way up the cab out there in the slough. Then he walked back to camp and demanded his pay. Isbister was there and wanted to know how badly the shovel was bogged in.

"Bill, with his usual drawl said, 'Well, just to help you find it, I cut a 20 foot pole and stuck it in the mud where the shovel was last seen'. It turned out to be a very expensive decision for Isbister. Most good loggers were extremely independent. Any unnecessary interference from a boss and they'd just quit."

Ken Hallberg was 59 when he retired in June, 1974, as general manager of the Renfrew Division for B.C. Forest Products Ltd. He is enjoying retirement at his home in Nanaimo. He and his wife Elvira enjoy travelling. He keeps in shape cutting wood and looking after their lawn and garden.

In 1987, at 73, he logged off some good second growth timber from his tree farm near the west end of Cowichan Lake "just to keep in practice".

Trainload of logs in Camp 6, 1932.

Mauno Pelto and Jim Shaesgreen, Winter 1948,
discussing problems of salvage logging which was just
starting at Ladysmith.

CHAPTER 11
Mauno Pelto

Mauno Pelto came to Cowichan Lake in August of 1929 with his family from Finland. His father was hand falling for Camp Six, and had a nice three-room house in the married quarters.

"I was 11, my brother was younger and Mother gave us a good scrubbing, put us in spotlessly clean clothes, then walked us over to the camp's one-room school. Miss Fox, the teacher, met us at the door and Mother just pushed us youngsters forward, curtsied with a smile, turned and walked home without a backward glance."

There were 36 children—a few in every grade from one to eight. A big drumheater was at the back with wood stacked neatly in both corners. There were windows along the south side, and a four-foot blackboard behind the teacher's desk took up most of the west end wall.

"I had passed into Grade Five in Finland. The only difference was, when I came over here I couldn't understand a word the teacher was saying—not one solitary word," Mauno remembers. "It was embarrassing."

After his first week, Mauno told his father he didn't want to go to school in Canada. "Pack your clothes," he was told. "You go back to Finland next week and finish your education there." That put an end to any such foolishness. Mauno was back in his class on Monday, to stay.

"There were three of us that knew little or no English, a 10-year old girl from Poland, my brother, and me. Miss Fox took a special interest and stayed after school every day to help us. Within two months we had learned enough English to do our school work, and could understand what was said when we played games with the other boys and girls."

Miss Fox will always be a very special person to Mauno. He believes to this day she was the best teacher in Canada. She knew how to make young people want to learn. A few years later she married the grade shovel operator to become Mrs. William Lloyd, and together they went on to raise a large family and become oldtimers at the camp.

Mauno grew quickly. Most of the children in his class stood only to his shoulders. Within four years he was more than six feet tall and had passed most of the Grade Eight subjects. Mauno admits his English, spelling, and composition were not much above Grade Six level. His younger brother went on through high school with top marks, while Mauno quit school at 15.

He had watched the sleigh builders put a big Willamette steam donkey on a new sleigh. Something told him it was the time to go and see Bert Peck.

"You're putting a new sleigh under that big machine so it must be going out in the woods. It needs a whistle punk. How about making me the punk?"

"No, you got to go to school," Peck replied.

"I'm finished school," I told him, "and would very much like to have the job," Mauno said. Getting no further answer he walked away so the rest of the crew couldn't see how hurt and disappointed he was.

The machine was almost ready to go. Mauno was there

watching every move. The engineer had steam up and had tried the whistle several times to make sure it was working. There was so much noise and commotion the boy hadn't noticed that someone was standing right behind him. Bert Peck tapped him on the shoulder.

"If you want the punk's job, it's yours," Bert said with a big grin.

"Just like that, I had my first logging job," Mauno remembers. "It was almost like being back in Finland because all the crew spoke my language. I felt right at home and really enjoyed the work."

It was mostly skyline logging, and within a year he was promoted to setting chokers and working on the rigging. Mauno learned fast, including the loggers' woods language.

There was only one grade shovel in the valley, but Bill Lloyd managed to keep the main rail lines ahead of the yarding. There were three trackside steam skidders that could stretch out half a mile or more on the skylines and big gas cold deckers could reach out another 2000 feet to build coldeck piles. There would be as much as 14 million feet of logs in some of the bigger decks. They could break into these massive piles and keep on logging no matter how much it snowed. In the coldest weather fires would be needed to keep pumps thawed and water lines open for the steam skidder boilers.

Mauno was 20 when he started rigging back-spars with Henry Norman.

"I worked under him, and learned how to move those big machines out over the felled and bucked timber and up or down the steep canyons. He was one of those guys who was no hell with a pencil but the knowledge he carried in his head was unbelievable. He bossed on this same machine for something like 15 years and there was never one mishap."

Mauno got itchy feet as most loggers do. There was no road and it was a seven-mile walk out to Youbou along the rail line; and then, when you got there, there was nothing to do for a 21 year old.

He had been invited to join Comox Logging at Ladysmith. They had just started one of the biggest truck logging shows on Vancouver Island, which was a whole different setup for him. The crew lived in the town. Trucks had replaced the steam locies.

"I took a job as rigging slinger for a hooker I'd worked with. The big difference with trucks was that there was little need for skylining, so the equipment was much lighter. It was unbelievable, the difference in jobs, but the money was the same—$5.65 a day was the second rigger's, or rigging slinger's, rate.

"This was 1937, and Comox Logging was in a hurry to clean up the big blowdown from the hurricane of 1934. The first time double shifting was tried in the woods. It went on from May to September. If you happened to be working on a cold-deck machine and the afternoon shift finished up the setting, it might take half an hour next morning to find the machine, and another hour to find the tail blocks and straw line extensions. Or the other crew could rob the front end of the show so they'd look pretty good. Then you were cleaning up the back so you looked pretty bad."

John McQuinn was from Courtenay, the head man for Comox Logging at Ladysmith and Nanaimo Lakes until he was promoted to general manager. Under his supervision the company put in over 108-million board feet at Ladysmith that year with the trucks. The windfall situation and the double shifting put Ladysmith on the map as the largest truck logging outfit on the West Coast. When Mauno first started, there were windfalls as far as the eye could see—miles of them. A nasty situation for bucking crews. It needed a tremendous amount of knowledge and experience to cut logs among all those huge roots and criss-crossed fallen trees. Those old Scandinavian hand buckers knew their stuff. They worked in pairs and once they put their mind to the job the safety end of it came easily.

"Another logging show involved cleaning up one of mother nature's forest fires. In 1938, after the big fire back of Courtenay cooled down, four of us went with Art Qually to cold deck the burned timber at Camp Three. We logged in that black stuff for the next two years. We became black men.

"I met my wife there in the fall of 1938. We'd been dating for a couple of months, and this Saturday evening she exclaimed, 'Oh, my goodness! You've got blond eyebrows. I thought they were black'." Babs and Mauno were married shortly afterwards.

In June, 1939, Comox Logging shut down Camp Three for fire season. Mauno was fed up coming home looking like a black man. Victoria Lumber Company was starting a new

124

camp at Fanny Bay. He went to Thor Christenson, the engineer and camp super and was hired to go second rigging on their big skidder. They had just finished rigging the spar and were hanging the heel boom when the locie chugged up with a shiny new cold-deck machine on a flat car. Mauno asked if he needed a hooker for the new machine.

"I'm looking for one," the foreman replied.

"Well, you're looking at him. I'll take the job."

"Can you do it?" the foreman asked, looking Pelto over carefully.

"I was only 22 and just beginning to shave a few whiskers that grew once in a while."

"'The kid can do it, don't worry about him," a nearby logger told Claude Germaine, the side push.

Pelto recalls, "My first job was to move this cold decker out over the felled and bucked timber to the back end of the skidder setting, then raise and rig a spar tree. I remember the engineer, an old-timer. He kept looking at me and I knew what he was thinking. 'What the hell is going to happen here, when this kid starts raising the spar tree?'

"We had the tree in place and we were ready to raise it when the engineer left his machine and walked out,

"'Have you ever raised a tree, before?'

"I said to him, 'For your information I've rigged with Henry Norman, Matti Joupila, and Herman Carlson'. This seemed to ease his doubts and we went ahead and raised the tree. No trouble. I didn't tell him that I had not raised a tree using a ginpole before, nor that I'd been awake until well after three that morning deciding exactly how and where every line and block would be set. I also didn't tell him that it was a tough decision to make, whether I should quit and go look for another job, or raise this tree. My reason for staying was serious but simple. If I ran away from this one I'd be running for the rest of my life. From then on he trusted my judgment and we worked well together."

After Germaine was promoted, the head rigger quit and went with him. Jack Long took over and he came to Pelto that evening and said, "Hey kid, could you high rig for us?"

"Sure, no problem."

Mauno did the rigging at Fanny Bay for the next two years.

Stan Smith was the side push and they worked well together. When Copper Canyon was getting ready to start up, Smith was slated to go there as superintendent. He wanted Mauno to come with him to back rig on their big skidder. It was wartime and most camps were short handed. Bill Nummi was head rigging and his twin brother Tom was the donkey puncher. They were rated as the best skidder team on the coast, but Mauno had a personality clash with Bill Nummi.

"I'd been there about a month and we needed some big trees cut down to make tailholts for the next back spar," Mauno said. "It was a Monday morning and I told Bill Nummi that I would be willing to work late if he would send out some fallers that evening to do the job."

"You know what you can do with those tailholts?" came back the surly reply.

Young and fiery, Mauno snapped back, "There's only two men in this camp right now that can rig on this skidder. I just quit, so you're on your own," and he took off his gloves, picked up his lunch bucket, and started walking down the track.

"I'll give you the hand fallers," Nummi hollered at him.

"It's too late, I'm quitting right now!" Mauno yelled back and kept walking.

"You can't quit for at least seven days because the war has you frozen," Nummi told him when he caught up. Mauno had forgotten about the war freeze.

"I'll do anything else for the next seven days, but I will not rig on this skidder again!"

Mauno Pelto left Copper Canyon and went back to Comox Logging at Ladysmith, where he hooked and rigged until he was seriously injured in January of 1947. They were loading boomsticks and there was ice and snow everywhere. He was clearing the back set of tongs and was standing on a boomstick, when it took off sideways. He hit the ground first and the boomstick came down and flattened him. It broke his pelvis in four places, fractured his lower back, and pulverized his hip joint. If it hadn't been for the deep snow he would have been killed instantly.

Manager Jim Sheasgreen was very concerned about the injury when he came to visit Mauno in Ladysmith Hospital that night. The next day a Workmen's Compensation Board doctor came from Vancouver to examine him, and Mauno was taken by plane to Vancouver General Hospital that same day. Two months later, after half a dozen bone operations, he was able to hobble around on two canes. He was taking therapy in Vancouver on special equipment and getting home on weekends. About three months later he met Jim Sheasgreen on the ferry.

"Mauno," he said, "I've got just the job for you."

"I'm on two canes. What the hell could I do for you?"

"We're starting a small log salvage operation at Ladysmith. We're planning to re-log most of our old logging slash," Jim explained. "This way we can recover all that small wood and sell it to the new pulp mills. We'll also be pre-logging in the standing timber, taking out all the small trees and windfalls before they get broken or pulled over with the heavy rigging. There's going to be a lot of new light equipment. We're planning to use young people. You can just watch, drive around in a comfortable pickup and look after things. I've got a new 4x4 you can have for your new job," Shaesgreen offered.

Mauno agreed to give it a try and started by the first of June. He was put on a monthly salary and told not to overdo it.

There were a lot of good young men around Ladysmith in 1947, home from the war and eager to find jobs. The company brought in some light, fast winches and Mauno, with some minor changes, had them mounted on army surplus vehicles, either half tracks or all-wheel drive trucks.

The waste in logging up to then had been enormous and Mauno recalled a couple of years earlier walking from the back end to the front of one big slash. His feet hardly ever touched the ground. He'd be walking on young trees flattened to the ground, three and four feet deep, up to 18 inches at the butt and 60 to 70 feet long. This good wood had previously been left to rot or be burned. It was this wood previously wasted that they were going after with the salvage logging equipment. It was the beginning of better utilization of our forests. The pulp mills could use, and even preferred, this small timber.

Mauno's salvage operation wound up with four light, high-speed yarders and nine D-4 cats with wheel arches. Once his crew of young men got on to the light rigging, they took great pride in this new phase of coastal logging—salvage.

"We were raising spar trees prior to putting steel towers on these army trucks," Mauno remembers. "I'd just set these young fellows up and explain what to do. They'd always compete to see which crew was going to get the most production.

"It took a little while before we realized what size log should be left, and what should be brought in. We found a piece of 20 cubic feet was okay. Anything less had to be left in the slash."

Mauno always showed a reasonable profit on his re-logging. In pre-logging (taking out the small trees before falling the big ones), they would have a much better pulp log because the smaller trees had not been broken up by logging the bigger timber. If the material was good, they could put a load on a truck in less than 10 minutes with their portable conveyor, but there was no way to actually lift the bigger chunks. Mauno found it necessary to rig up a heel boom on an old grade shovel to load everything, and he discarded the conveyor system.

When the shop completed a set of air tongs for one of their 3/4 yard shovels, loading improved. The air tongs opened and closed on the logs with an air cylinder and eliminated the need for the tong man and head loader. The shovel operator did it all. Production doubled at the landings. When bigger machines and hydraulic tongs were used, this system completely changed the loading concept for all log sizes.

Mauno spent seven years on salvage and pre-logging. He was asked to speak and give demonstrations at many logging conventions because he was the expert in this new type of timber utilization. And being an expert, Mauno always gave full credit to his men.

"Once these youngsters caught on, they were just an excellent crew. Many of these kids worked with me off and on for 30 years. Some became foremen, others became managers. The whole situation was very, very, gratifying."

Pelto left salvage operations in the mid-1950's when he was sent to Jervis Inlet to manage the Saltery Bay show for Comox Logging. He took over Nanaimo Lakes in 1958 as general manager and in 1960 he was sent to Sandspit on the Queen Charlottes, to reorganize and put in some new equipment.

Sandspit was a camp with 120 men plus the barge loading operation at South Bay. He remembers one year they sent out

93 barge loads averaging about a million feet each. They also did salvage logging with self-loading trucks, strapping the load at each end to make one big bundle.

He attended the opening of the new nursing home at Queen Charlotte City and he recalls, "The Haida Chief gave the dedication speech. He took his audience back a thousand years, from the days of the big ocean-going canoes up to the present when aircraft brought his people home like soaring eagles. He then filled in the thousand year gap in a very entertaining way using many illustrations and legends."

Mauno realized from the beginning that when dealing with the Haidas he would be involved with some very talented people.

"I suppose that's why we got along so well."

Mauno was chosen to open up a new logging operation at Kitimat on The Mainland. The new camp was built at the head of Douglas Channel, about 150 miles northeast of Sandspit. It took four years to get things running smooth. In 1968, he was shifted south to Vancouver as a logging advisor at Crown Zellerbach's head office. He appreciated this major promotion, but didn't like big-city living. He toughed it out until 1975, then asked to be transferred back to supervise the Nanaimo Lakes camp on Vancouver Island.

The general woods foreman at Crown Zellerback's Nanaimo Lakes Division was Torchy Kulai, a long-time friend. He had been the whistle punk for Mauno on his first skidder hooking job 35 years earlier. Mauno spent six good years at Nanaimo Lakes before his retirement in 1981. He always liked to be where the action was.

A man respected and liked throughout the industry, he has never failed to give full credit to the men who helped him make changes and accomplish goals. These goals were many and varied. Although none of them were easy, all were worthwhile. But his greatest asset remains his ability to get full cooperation from the people he worked with. His solutions to problems, and his relationships with his crew, were direct, simple, and usually successful.

An example was one Christmas eve in the kitchen of their home in Ladysmith. The family were in the living room, when a

RETIRED LOGGING MANAGER.

MAUNO PELTO
OF NANAIMO, B.C.

Mauno retired 1981. Picture courtesy of *Loggers World.*

130

loud knock came on the back door. It was cold with two feet of snow outside, and when Mauno opened the door, four of his rigging crew stood there shivering.

"Come on in, boys, and a Merry Christmas to all. How about some hot rum?"

"Sure," and in they clumped.

"I'll clear the table, and we'll sit here," Mauno said, and with one sweep of his big left arm everything went off the kitchen table, towards the sink, and onto the floor. Turkey, baking pan, pots, everything. He lifted a tray with glasses and a full bottle of overproof rum from the drainboard to the table.

"Now we've got room to do some drinking," he grinned.

"Sure do!" his rigging slinger agreed.

Mixing some hot water, lemon, cinnamon, wild honey and a bit of butter, they soon polished off the 40-ouncer.

"Get your coat and come with us," his donkey puncher invited. "We should visit the rest of the gang."

"Sounds like a good idea," Mauno agreed, and they headed out into the snow towards other houses.

This, in a small way, illustrates Mauno's direct approach, and the general good fellowship amongst loggers.

Mauno and Babs live in a quiet valley a few miles south of Nanaimo. They enjoy cruising the coast in their boat, fishing, and fixing up the flower garden. They are near most of their old friends and logging buddies and visits are many and pleasant.

Emblem family. Thelma and Wally standing. Wally
did the welding on the big steam whistle at the
Chemainus mill for Bob Swanson.

CHAPTER 12
Thelma Godkin
(née Emblem)

Thelma Emblem's first job away from home was helping an
elderly lady in Ladysmith. She had just graduated from Grade
12 and her mother had arranged the job. The lady thought she
should be able to do everything around the house. Thelma was
18 but she had never done housework, not even at home. She
had always worked with her Dad clearing land, cutting wood,
planting the crops, and helping with the chores. Her first job
lasted one day.

Wally, her father, suggested she might like to go on to
college, but Thelma didn't want that either. Being a foreman at
the Chemainus mill, and with many of the men already gone to
war, he arranged for Thelma to work in the planing mill.

The safety regulations on the notice board stated "Ladies
with long hair must do it up so it can't get caught in the

machinery". Thelma didn't agree, and the foreman never enforced it when she told him, "I'll quit rather than have my hair tied up in rags."

"On my first day there, they were planing kiln-dried cedar. You know what cedar is like. It was down my back and everywhere else. Mother had decided to get clean sheets out of our cedar chest and put them on my bed. I broke out in a rash and didn't sleep a wink. Next morning I went to work with big red blotches all over my hands and arms. It was just a case of being allergic to cedar."

Thelma's job was called 'racking'. The finished lumber came out onto conveyor chains where the inspectors marked and graded it. It then had to be stacked by lengths onto the racks and tied in bundles with a strong brown cord at each end.

"A handsome young European gentleman was doing the grading in our area, and this older woman was after him. She had one walleye, so you never knew whether she was looking at you or somewhere else. She was a real vixen, and if any of us younger girls even talked to the chap she thought we were making a play for him. She was very jealous and let us know she would tolerate no competition."

Thelma didn't like being inside with all that noise, not knowing if the sun was shining or if it was pouring rain. On her days off she could usually be found down at the lagoon chatting with the guys who drove the logging trucks. Grant Hawthorne, the foreman, asked her if she'd like to sign on as a whistle punk. She quit the mill to work in the woods.

"What did your mother say when you told her?" I asked.

"My MOTHER!!!! Well, she first had to warn me about loggers having a reputation for being rough-and-ready guys. Then she admitted that I'd liked cutting wood and working outside with my Dad from the time I was three years old.

"'You'll just have to get yourself some good rain clothes and a pair of caulk boots, then learn how to take care of yourself,' Mother told me."

Thelma went to work at Teddy Robson's camp in the spring of 1940, riding with the crew in a beat-up crummy. The men let her ride in the front seat because it was more comfortable than the benches in the back.

"I found the loggers much more courteous and considerate than the men I worked with in the planermill. I just seemed to fit in better with the woods crew, and liked it right from the start", she admitted.

Thelma wore the same kind of clothes all loggers wore—old tin pants, a bone-dry coat and a waterproofed hat. Every weekend they painted their outside clothing with a solution of hot wax mixed with paraffin oil. A few applications and the pants could stand in a corner by themselves. Hence, the name 'tin pants' The legs looked like stovepipes.

It was difficult for Thelma to find the right size clothes and a pair of logging boots to fit. There just weren't any size four boots around. They searched the whole district. Finally Ladysmith Trading found a pair of leather work boots in their basement that were small enough. Johnny the Jazz, an excellent shoemaker, put on heavier hard leather soles and drove some logging caulks into them. He gave her a mixture of seal oil and bear grease to put on the boots every weekend and showed her how to rub it in. Those boots didn't smell too good but they kept the water out and lasted three years. When it began getting colder in the fall, Thelma bought herself a grey wool, double-backed cruiser's jacket to wear when it wasn't raining. This was much warmer than the stiff tin coats.

"I felt like the tin man in the Wizard of Oz. That tin coat was most uncomfortable, but very necessary when it was pouring rain,"she remembered.

Thelma started as a whistle punk on the cold deck machine. She can still remember the signals:

HIGH LEAD WHISTLES

Ahead mainline	THREE SHORT
	(Prior to 1950—One short.)
Ahead on straw-line	THREE SHORT—pause—ONE SHORT
Back on the haulback	TWO SHORT—pause—TWO SHORT
Slack haulback	TWO SHORT—pause—A SERIES OF SHORTS
Slack mainline	SERIES OF SHORTS
Slow	ONE LONG whistle precedes any signal
Stop all lines	ONE SHORT

Tighten lines	THREE SHORT—pause—TWO SHORT
When butt rigging at tree to send out strawline	THREE SHORT—ONE LONG
When butt rigging is at tree	TWO SHORT—followed by a NUMBER OF LONGS indicates the number of chokers required to be sent out

Grant promoted Thelma to the home tree to punk whistles at the landing a month later. She was now accustomed to wearing caulk boots, and walked just like any other logger. Grant hired Dolly Mae, a young girl from Duncan, to take over on the cold deck.

"A Chinese crew, 10 of them, did all the falling and bucking. There were no power saws in those days. It was all done by hand, using saws the guys called 'Swede fiddles'. One of the older Chinese was kept busy just filing saws and sharpening axes. Spring boards were used to fall most of the bigger trees. The Chinese fallers seemed to have about five different straw hats. When one wore out, they just put a new one on over the old one. I can still picture that in my mind," Thelma laughed. "They lived in one small bunkhouse and always walked in a line, one behind the other. Each one had an oil bottle hanging out of his back pocket and a sack with sledge and wedges hung over one shoulder, with their axe and crosscut saw over the other. It was the way they worked in those days."

Thelma started in 1940 and worked in the woods all through the war. Most logging crews were a mixture of old men and teenagers—either too old or not old enough to go overseas. In 1942, they finished dumping logs at the Ladysmith lagoon and moved to Mount Hall.

"That's where the forest fire burned us out," Thelma remembers. "Everything was tinder dry, and it was scary. I had never before seen a crown fire, and didn't realize that it could travel so fast. It just roared through the tree tops, flashing from one tree to the next. It burnt all our machines and most of the bridges. We eventually had to run out the other end to save our lives. All I could do was pack water from a creek by the bucket full. It was so hot and smoky we could barely breathe."

After the fire jumped the road, the crew piled into the crummy and made a run for cooler air. The driver was a big colored fellow called 'Feet'. His boots were size 15.

"I don't know how he ever got us out through those flames, but he did. We went through places that were still burning. We were suffocating. I thought we were all going to die," Thelma said.

"It rained the next day but the crew were off for a couple of weeks while the men repaired the machinery and rebuilt the bridges. When we started logging in the burned area that black soot would get right into our skin. We'd come out and our faces would be blacker than a coal miner's. The fire ravaged more than trees and loggers. After that big forest fire there was a young deer that haunted me for over a week. It was less than half grown and it would stand looking over this log at me. It would even nibble at a bread crust as I held it in my hand."

When the crew returned to log the burnt-out Mount Hall, one day, by accident, a smoldering log was loaded onto one of the trucks. The speed of the truck fanned the log into flames. By the time the logs were dumped into the salt chuck at Ladysmith Harbour the whole load was blazing 10 feet high. As the logs hit the water, a cloud of steam rose a hundred feet into the air.

After all that burned over timber was hauled off Mount Hall the camp closed down, and Thelma was offered a job on the Malahat with Kapoor Lumber Company, near Shawnigan Lake. Jimmy Crone was camp superintendent. He put her punking whistles on the big slackline skidder. It was such a long drive from Saltair to the top of the Malahat and back she quit. The very next day she went to work at Youbou in the cookhouse as a flunkie, or waitress. Their day started at five and would finish after nine in the evening, so it ended up being a longer day than driving to the Malahat.

"I'd never do that again, even though we could sometimes catch a couple of hours sleep in the afternoon between lunch and the evening meal.

"About a month later I was offered a job at Copper Canyon. That was one of the best jobs I ever had. At first they put me punking whistles on the unit. Jimmy Gammie was the hooker and Ollie Parka was head loader. Those two were the steady guys. The second loaders and the chokermen never stayed long. They'd either quit, or were sent 'down the road'—that's the expression they always used when you were fired. During the war there were few good loggers to be hired. All the key men, such as donkey punchers, hookers, high-riggers and head loaders, were frozen in their jobs. This class of logger wasn't even allowed to join the army."

She worked several months on the unit with Gammie. It was a good setting because the ground was flatter than either the Malahat or Mount Hall. It was a nice change to be working on a railroad show.

"The timber was huge at Copper Canyon. I rarely missed a day because I really liked working there. I was filling a very responsible position. You could injure or kill somebody if you blew the wrong signal, or didn't do exactly what you were supposed to. I had a good pair of leather gloves, and would help pull out the straw line when they had to change roads. The signals were exactly the same as I'd used with the other outfits I'd worked for, so I didn't have to learn all over again. Then I went on the big skidder to work with the Nummi twins.

"That was my biggest promotion with much more responsibility. Tom Nummi was the engineer and his twin brother, Bill, was the hooker. They didn't seem to like women, and they just tolerated me until they realized I had experience and could be trusted. I'd studied the signals every night for a week. It was quite an honor to be asked to go on that big skidder. It was a Ledgerwood, weighed 120 tons, and was the biggest thing in the woods. The main signals were okay, but then they'd holler at me from the back spar. When Raymond Roy was the back rigger he would be yelling at me to send more line back, and someone else would be screaming for lines in. They wanted the lines going in and coming out at the same time. It was a bit confusing at first.

"Changing road was my toughest time. I wasn't used to all that power and the massiveness of the Ledgerwood. I was used to turns being dragged into the landing by ordinary highlead, but that monster just picked the logs up and danced them through the air. There weren't just two or three little logs at a time; they'd hook on half a dozen huge logs. These would dangle along under this great carriage on the skyline and fly

137

through the air right into the landing. The carriage would race back, WHAM, it would stop, and down would come all those chokers.

"They had two sets of chokers. One set out in the woods and one set going in. When they came back they just dropped one set, hooked up to the other, and they were gone again. In the meantime, the other guys would be getting the next turn ready. The men were working right under the skyline. If a wrong whistle went in, the rigging could have come right down on top of the crew. It was just too much responsibility."

These are the signals used in most camps, with possibly minor changes in individual cases. They were kindly provided by Thelma, Mauno Pelto and Ken Hallberg.

SKIDDER (Skyline Operation) WHISTLES

GO SLOW when	Any signal to move any cable is preceded by one LONG whistle
For an accident	SEVEN LONG
Unsafe conditions	BUNCH OF SHORTS continued until the emergency is taken care of
Fire	ONE LONG—BUNCH OF SHORTS repeated
Starting whistle	ONE LONG—usually a bull whistle
Tighten skyline	TWO SHORT—TWO SHORT—TWO SHORT—ONE SHORT
Slacken skyline	TWO SHORT—TWO SHORT—TWO SHORT
Wind in receding line	TWO SHORT—TWO SHORT
Slack receding line	TWO SHORT—TWO SHORT—SEVERAL SHORTS
Wind in skidding line	TWO SHORT
Slack skidding line	TWO SHORT—SEVERAL SHORTS
Wind in transfer line	TWO LONG—stop—ONE LONG
Slack transfer line	TWO LONG—SEVERAL SHORTS
Wind in strawline	THREE SHORT—ONE SHORT
Slack strawline	THREE SHORT—ONE SHORT—SEVERAL SHORTS

138

Wind in slackpulling line	ONE SHORT (when line is stopped)
Slack the slackpulling line	ONE SHORT—SEVERAL SHORTS
Stop any moving line	ONE SHORT, except when carriage is returned to hooker or back rigging crew; then one short means stop carriage and lower chokers to the ground by winding in slackpulling line and paying out skidding line
Stop pulling slack	ONE SHORT
Start again	ONE SHORT
Pull logs up to carriage	TWO SHORT means slack the slack-pulling line, hold receding line and wind in skidding line
Move logs towards head spar	THREE SHORT means wind in skidding line and slackpulling line, put receding drum into interlock which will pay out line at about the same speed as skidding line is winding in
While carriage is moving towards head spar, to stop and pick logs up closer to carriage	TWO SHORT
Pick up slackpulling line while carriage is on its way to head spar	SEVERAL QUICK SHORTS
To shake the carriage to free chokers	TWO SHORT—ONE SHORT
Calling head rigger	TWO long—ONE SHORT

When carriage is at head spar

Check rigging	TWO SHORT

139

Eye splice needed in tong line	ONE SHORT—ONE LONG—ONE SHORT
Send out water bag and/or lunches	ONE SHORT—ONE LONG
Send strawline coils and or prearrange rigging to back end	ONE LONG—TWO SHORT TWO SHORT and ONE SHORT for each coil
Chaser indicating they are sending coils or rigging to back end	ONE LONG—TWO SHORT—TWO SHORT
For longer tongline	TWO SHORT—ONE LONG and ONE SHORT for each 10 feet of line
Shorten tongline	TWO SHORT—ONE LONG—SEVERAL SHORTS and one SHORT for each 10 feet of line
Calling backspar rigger to head spar	TWO LONG—TWO SHORT
Call backspar rigging crew to head spar	TWO LONG—TWO SHORT—FOUR SHORT
Calling hooking crew to head spar	THREE LONG—FOUR OR FIVE SHORT
Number of chokers to return	TWO SHORT—TWO SHORT and ONE SHORT for each choker plus ONE LONG for a bull choker
After pulling cable	ONE LONG (usually with the bull whistle) meant to chain it at back end and tail-holt the sky line

---

After being on the skidder for a year, Thelma was a nervous wreck. In the interest of safety for the rigging crew she decided to quit. Next to the hook tenders, the high riggers or the engineers, Thelma was considered the most important person on the skidder crew. Bill Nummi was rated as one of the greatest hook tenders and riggers on the coast. It was an honor for anyone to have worked with the twins.

"I didn't get to know them very well because they were so quiet and kept to themselves."

"Well you certainly wouldn't have been there that long, if they didn't trust and respect you," I suggested.

"They did trust me. After I quit, Thor Christenson, the logging manager, came to our house and said 'Thelma, please come back. Bill Nummi sent me to ask you to come back'.

"You go back and tell the crew I'll come back next week until they get someone to take my place."

That next weekend there was a big windstorm. The crew went as far as they could go on the speeder. There were trees down everywhere. The men were cutting out the windfalls and clearing the track.

"I was just standing there watching them when Bill Nummi walked by. It was a funny experience. I was never sure if it was Bill or Tom until they spoke. They were identical twins and even dressed alike. Bill never looked at me but he knew I was there. He always called me 'Poonk'. He never did call me by my name. I heard him say, 'Poonk, pick up some branches and make a fire for lunch'. He didn't look in my direction or change his pace in any way, but I knew what he wanted done and I did it. They never at any time used bad language in front of me, nor would they allow it. I'm certain that if I'd allowed any hanky-panky at all Bill would have sent me down the road."

Thelma, in a way, was intimidated by The Nummi twins because they were the bosses of that skidder crew. No one ever questioned that, not even the superintendent. After some weekends, there would often be write-ups in the newspaper about their escapades in town. They were tough guys to argue with. Those who knew them were awed by their reputation. They were hard drinkers and backed off from no one if they'd had a few. It was usually some stranger in town who would say the wrong thing and BAM, it was bye-bye for the night. Thelma recalls, "Bill usually had a bad hangover on Monday mornings. I thought he always walked sideways, but he didn't."

In July of 1966, the Nummi twins were killed in an accident on the main highway going north. It happened when their car struck the rock cut near the top end of Ladysmith Harbour.

This poem appeared in *The Ladysmith-Chemainus Chronicle* on July 28, 1966, written by Herman Anderson, a long-time friend of the twin loggers.

IN MEMORIAM

The quitting whistle echoes from the logged-off hill
Its requiem for old-time logger Bill,
Re-echoes down deep canyons wide
Its sad refrain for Bill who died,
Not in the woods he loved so well,
But in the weekend traffic's rush to Hell.

The B.C. woods will never be the same
For Bill has gone and with him goes the name
Of Logger, the roughest, toughest breed of men
That we have seen and will not see again.
Hard hats in hand we give our last adieu,
We know you're lining up your old-time crew
To log again as you did in days gone by,
We hope you'll take us in when our turn comes to die.

Unhappy Bill to the Big Push said;
'We'll never get any logs round here
Till we get the best damned engineer
The B.C.-Washington woods have seen
In this old age of wood and steam.
You phone our Heavenly Union Hall
And give my brother Tom a Call.'
Tom got the message, toolbox in hand,
Fare-advanced, he goes to that Promised Land
Where you'll never see any sidehill shows
And at four the slack-off whistle blows.
The bunkhouse is a logger's dream,
The cookhouse something you've never seen,

142

With kegs of rum and quarts of beer
And no hangovers in this liquid cheer.
Among old-time friends and with great big grins
Sit Bill and Tom, the skidder twins,
Modern traffic once split them in twain
But these boys will never part again.

"At Copper Canyon we never had breakdowns like some of the gyppo outfits did. We might break the mainline or haulback occasionally, and that's about all. It was nothing to move the skidder to a new setting, because it was on a huge rail car and it moved along the track. The spar tree would usually be up by the time the skidder got there. The yarders were on skids, and that was quite some experience for me to give the signals while those machines pulled themselves through the stumps and over the felled and bucked timber. Sometimes they'd just tell me to go make the lunch fire and keep out of the way. I'd help them rig the spar tree though, and I had to be letter perfect with every signal or whistle. I'd never let anything distract me. No one was ever hurt because of any carelessness on my part.

"To this day, I am very proud when I look back on my record as a whistle punk. As far as I know, I was the first girl to actually work out on the rigging. There were other girls who worked in the cookhouse or drove the crummies, but not out where they were doing the logging. At first I was scared, but those were neat old days. Every day was another challenge. Safety was my important thing. You know, Tom Nummi, the engineer, must have been under tension every minute of every day. When you think about it, he had to be right the first time. There was no time to hesitate and there could be no mistakes. The whole crew had to know all the signals, and what every single one of them meant. I had to be able to distinguish which crew was setting up the turns and who was hollering the signals to me."

Sometimes Thelma would blow 'stop', because she could see a hangup coming. One time, on another machine at the Malahat the engineer gave a great reef just as she blew 'stop'. It was too late. The top of the spar tree snapped off and came down with all the rigging onto the landing. The chaser just dove under the machine. It was a terrible mess, but nobody was seriously hurt.

Thelma Godkin (née Emblem) pictured at Ted Robson's Mount Brenton logging show in 1940: The first lady whistle punk on Vancouver Island.

The crew just looked at each other when the landing crew came crawling out from under the smashed tin roof that had been over the machine. That was the high lead side—Bill Nummi's trees never came down.

Wally Emblem was proud of his daughter, especially when she worked on that big skidder at Copper Canyon. When the nervous strain became too much for safety she would sometimes swap jobs with one of the rigging crew, and set chokers for an hour or two.

"Electrical storms were really bad with all those steel cables in the air. One day a flash of lightning struck the skyline. You could hear it hit and watch it run. It didn't burn the cables, it just danced along to the back end, then ran down the cable to the tailholt stump and started a fire. Luckily, it began to pour rain and the men put the fire out with shovels.

"Sometimes it would get so hot and dry up in the woods during the summer that the crews would have to go on what was called 'early shift'. Some called it 'the hoot owl shift'. The order would come through the night before to go on the early shift. That would disrupt the whole camp. The crews would have to leave home before three the following morning. Mother would always be up to get my breakfast. I'd tell her not to, but she always did. The crews had to be out of the woods by two o'clock in the afternoon. Usually, after about two weeks if there was no rain they would just shut the camp down.

"In those days my wages were $5 a day. That was pretty good for a young girl not too long out of high school. We worked six days a week. On Saturdays we got time and a half. Sundays were at double time if we had to go out on some special job."

Some of Thelma's friends thought she was insane when she started to work in the woods. When the crew sat around eating lunch, some of the younger men would tease her, but it was just fun.

She boasts, "I could make a fire quick as a wink—rain or shine I rarely had to use more than one match. If it took two matches, that was a disgrace."

Thelma Emblem met her husband while working in the woods. The Godkins are presently living in Saltair and enjoying their retirement. In her spare time, Thelma dabbles in oil painting, does some writing, and enjoys reminiscing about her logging days.

145

Bill Moore talking timber in his home at Winter Harbour
on the west coast of Vancouver Island.

CHAPTER 13
Bill Moore

This memoir was written by Bill Moore, and gives an insight
into the way he looked at logging as a child, and on through
life.

I knew a Logger—
His name was Albert.
He ran a small A-frame float camp
out on the West Coast.

His men were hungry thirty loggers.
Top man got Six-fifty a day
Jerk wire whistle punk got two six bits.

He was a kind man
tall and thin

and his crew stuck with him
year after year.
He logged for seven dollars
and fifty cents a Thousand
  in 1934
and swung the logs three or four
  four times
  with steam donkeys.
He asked no favours
and worked hard
  every day of his life.
I can see him yet—
wearing his old battered felt hat
Standing on the felled and bucked
  and
Sizing up the lay of the land.
  He was a logger
  and
  He was my father.

In 1901, the government amended the B.C. Land Act so that any incorporated company empowered to manufacture pulp and paper could obtain a lease of Crown timber for 21 years. They must build and equip a pulp or paper mill capable of producing not less than one ton of paper a day for every square mile of timber leased.

Oriental Power and Pulp Company Limited leased some 85,000 acres in the vicinity of Graham and Fraser Reach and at Swanson Bay they planned a sawmill to produce 100,000 board feet of lumber a day. Their plans also included a sizeable pulp operation and a shingle mill.

Canadian Pacific Sulphite Pulp Company bought this lease in 1906 and started the town and mill construction. They first put in a small sawmill to cut the lumber to house their employees. By 1909 they were actually producing 25 tons of pulp a day, yet this company got into grave financial trouble and was taken over by Empire Pulp and Paper Mills Ltd. With capital of $2.5 million, Empire updated the mills and were employing about 250 men by December, 1916.

According to The Victoria *Times* of May 12, 1917, Empire was purchased and taken over by the Whalen Pulp and Paper

147

Co. with capitalization of $10 million. By 1918, the town of Swanson Bay had a population of 500, which included the mill staff and their families. They were exporting 100,000 board feet of lumber daily, plus pulp and shingles, to Japan and China.

After the First World War, Albert Moore (Bills' father) cruised timber and became The Whalen's logging manager. His headquarters were in the new town of Swanson Bay, about 100 miles south of Prince Rupert and the same distance north of Ocean Falls. Young Bill Moore spent his early childhood in this town and got to know what it was like to live where the rainfall was between 200 and 250 inches a year. Bill suspects Swanson Bay invented rain.

A serious depression followed the First World War. By 1920 Whalen's Lumber and other sales to Japan had disappeared and in 1925, B.C. Pulp and Paper Company Limited was formed to take over all the Whalen interests. Swanson Bay was closed forever. The families moved to other camps and the town was flattened by the heavy snows and wind. Nature reclaims men's dreams and hard work in a relatively short time.

Bill's closing remarks in the British Columbia Lumberman, July, 1974, were:

"Times change—so do people. Swanson Bay has vanished—swallowed by the alders, salmon berries and salal. Ocean Falls is hanging on and there are reasons and people that won't let Mother Nature devour her. Which only proves that the forest around us is a very interesting place that holds countless stories yet to be told."

Bill's father went on his own as a gyppo logger in 1928. He acquired an old Willamette skidder from B.C. Pulp and Paper, built a big A-frame spar on a float, put the skidder aboard and lashed it down. He began producing booms of spruce and hemlock every week for the Port Alice pulp mill. (Port Alice is on Vancouver Island, directly west of Port Hardy.) This mill had been operating for 10 years and was having problems procuring sufficient logs to keep it going until Albert Moore started contracting for them with just one small cookhouse, a couple of bunkhouses, and his A-frame. That was the beginning of their float camp for a 25-man crew. As it grew, the camp was all coupled together with boom chains and was moved along the shoreline with the A-frame.

Two other steam pots up along the mountain were building cold deck piles to be skylined down into the chuck. They were logging the west arm of Quatsino Sound. In the mid-thirties a small gas-powered Fordson was brought in to clean up some of the poorer pockets of timber and tightline the logs directly into the inlet. Albert Moore tried many methods of logging from 1928 until 1935 because the gas engines were commencing to replace steam power.

In 1931, he bought a gas-powered monster from Morrison Tractor & Equipment Company in Vancouver for $3,000. It was called a "caterpillar" and it was the first crawler track machine at Quatsino Sound. Bill, now 10, spent most of his summer holidays following and watching this machine drag logs to the beach. It rained most every day, but the caterpillar managed to wallow through the mud and haul the logs to the water. His dad designed a steel pan, and hooked it up behind the machine to prevent the logs from plowing. This was several years before track arches were used or even thought of.

The A-frame would only work back as far as the main line would reach so Albert hired Harold and Claude Germaine and one of their cousins to build a log chute down over this bluff. It was steep and started about 600 feet up from the beach. They used Gilcrest jacks and B.B. winches to place the two big side logs, then smaller logs were manhandled into place to form the bottom. They moved the Washington steam yarder to the top of the chute. It had a massive main drum that carried over a mile of one inch line to reach the three cold deck piles strung out along the back end. When the skyline cable was rigged, the logs were swung into the hometree at the top end of this chute. A small 9x10 Willamette winch was hooked up with steam pipes from the big donkey's boiler and this was used as the "kick in" machine. It pulled the logs from where the skyline dropped them into the apron to start them down the chute. The bigger logs and boomsticks would come down at 40 miles an hour or more.

"I don't remember if we ever had a fire in the chute," Bill said, "but we sure had lots of smoke flying around at times. I sat in a rowboat out in the bay and watched. Some of the boomsticks would act like torpedoes. They would speed under water and not come up until they were outside the boom pocket. It was my job to put them back in."

It wasn't long before B.C. Pulp and Paper wanted to log in Winter Harbour, then nothing more than a lonely fish camp with a one-room general store. Union Oil had some fuel tanks on a log raft for fish boats.

In August, 1936, Moore's crew towed the A-frames and the rest of the equipment, including the buildings, out into the swells of the Pacific and around into Winter Harbour. It was necessary to uncouple the house floats, to manoeuver them one or two at a time, through the narrows. It was a tough and dangerous move because even a minor storm could have demolished their total outfit. The two Johnson brothers had been sent on ahead in their float shack to start the felling and bucking. When they needed groceries it was a two mile trip in a rowboat.

The price for logs delivered to the Port Alice mill was $7.50 a thousand. The booms had to be towed out into the ocean swells, then back through the inlet to the pulp mill booming grounds. In a matter of minutes those outside waters could change from calm to a raging storm, and most of the heavy floating hemlock would be lost. Those heavy logs would bob along until they came out under the boom sticks, to drift off towards Japan.

At 14, Bill was in school in Vancouver, but working with his dad during the summer holidays, and he recalls, "Our three old steam donkeys were worn out and forever breaking down. Dad was like most old loggers; he loved stretching the equipment out to the very limit. Though we got lots of wood to the pulp mill, the bills kept piling up. There certainly was not enough money in it for a gyppo logger to break even at $7.50 a thousand. I realized this by the time I was 16.

"After finishing school I worked full time, seven days a week, at just about every job there was. If someone got sick or hurt I would take his place to keep things going. As Dad got older, he just seemed to wear out. His health failed rapidly and he died in 1943.

"B.C. Pulp and Paper didn't waste any time telling me about all the outstanding mortgages. They also let me know they needed logs and were expecting them from our camp."

The pulp company arranged for Bill to take over and told him that, according to their books, the three steam donkeys had never been paid for. That was going back over 15 years and there was no way he could prove otherwise, so they charged his account $1,000 for each machine. Bill put up such a fuss they eventually deducted the $3,000 off the mortgages.

"There was nobody else to take charge, so at 21 I had to take over. It was on-the-job training where we paid dearly for our mistakes." It took almost two years to square off the old debts by saving every nickel. Many evenings I'd be making chokers, or doing other repairs in the blacksmith shop until well after midnight. I'd take the steam engineers out at six every morning so they could fire up their machines and be ready for the eight o'clock start.

Bill had just finished building an A-frame float when the company called him in to discuss future logging plans. B.C. Pulp and Paper informed him that A-framing would soon be over. Their maps showed most of the shoreline had been logged, and by the following year he was told it would be all truck logging. They produced maps indicating where the roads would go, and where the new log dump would be built.

"That scared the hell out of me. Our crew were good A-framers and knew every move. It was a joy to watch them work," he said.

From 1943 to 1947, Bill lived on a salary of $100 a month and it was at that wage he courted Beverly North. They were married in 1946. By Christmas of 1948, they were square with the world and had $18,000 in the bank. Bill decided it was time to get out of steam.

Old Garish, one of Moore's earliest employees, had come from Maine as a steam donkey engineer and Bill recalls, "He was a skinny old guy, a marvelous man, and a fine donkey puncher. I told him I was going to Vancouver to buy a diesel donkey. 'You come with me, I'll need your advice.' We'd never seen one and didn't even know what they looked like. He said he'd been a steam man all his life and was scared to death of them new diesel machines!

"Someone told us Finning Tractor would be the place to go. We walked into their Vancouver office and I told the man behind the desk, we wanted a diesel donkey.

"'What kind do you want?' Harold Hall asked me.

"'I don't know.'

"'Well how big do you want it?'

"We want one something like our old 11x13 Willamette. 'It's got to be able to pull logs like that,' Old Garish stated with authority."

After looking at several machines, they bought a BU 135 Skagit. It cost $17,000 and Bill wrote out the cheque. That left less than $1,000 to build a sleigh and buy groceries, but this cash purchase changed everything and they never looked back. The switch from steam to diesel power cut the logging costs almost in half.

"I'll always remember that year with our first Skagit. Garish ran it, but was always a bit nervous. It sure produced logs once he got the throttle open. On Sundays, he would ask me to help him service this 'diesel monster', as he called it. We'd read the instruction book, one page at a time, change the oil, put in new filters, adjust the clutches and brakes, then Garish would spend the rest of the day polishing and admiring. That's how he spent his Sundays. Clean fuel, proper oil and grease, plus a good warm-up in the mornings became a ritual with Garish."

By the end of that year they had bought a new 10-10 Lawrence for $5,000 and the next year another BX 140 Skagit. It was a whole new world. A great future lay ahead.

Alaska Pine, in 1952, helped Bill with the first mile of truck road. Bert Peck and George Percy were their logging managers, and they would drop in to see how things were going. It was arranged that Bill could pay for the cost of the road building on a stumpage basis. A new and different contract was drawn up and they were into truck logging. Again a big change, a different way to get logs in the water.

B.C. Pulp and Paper had applied for Tree Farm Licence #6 on the northwest part of Vancouver Island. That licence was granted and the Koerner brothers bought out B.C. Pulp and Paper and amalgamated with Alaska Pine. They also took over the pulp mills at Port Alice on the Island and Woodfibre in Howe Sound on the mainland. The deal included all lands and timber holdings of both mills. They acquired timber in the Queen Charlotte Islands, Swanson Bay, Port McNeil and Quatsino Sound. Their timber supply was in the billions of board feet.

Before Bill started logging the tree farm timber, contracts would change almost every year. Some were just letters of intent, saying: this year you will log a certain portion according to this plan, and you will receive so many dollars per thousand for doing it. Later Bill hired a good lawyer to help negotiate a five year contract. Things worked much better with the longer range planning.

"How many times has Management Licence #6 changed hands since it was granted?" I asked Bill.

"We are now working with Western Forest Products. It was formed by B.C. Forest Products, Doman Industries and Whonnock Lumber. When #6 was granted in 1948, the cruisers estimated it contained approximately four billion feet of timber. When it sold the second time, other cruisers estimated it contained nearer 10 billion board feet. It still has the same boundaries, and loggers have been cutting on it for years.

"At first, some 30 per cent of the tree farm timber was left on the ground to rot. They ignored the cedar, considering it a big nuisance. When the forestry started to scale this wood and charge stumpage, they began loading it on barges and shipping it out. It wasn't unusual to see six-foot #1 Hemlock logs go into the chippers at the Port Alice pulp mill.

"Criminal!" Bill snorted in disgust. "Wasting good timber was certainly not the intent of any tree farm licence."

Bill's float camp at Winter Harbour was getting heavy in the water by 1952. They rented some land from the Indians and moved the houses ashore. It was a nice bit of property with a good beach and near a stream. When the land was cleared it made a beautiful camp site. The Indian band would only agree to a one-year lease with no guarantee of renewal so all the buildings were left on skids.

"In 1967 we put on a music festival. I love all kinds of music, and it has always been a part of my life," Bill said. "We invited people from Vancouver we knew would be interested. When Pacific Western Airlines were asked for some free air tickets they offered us one of their DC 3s, with a pilot, for the entire weekend. We kept it busy from daylight to dark.

"Ray Williston, the Minister, Dan Campbell, our MLA, two aldermen from Vancouver, Jack Webster and many other dignitaries were invited. All the mayors and boss loggers from Victoria to Port Hardy were brought in for the celebration. Tables and benches and a covered stage were built in the ball field. A chap from Alert Bay brought over and installed a good public address system. It was really neat," Bill recalled with obvious pride.

It was known as The Downtown Winter Harbour Music Festival, and was such a success they did it again in 1969 and 1971. Lance Harrison, Barnie and Thora Potts, Pat Morgan, Fraser McPherson from Vancouver and The Pat Kelly Trio from San Francisco were just a few of the big names to arrive in 1971.

"The vice-president of Standard Oil, Dermot O'Reilly, along with Jack Monahan and Gerry Holmes set up a free bar out on an old cedar stump down by the creek. They were out of booze within an hour.

"The ladies from camp tried desperately to keep the masses fed. It was a social thing, so we only charged a dollar a carload to get in. We had over 2,500 people at the little camp in 1971. The hippies arrived with their pot and all kinds of other stuff. It was crazy. Two nights before the festival started, the ladies were cooking for over 150 early arrivals. Campers of every description came. It was a madhouse. My wife was crying that night. It was just too much for Winter Harbour, so we never held another one."

Bill realized a long term deal with the Indian band was impossible, so they decided to move the camp off the reserve. Bill's father had bought some 250 acres of crown grant timberland with about a mile of shoreline at the south end of Winter Harbour in 1935 from Ben Leason who had pre-empted it around the turn of the century. Old Ben, at one time, also had a clam canning factory to augment his photography business.

Moores' floating camp before it was towed out into the Pacific Ocean and around into Winter Harbour.

154

It was a tough piece of ground to clear and move the camp on to, but at least it would be permanent. Roads had to be built and it was expensive to grade the site. They built a cookhouse, shops, log dump, bunkhouses and more family quarters. It cost almost a million dollars. A school was next on the list.

Bill started their own home in 1973 on a six acre island, linked to the shore by a short causeway.

"Thank God we did the whole thing then. We never could have afforded to do it a few years later. We finished it all just before building costs went sky high."

"Bill, what do you think is going to happen now? The Indians seem to think they can lay claim to all of Canada," I asked, stating a problem that concerns all British Columbians.

"Well Joe, we have some gutless politicians who won't step in to say or do anything. Our grandfathers and great-grand-fathers won the damned war a long time ago! No one seems to know the answer, but we'd better find one pretty quick."

Bill also holds some strong opinions on tree farm licences, saying "I don't believe all tree farm licences are treated as tree farms. Some companies use them as a source of raw material, and not like a farm that must produce our next crop of trees. Proper thinning and various silviculture practices need to be up-dated. They go through the motions, but the new growth is so thick in our part of the country it can't possibly grow properly."

Bill Moore is still logging at Winter Harbour in a very substantial way and intends to carry on for at least another five-year contract period. His continuing advice to loggers is summarized in various articles he writes for timber magazines: "Keep out of the bite."

155

Norm and Gladys on the *Reverie* before sailing the
Atlantic Ocean in the 1960's.

CHAPTER 14

Norm Madill

Norm's Dad, Sam Madill, was born in the village of Minne-
dosa, directly west of Winnipeg and south of the Riding Mountain National Park. An ambitious fellow, it was there he had
apprenticed as a blacksmith, machinist and wheelwright. When
he came west, Sam worked for several years in the Fraser
Valley before moving to Nanaimo in 1911 to begin working for
the Wilkinsons in their blacksmith shop. After a couple of
years there, Sam went to work for himself.

His first shop was on Ravine Street, next to Akenhead's old
livery stables, and just south of a thriving red light district.
When the circus came to town in those early years, they set up
in an area near his blacksmith's shop. Their horses had to be
shod and work done on the wagons and other equipment.
Norm can still remember watching the clowns and eating the
colored candy floss.

"Our first shop building was only 30 feet square, with a steep, cedar-shake roof and a heavy front door that slid open on tracks. I spent most of my summer holidays cleaning up horse manure and turning the bellows for the forge.

"Dad used to take me with him out to the farms so I could hand him horseshoe nails as he shod the big teams. In the winter he'd put sharp cleats on the steel shoes so the horses could work on the frozen ground and ice. The Beban family had a string of good race horses and it was a thrill to go there with Dad and see the beautiful stables and race track. Mrs. Beban would always bring out tea and cookies to where we were shoeing their horses. Frank Beban was in mining, sawmilling, and logging long before we came to Vancouver Island," Norm recalls.

Sam and his sons were doing a roaring business welding and repairing road equipment for the Provincial government after the war. They were also building bunks, bulkheads, draw bars, and water tanks for the logging trucks. They also designed and manufactured one of the first steel-heel booms for loading logs with a power shovel.

All this work forced them to look for larger premises, and they bought the Newcastle Shipyard building next to the old ice arena and remodelled it into a heavy duty machine shop. One end was equipped as a blacksmithing area where old Sam continued to hammer out logging hooks, tongs, and other equipment. In the other end, near the water, they began constructing steel boom boats.

These little boats could turn around in their own length and go backwards as fast as they went ahead. When it came to sorting logs in a bull pen and pushing them into the various pockets, one of these powerful little dozer boats could do the work of half a dozen good boommen with pike poles. They were powered by Chrysler gas engines, but were soon changed to the more reliable diesels. The Madills' new shop built hundreds of these dozer boats which revolutionized booming methods. Norm did all the drawings on the weekends, and was responsible for the design. Some 40 years later this type of boat is still in use.

Madill's also did some revolutionary labor relations. It was Norm and their accountant Oscar Harder who devised a system whereby all the men involved in the shop work could share in the profits. Oscar went on to make his system agreeable to the workers and the federal tax department. It was the boom boats and the new concept of profit-sharing that started the Madill organization on the road to becoming a successful public company.

Joe Cliff, a boss logger for Comox Logging had built a portable banjo-headed spar at Nanaimo Lakes. It was one of the very first steel spars in British Columbia, and it marked the beginning of the end of the legendary high riggers and wooden spar trees.

Adopting Cliff's design, the Madills built their first spar the following year. It was bought by Baikey Brothers of Campbell River.

"It had the banjo head, but we used better steel and it was much lighter than the one Joe Cliff had built at Nanaimo Lakes. We mounted ours on a standard logging truck which made it quicker to move and set up. We used mechanical winches on the guylines, but soon found out that the banjo head part was just too cumbersome. Then I designed and patented a double acting fairlead on a swivel. The biggest job was getting this fairlead patented. We had to submit drawings and then write up a legal description. It took about a year to get it put through. This fairlead was built right in our own shop and mounted on the top of the next steel spar. The fairlead system was the making of the steel spars," said Norm.

"Tom Carter of Van West Logging purchased the second spar and helped us get the bugs out of it. Because of his logging knowledge he was a great help when we started the third, which had a long hydraulic cylinder to assist in the raising and lowering of the 90-foot spar. We installed hydraulic winches for tightening the guylines.

"We couldn't afford a qualified engineer, so my younger brother Chuck did the selling and I did most of the design work and looked after the shop crew. It was a lot of long hours and hard work for both of us. In 1962, I was 45 years old, and feeling the increasing pressure of the unions on our workers."

Oscar Harder was doing the tax work for both S. Madill Limited and Garner Bros. Ltd. The two companies had been doing substantial business together for the past 15 years. Oscar phoned me in Duncan about noon and asked me to a meeting in Nanaimo that evening with Norm and Chuck.

As we drove up in his car, Oscar explained,

"You know, Joe, Norm is president and general manager of Madill's and he's planning to leave on an extended holiday. While he's away Chuck will be taking full charge. Since you have been doing a great amount of business together, I felt you should have a chat."

We joined Norm and Chuck aboard the Madills' sailboat the *Reverie*, had drinks and some sandwiches, then Norm said, "I'm leaving in the morning at daylight to sail down the coast and go through the Panama Canal. I expect to be away for some time so Chuck will be taking complete charge of everything, and you can carry on with him as you and I have done in the past."

I stood up amidships and could almost touch both gunwales with my finger tips, saying "Norm, you're surely not going out in the open Pacific in this narrow gauge contraption." Then Oscar told me this was one of the most seaworthy 50-foot sailers in the world.

"She was built in India by a retired British Army officer and is narrow because she had to be moved 600 miles over their rail line to get to the ocean. At the coast she was loaded on a ship and taken to England to be fitted out with sails. Reverend John Antle of the Columbia Coast Mission bought her in England and sailed her across the Atlantic, through the Panama Canal and up the coast to Maple Bay."

"If an old man could do that," Norm said "I sure as hell should be able to take her down the coast and through the canal." We all drank to that.

Norm and Gladys spent several months in and around the Florida Keys, repairing the sails and preparing for the next leg of their journey. They knew it was going to be a rough one— crossing the Atlantic from west to east. It took them 24 days to reach the Azores.

Norm said, "This crossing was no picnic. The *Reverie* with its narrowness, seemed to go through the waves rather than ride over them. We hit one bad storm where we tacked for a full week with the sails reefed and in winds around 60 miles an hour. One of us had to be at the tiller at all times. You can imagine the problem of preparing meals and getting sleep under these conditions. During this storm we saw no ships of any kind. By the time we tied up in the Azores we were exhausted. It was like a dream to soak in a hot bath and get some much needed sleep. After resting for a few days, we sailed on to Gibralter. It took us another six days to cover that 900 miles.

"We spent over a year cruising the Mediterranean, Spain, France and Italy. With her big, long bowsprit and a boom coming out over the stern, the *Reverie* was the curse of the Mediterranean where everyone normally ties up stern-to. We then cruised down to Malta and sailed around for awhile. We had an offer for our boat and we sold her.

"After that we went to Holland where it took two years to have a motor-sailer built. I did the structural drawings for her, but an English architect drew the lines and did the sails. The steel hull was contracted to a firm called Van Lim. They were building Henry Ford's *Santa Maria* in the same yard, right alongside our *Reverie II*. Ours was a 55-footer, but twice as roomy as the *Reverie*. We lived in a cottage near the shipyards for the first while, then moved aboard the new boat until she was finished. Those were two of the coldest winters in Holland in over 50 years. The ice on the canal was over 18 inches thick, so we drove our camper out and parked there beside the boat all winter."

The *Reverie II*, like the *Reverie*, was also fitted out in England. Norm and Gladys courageously faced the open ocean again, and sailed their new boat back across the Atlantic. They must have enjoyed the challenge, because they were to sail her again back to Europe. The second crossing took only 19 days. Norm sold the *Reverie II* before coming back home to live on Vancouver Island.

After Norm started his lengthy vacation, Madill's carried on, but Chuck was doing such a good job of sales and management that this shop also became too small to keep up with the business coming in.

A larger new shop was built three miles north of Nanaimo, on the corner of the Island Highway and Bowen Road. With bigger and better lathes, welding equipment, presses, and a smart, young permanent engineer, the steel spars, boom boats,

A skidder landing a turn on a skyline. Photo courtesy of Bob Swanson.

A Madill portable steel spar with its own loader attached. A marvelous idea
that didn't prove to be a big hit with the loggers. It does demonstrate that the
Madills were willing to spend their own money to develop new and better
logging equipment.

Madill's first steel spar, for Baikie Bros. Logging, being set up at Campbell River. The banjo head was not satisfactory and was later replaced with swivel fairleads.

A late model Type-044 Madill yarding crane in action. This machine is powered by a 535 h.p. diesel engine and is a real log-getter. There is not much left of a million dollars by the time such a unit is completely rigged with lines and other gear, then moved and set up in the woods.

Sitting on this huge 14′ spruce log near Alliford Bay on the Queen Charlotte Islands in April of 1959 are Archie Rafter and George Naylor, managers for Crown Zellerbach. The top of this tree had blown off 165′ up, where the diameter was still 5′. It was felled and bucked by Frank Landry and Rudy Simonson in 7½ hours. The six 25′ logs scaled out at 51,004 board feet.

Grandfather Joseph Richards stands at base of Westholme tree sometime prior to 1900. This tree grew about 150 yards southeast of the present Westholme school. The top of this tree had blown off about 180′ above the ground and measured over 4′ in diameter at the break. Granddaughter Phyllis Richards has original photgraph with notes declaring the tree to be over 300′ high, and growth rings counted at over 1500 years old. Photo courtesy of Phyllis Richards.

Westholme tree blew down November 24, 1913 and blocked what was then the Island Highway. It was the largest Douglas fir ever recorded according to *The Cowichan Leader*, November 1913. Indians took the bark and cut the tree for wood. Joe and Fred Richards are standing on the tree, while Billie Thomas and a 1912 Model-T Ford are in the foreground. Photo courtesy of Fred and Frank Holman.

This is one of the early Madill portable steel spars, serial #41027. It was donated to the B.C. Forest Museum by Pacific Logging Ltd. *Note*: The swivelling fairleads at the very top were designed and patented by the Madills.

A view of heavy track arrangement making the S196C Madill spar mobile. (Opposite page)

D-4 Cat, and specially designed rubber tired arch, yarding salvage logs out of the Ladysmith logging slash.

This is a portable chain elevator designed by Mauno Pelto to load the salvage timber. This system worked well enough until loading was improved by using airtong shovel loaders.

Salvage pulp logs being unloaded off a special truck at Ladysmith Harbour.

A self-dumping barge being unloaded, by pumping water into one side of the barge, for Crown Zellerbach in Ladysmith Harbour.

Dynamite explosions were used to loosen log pile and spill logs into the water. Fred Holman crouched at the end of the barge while setting off the blast, then hung on while the barge skittered across the water for some hundreds of feet before it settled down.

A-Frame lifting a full load of logs (approximately 110 tons), then lowering into booming grounds at Kelsey Bay. Photo courtesy of *Loggers World.*

Torchy Kulai, General Woods
Foreman for Crown Zellerbach
for over 30 years.
Photo courtesy of *Loggers World*.

Flying Grapple. This is the
grapple considered by some to be
the best in the business.
Note choker hookup directly
behind the grapple.
Photo courtesy of *Loggers World*.

A set of Triples, on a main haul road, heading for the log sorting yard. Truck engine is a 500 H.P. V-12. Photo courtesy of *Loggers World*.

Side view of a "snorkel" on an American loader, used for short yarding and truck loading. Photo courtesy of *Loggers World*.

Top. The mill buildings that were at Swanson Bay in 1925.

Centre. Swanson Bay where Bill Moore spent his childhood.

Right. This concrete structure is all that remains standing of Swanson Bay. The rest is now a forest of alders and salmonberry bushes.

A Madill small dozer contraption being tested near their old shop in downtown Nanaimo.

Hundreds of these small boom boats were built by Madill's, and became a way of life at booming grounds in many parts of the world.

and other new logging equipment was being manufactured in volume. The name of Madill could be seen on logging equipment in about every country in the world where logging was being done. It was not unusual to see a barge heading north for

Alaska every spring with half a dozen or more Madill spars aboard.

The Madill family is presently in its third generation of logging equipment construction. One of their latest pieces of yarding equipment is a grapple yarder—Type: 044, Model 60500, with a 535 horse power Diesel engine and a 70-foot long tower all equipped for grapple yarding. It will cost the logger just a bit under $1 million! This machine is designed to work and yard without chokermen or other men hooking up the logs. The operator spots and closes the grapple with push button controls from his high cab, a far cry from the old steam skidders with the skyline and 20-man crews. This machine is mobile on tracks and moves along a road by pressing a button.

The logging industry will always owe the Madills a debt of gratitude for their willingness to experiment and improve. There are no new types of equipment they won't try if they believe it can work.

Joe Frumento, born 1923, recently retired as General
Manager of Doman Industries Ltd.

CHAPTER 15
Joe Frumento

Joe Frumento's career has covered many facets of forestry. His
great-grandfather Giovani Ordano arrived in San Francisco
from Genoa, Italy in 1852. He was so impressed by the west
coast he returned to Italy on the same ship, gathered his
belongings, and came back to California. He made his way up
the coast to the San Juan Islands, where he worked for the
Hudson's Bay Company and first met Sir James Douglas.

Giovani soon started his own business at Friday Harbour,
on Orcas Island. He bought salmon from the Indians, smoke-
cured them by his own special process, and sold them to the
British Navy at a good profit.

Giovani became involved in the ruckus that started the
famous Pig War. Cutler, his neighbour, was a declared American who shot a pig owned by Charles J. Griffin, also a neigh-

bour and a declared Canadian. This brouhaha called the Pig War eventually led to the location of an agreeable boundary between British Columbia and the State of Washington through the American San Juan Islands and Canada's Gulf Islands.

"When great-grandfather Giovani declared himself a Canadian he was ordered to head north within 48 hours or be jailed. He and a Catholic priest piled their belongings into a big canoe and paddled north toward Cowichan Bay. They were the first white settlers to live there," Joe declares.

This priest worked with the Cowichan Indians and helped them to build the first Church in the Cowichan Valley. It is presently known as The Old Stone Church and stands on a rock ledge overlooking Cowichan Bay. The Duncan Chamber of Commerce re-roofed this old landmark and it is now a tourist attraction.

Genoa Bay was named by Giovani after his birth place. He and the priest camped there for several months before moving on up to the main Indian settlement on the Cowichan River. Giovani built the first trading post in the area near where the little white wooden Catholic church now stands. He soon had a thriving business going with the local Indians.

Giovani batched and tended his trading alone for a while, then latched on to a young Indian lady to help with the housekeeping and other chores. A daughter, Antoinette, was born. She was Joe's grandmother. Two boys and another daughter followed.

The couple worked together at the trading post, and Giovani amassed quite a sizeable fortune.

"He had a good Italian system going," Joe said with a big smile. "He bought smoked fish from the Indians for five cents and sold them to the British Navy for fifty cents — by his standards that was a ten per cent markup."

Some years later Giovani took three of his children to Italy so they could marry and bring Italian spouses back to Canada. Antoinette married Pasqualli Frumento, better known as Pete. They had four children. One was Joe's father, David Austin Frumento, and when the First World War started he enlisted, went overseas with the Canadian Army, and was badly wounded in action. He was sent to a hospital in England to recuperate, and there he fell in love with his nurse, Harriette. David and

Harriette were married just before the war ended and their honeymoon trip brought them home to Cowichan Bay. They had three children—one daughter, Lillian, and two sons, Pat (the elder) and Joe. Shortly after Joe was born, his mother and father separated and eventually divorced.

"When I was six my mother married Domingo Ambrigo Ordano, my great-uncle, so he became my stepfather," Joe explains. "That's how the Ordanos and Frumentos became related.

"My Mom was a great lady. You had tea with her many times. She was of good English stock and came out here determined to make a success of it. But unfortunately, her first marriage didn't work out. I think in the long run it was better for her. My stepfather was a very fine gentleman, a very honest person, and a strict taskmaster. You had to toe the line. Although he lectured us a lot, he never laid a hand on us. I've met a lot of people, including your brother Tom, who did business with him. Did you know that Domingo loaned your brother Tom some money? This was when Tom was first getting started. My stepfather rarely picked a loser. He could judge people. His deals were straightforward and he honored any commitment he ever made.

"We lived in a big house by the Koksilah River near Cowichan station. Joe Kerrone was doing some horse logging there. We owned a big barn that he rented for his logging horses. I would clean out the stables for him, then go out to meet the teams on their way home. He would always stop them and put me up on the lead horse, and let me ride the last quarter of a mile to the barn. I remember sitting on that big lead horse and imagining myself as 'the teamster'.

"Mr. Slater hauled Kerrone's logs from Cowichan Station on an old White logging truck and trailer. It was a chain-drive, single axle with solid rubber tires. That old truck hauled those big logs up the hill right in front of our house. We could see them from our front window," Joe remembers. "The chain drives would just wind the front wheels up in the air until the truck got over the steepest part of the hill.

"The logs were dumped at Cowichan Bay and boomed on contract by Domingo. When things got tough in the early 30's, My brother Pat quit school and started to work full time with our stepfather. Joe was only 12 when he learned to run the swifter winch and work along with brother Pat during the summer holidays.

MacMillan Export hired Domingo to sort the logs they were using for plywood. Jack Sexton was in charge of log buying and sorting and he would go over and show Domingo how he wanted the logs sorted for the various mills. This took a lot of time so he usually stayed at the hotel, just up from the wharf.

Domingo also had a boatworks and built and rented out fishing boats to the tourists. Mrs. Ordano invited Jack to stay in their guest room instead of paying at the hotel. They had a two-storey house and she offered Jack an upstairs room. Jack remembers: "The first night there Domingo suggested we should go fishing first thing next morning. Sometime during the night I got a tap on the shoulder.

"I slid out of bed, dressed in a hurry, went down to their kitchen, then sat around drinking coffee for almost an hour. Glancing at my watch, it was a bit of a shock to learn it was not yet 3:30. We drank more coffee until it started to get daylight. We then went out and fished for over an hour, but caught nothing."

'Killer whales in the bay—that's why the salmon won't bite,' Domingo told me."

That evening they tried again and Jack landed two huge spring salmon. One weighed 38 pounds and the other was over 40. Somehow the Victoria radio got hold of this news and put it on the air: Jack Sexton of Vancouver fishing Cowichan Bay on Thursday landed two huge 40 pound springs. Domingo had probably phoned the radio station to bolster his boat rentals.

Jack got a reprimand when he arrived at work next morning. "You're supposed to be marking logs, not fishing," H.R. said. Then with a smile, "I wouldn't mind having a couple of slices of that salmon if you can spare it."

Domingo also did contracting for Victoria Lumber which owned the big mill at Chemainus managed by John Humbird. They had logging camps at Shaw Creek and McKay Creek, near the Cowichan River. That timber was all hauled down to Cowichan Bay on the C.N.R. Some of the better eight-section booms would scale out at over half a million board feet.

Domingo and John Humbird made a new contract every

spring. Domingo would do all the booming and sorting for them and John would come down to discuss the contract. Joe recalls them sitting in their living room, sipping tea and devouring short-bread cookies, arguing whether the price for booming should be 18 or 19 cents a thousand.

Joe learned early that when you work in a family business you don't get paid much and the day never ends, so at 17 he left booming and worked for the Hillcrest Lumber Company just west of Duncan. Lem Traer was camp boss and put him to work on the rigging with a cold deck crew. Joe was soon promoted to the track side on their Washington skidder. Traer then put him second rigging with George Parlee who was their number one hook tender and did most of the high rigging.

"After that, I went over to head load for Neil (Cougar) Smith. He swore at me one day when I did something dangerous. I got mad and quit. Old Cougar was an all-round good logger, and later became a prosperous gyppo. He and his sons have done very well in the logging business. They were all good men in that family.

"I later went hooking for Blainey Clarke on the west side of Shawnigan Lake, until the Second World War started." Joe made plans to go to England and join the Royal Air Force and it took him almost a month to make all the necessary arrangements. He booked passage on the *Anglo Canadian*, an old tramp steamer that was scheduled to sail from Cowichan Bay on September 28, 1939. He missed the ship because it had sailed five days early. He was working in the woods and couldn't be contacted. Most of the young men who went over on that ship didn't come back. It wasn't until 1940 that Joe got his call to join the R.C.A.F.

He spent four and a half years overseas, coming home in August of 1945. "I'd seen a bit of the world and was glad to get back working on the booms for the old man again. We worked together from 1945 to 1950, and during that time I got married.

"We handled all the MacMillan logs, and the booming for Virgil Stoltz and Gerry Wellburn. Our family operation had no workmen's compensation or unemployment insurance, and this worried me in case there should be an accident."

In the spring of 1950, B.C. Forest Products had a major break-up of log booms in the Victoria harbor. They needed experienced people and Bill Hemmingsen called Joe to come down and help straighten up the mess. They appreciated his knowledge of logs and booming and offered him a steady job with a good monthly salary. In less than a year he had learned their log requirements and became one of their log buyers. This was a management position and soon Joe was transferred to head office in Vancouver.

B.C. Forest Products, building the Crofton Pulp Mill in 1958, brought him over to set up the raw material supply department, and supervise the log sorting and storage facilities.

"I was there during the start-up, and it was a once in a lifetime experience. Few people ever have this opportunity. Pulp mills are like anything else. When you first start them they never run right. We just slept at the mill for three weeks and tried to iron out the problems as they arose."

Joe's responsibilities included supervising the log and chip supply, and overseeing the operations of the wood rooms as well as all the storage and log buying. In 1967, they told him he would soon be going back to head office in Vancouver. He discussed this at home and his two children laid down the law: "If you go over there you'll have to go by yourself!" they both declared.

"While I was at Crofton I'd got to know Herb Doman pretty well. When he heard I didn't want to move back to Vancouver he asked me if I would consider joining his company. Herb was a Duncan boy who had built a sawmill at Ladysmith and was having some problems. I thought about it overnight and said yes. At 48, it's not easy to make a change, but I didn't want to live in Vancouver again."

Herb Doman and Joe worked well together and the sawmill soon started making profits. Joe was made responsible for log buying and complete management of the sawmill operation, and then was promoted to general manager. Doman's only had this one good sawmill at that time, and despite some flaws in the equipment it was basically good. During his first year at Ladysmith, the mill produced 30 million board feet of lumber. The second year it was up to 80 million, and the third year production was 120 million board feet. Ladysmith Forest Products proved to be a good mill, and made a lot of money. It was this operation that was the beginning of Doman's success.

During the early 70's Doman's built two new mills. The first was a dry-land mill on the highway at Chemainus. Before Chemainus was operating smoothly, the foundation for the Cowichan Bay mill was poured on May 12, 1975 and it started up on January 2, 1976. The Cowichan mill was built in record time at a cost of nearly $10 million.

"Damned near broke the company," Joe remembers "but we struggled through because the markets were in an upturn."

The Cowichan Bay mill was rated as one of the most up-to-date mills in the province. On a two-shift basis, it produced better than 135 million feet of lumber every year. A lively sawmill and a good money maker, it still has one of the highest productivity levels per man-hour of any sawmill in North America.

Doman's also had just started a logging operation in Jervis Inlet. Teddy Robson had originally owned the timber licences. Tom Garner bought them and later sold to Andy Olson and Doman's bought Olson's out. Joe said, "Andy had this old Cummins operated dump machine there. I asked him where it had come from."

"'Hell, that's one of the old steam yarders from Hillcrest,' Andy replied."

Joe at 17 had worked on that same machine when George Parlee was his boss. The old steam engine had been replaced with a diesel, and it was still doing a pretty good job. It's not just the loggers that go from one camp to another.

Joe said: "Herb didn't think the company was big enough, so we tendered on a timber sale in Rivers Inlet. Our bid was accepted, so we grew a bit more. When the Pearce Royal Commission changed the forest act, this claim became a Tree Farm Licence. Doman's were fortunate in the selection of that particular area because once established as a tree farm they were assured of timber for 20 years."

Herb Doman then announced he had arranged financing to build another large log mill near Nanaimo, at Duke Point. They started in 1979 and put the mill into production in 1980. This complex is probably one of the most efficient large log mills on the whole coast. Duke Point presently puts out 160 million feet of lumber a year on two shifts. Joe is sure it could easily go up to 220 million feet on three shifts with a few changes and a better log supply.

"Our group has now amalgamated with B.C. Forest Products and Whonnock Lumber, so we're a consortium of three. Things happened very quickly once we acquired that Knight Inlet timber and finished the Nanaimo Mill. We had completed all but one of our commitments and that was to build a pulp mill.

"We were all gung-ho and actually very close to setting up a deal with a Japanese partner to build a pulp mill at Duke Point. Then, along with B.C. Forest Products and Whonnock Lumber, we took the opportunity to buy out the Rayonier interests here. It was a major move and we did it because the companies were all reasonably timber poor. We needed a better source of big logs," Frumento explained.

"The timing was very poor. The ink was barely dry on the purchase contract before the recession of the early 80's started. The market went down and bank interest rates went up. Once again it damn near broke us.

"However, our new consortium survived because of long hours and hard work. Herb Doman spent a tremendous amount of time either in Vancouver or back east trying to persuade his bankers to stay with us. I recall hearing Herb say many times 'You know Joe, I have to get over there. You stay here and run the mills. I'll see if we can hold it all together'. At one time Herb Doman had to let the banks hold some of the company's preferred shares as security. 'We were the only business in Canada with a debt that exceeded its annual total sales', Herb confessed to me. It took a lot of good people working and staying together to keep the company out of bankruptcy. Eventually, timber prices began to rise and in 1985 the group came up with a $40 million profit. It looks about the same for 1987. If we have three good years in a row, this company is assured of a sound financial future."

I asked Joe, "Did you have anything to do with the pulp mill at Port Alice?"

"Oh yes, we updated that pulp mill three years ago. Matter of fact, it was Herb's idea. The debt load on the company was way too high. I'm not talking about Doman's. I'm talking about the Rayonier operations that eventually became Western Forest Products. It was evident those old pulp mills would never work themselves out of debt in the condition they were in.

"The pulp mill at Squamish had never been modernized and was one of the oldest on the Pacific Coast. Herb came up with the idea of selling some partnership stock to raise enough money to modernize and update both these old pulp mills. Now, after many millions of dollars, Port Alice and Port Mellon are the most modern pulp producing mills in the world."

Joe recalls going up there when they first bought the Port Alice mill: "We had several big shots from B.C. Forest Products and Bob Sutter from Whonnock with us. We thought we'd better find out what we were getting into. We hired a helicopter and went over all the logging claims. We went up to the Queen Charlottes and down through Port McNeill, over to Port Alice, and finally ended up in Bill Moore's camp at Winter Harbour.

"Bill had a big sign up on the side of his house. It had a lot of company names on it—B.C. Pulp, Alaska Pine, Abitibi, Rayonier and a couple of others. Pointing to the sign, Bill's welcoming hello was 'I've survived all six of them so I guess I can survive you guys'.

"Bill Moore's a 100 per cent man and a good logger too. He has a great sense of humour."

"I've worked for several big companies. I feel that my promotions came because of the common sense I learned by working in the family business. Like most young people in those days, we didn't get much education. I completed Grade 10, brother Pat left school in Grade Seven and my sister Lil finished grade Eight.

"You've bumped into a lot of education. It must be pretty tough now, with all the college graduates going into management," I cut in.

"We pick most of our foremen and superintendents from the bright people that come up through the ranks. They know their jobs from the ground up. Nearly all our top sawmill people, who really got the company going, are practical people who have learned the job by doing it. Of course, it's a must to have some university graduates in our forestry division.

"I intend to retire on my 65th birthday. I believe in letting the younger generation take over the responsibilities," Joe added.

I have known and watched Joe Frumento and Herb Doman since they finished school. It has always been a pleasure to do business with both men. They should be as proud of their achievement as I am proud to be their friend.

Joe, tall, dark and handsome, married his first wife Catherine Rae in 1947. Her father was the first white child born at Squamish. Son Earl is presently a sawyer in Doman's big mill at Duke Point in Nanaimo, and their daughter Donna works in the Island Savings Union in Duncan as an investment officer.

Joe and his present wife Johanna, who loves gardening, are both enjoying retirement on their Quamichan Lake acreage. Though Joe at times does a bit of consulting work, he is pleased to be away from the hectic pressures of big business.

Joe with daughter Mrs. Donna Barry and son Earl. In front are grand-daughters Sarah and Jennifer.

Al Garner, President of Quesnel Division,
Prince George Truck Loggers'
Association, January 1969.
Courtesy *The Big Wheel* bulletin Jan-Feb, 1969

CHAPTER 16
Al Garner

In the summer of 1926, my six-year-old brother Al left Salts-pring Island to live in Vancouver with Mother, so that he could go to a better school and know the difference between country and city living. Mother had decided to leave Dad. Two of the ten Garner children stayed on Saltspring with their father.

Al recalls, "I started in Grade Two at Block 70 School and went on to Templeton Junior High. Part way through Grade 10, Mother decided we should move to Westholme on Vancouver Island. My brother Tom had offered me a job helping him build a gas donkey that summer. We moved this machine to Crofton and I had the job of blowing whistles and chasing at the landing. His timber was on the Crofton smelter property, near the beach at the very south end of the harbor. I worked there all the summer of 1936."

Al's next job was on Mount Provost, at a MacMillan tie mill, punking whistles on a Fordson donkey. It was a jerkline show and Al, though only 16, was soon promoted to the Number One side. He started this job at 35 cents an hour. After the Union organized the camp, the minimum wage was boosted to 50 cents. Al got 65 days back pay on this deal, about $78, a lot of money in those days.

"MacMillan laid us all off in 1938," Al remembers. "They had cut all the timber and were moving the mills to the Malahat. The older Garner boys had just completed a subdivision north of Chemainus. The lots were selling at $250 each with $10 down and $5 per month, plus 4 per cent interest on the balance. Mother picked a lot and Tom gave it to her. The boys built a nice three bedroom house and our family was able to move in. It was November," Al remembers.

"I worked on the steam boilers at the Chemainus mill on weekends, and through the week for Slim Hayes on construction. He had bought a lot and lived next door. Hayes was doing the cupboards in Mother's kitchen for his meals. He was like one of the family. When war was declared on September 3, 1939, he and I signed up for active service the same day.

Al did his training in Victoria with the 17th Surfside Battery. It was almost three years before he was sent overseas with the 6th Anti-Tank Regiment.

He was stationed on the south coast the afternoon before the D-Day invasion. They were rushing to finish waterproofing the electrical wiring systems on the jeeps and tanks that were to be on the landing barges. They had orders to have everything ready to move out at midnight.

Six of them were working frantically under a big oak tree when they heard a buzz bomb coming over. An aircraft gave chase and shot the engine out of this bomb . A deep slit trench had been dug near the tree. Al, was the sergeant and yelled, "Dive for the ditch".

He has only a vague recollection of hearing a crash before being buried alive. He doesn't know how long it was before he was dug out, but he remembers not being able to see because his eyes were full of dirt.

"They told me later that the oak tree had been completely

174

shattered and that we were buried under four feet of earth. Somehow there was enough air to keep us going."

Six electricians had been buried in that trench, but they all came out alive and were taken by ambulance to the nearest hospital. Al had metal shrapnel in his back and shoulders. The doctor got four pieces out but he still carries two chunks of metal in his back.

"The enemy had started sending these bombs over about a week before D-Day. We were right in line between the Channel and London. That bomb, carrying 1,000 pounds of explosives, was within 15 feet of us when it exploded. If we hadn't jumped into the ditch we'd all have been blown to smithereens."

Those slivers of metal in Al's back sometimes set off the buzzers when he is going through the security gates to board an aircraft.

"Takes a bit of explaining," he says.

After two months in hospital, Sergeant Garner was in charge of an airport workshop, looking after the landing lights. He well remembers the celebration when victory was declared. Al left for home in November of 1945.

Discharged in Vancouver he did some visiting, deciding what he should do. His brother Tom had timber on Galiano Island and was looking for contractors.

"He offered to finance me to go logging over there. With a rented D-7 cat, Paul Adank and I went as partners on the deal.

"Paul was my brother-in-law and had been falling for one of the other contract loggers. Tom showed us through the timber he wanted logged. We went right to it and had six sections in the water and boomed up before Christmas. Next spring Paul got an infection in one of his hands and wound up in hospital. He sold his half of the partnership to me. I was also now buying the D-7 cat and producing logs every day."

Al was working on the gulf side of Galiano Island and had a three mile tow down to the booming grounds at Whaler Bay. They would pile the logs up on the sloping rocks, wait for calm weather, then push them in with the cat on a rising tide. The tug boat would stand by with a string of boom-sticks, surround the logs, close the sticks and away they'd go to the booming grounds. It was only possible to dump safely on good days, so

175

Al built three landings, so they could work for a week or more if the weather was bad, then push in on a calm day. He was logging about 90 per cent old growth fir that sold for about $25 per thousand. Tom did most of the selling, then paid Al after deducting the stumpage and other government fees.

Al logged on Galiano for almost five years, where he met and, in 1948, married his wife Barbara. She had grown up on Galiano, moved away for a short time, and started dating Al when she came home to visit her sister.

When they had logged off the timber on Galiano, Al loaded his equipment and household goods on to a big scow and headed for grizzly bear country, at the head of Knight Inlet. Lloyd, his brother, had been logging up there for over a year. Lloyd and Al decided it would be better to work together and formed a partnership.

"That really was grizzly bear country. When the salmon were spawning in Simm Creek, we were challenged more than a few times," Al remembers. "After a big boar grizzly put the run on the crew a couple of times, they never walked to the logging show without a loaded gun. We'd dump the logs into Simm Creek and they'd drift down right past the bears as they fished the shallows. You'd go to walk by one of these old bears while he was fishing. If he decided that you were trying to cut in on his territory, he'd rear up to stand on his hind legs, let out a blood curdling roar, paw the air with those big front feet, snap his teeth. Believe me, it was time to get the hell out of there."

Finished at Simm Creek, they moved to the head of the inlet to log on the Franklin River, a big river with more salmon and many, many more bears.

By the fall of 1951, they had over a million feet in the water, boomed up, scaled, and ready to go. Log prices plummeted. By the time those logs reached Vancouver, the price they had to take barely covered stumpage and the cost of towing. Prices had dropped from $50 to $22.50 or less.

Overnight, Al and Lloyd were bankrupt and forced to close the camp. They had enough money to pay the crew's wages and that was all. There was no way to pay the regular monthly bills, so they had to go into voluntary liquidation.

"We managed to sell the camp building and booming equipment on a stumpage basis to Earl Laughlin. Earl and his wife

Grace were just moving in to log at Knight Inlet. He agreed to pay so much per thousand as he logged. They needed two years to pay for the camp," said Al.

The rest of their equipment was loaded on two big scows and towed to Vancouver where they hoped to sell it off to pay the creditors, and he remembers, "It took almost three years to come out of that episode and be free of debt."

Lloyd landed a job with Finning Tractor. He was to fly in parts and mechanics to make repairs on broken down machines in the isolated inlets from Vancouver to Alaska.

Al moved to Lac La Hache in the Cariboo and took a lumber hauling contract. He put a down payment on a used flatdeck truck and was in business again. He hauled all that winter, and learned how to operate at 40 below zero.

When spring breakup came, the side roads were impassable and the main highways were restricted to half loads or no hauling at all. Al figured it would be better to trade the flatdeck in on a logging truck and go to Quesnel to haul logs for Garner Bros. It was a 35 mile haul, partly on public roads but mostly on private. Al soon found the truck didn't have enough power and he traded it in for a new White. He could make at least one extra trip every day with the new truck.

The following year, Ian McQueen of Weldwood and Garner Bros. decided to put in an all-private road, with a skyline transfer across the Fraser river to the Quesnel mill. "That's when we went into the bigger Kenworths. The newer trucks could haul 90-ton loads on their eleven-foot wide bunks with seven-foot stakes. This was a whole new ball game. This private road did away with fuel tax, licence fees and insurance other than public liability.

Al again traded up to a bigger and better unit, a new, fully equipped Kenworth with a 350 horsepower Cummings Diesel costing $80,000. Winter hauling was a breeze. "To fix a road in the winter, we'd grade it up just before freeze-up, and if there were some potholes, fill them with water and they'd be solid until spring."

Bill Eastman and Al, together with Gerry Howe, formed a partnership in 1956 to take over the whole logging operation of Garner Bros. Cariboo Ltd. Gerry, Barbara and Al started flying lessons that year and became private pilots. They bought

177

a Piper, traded up to a Cessna 172, and eventually traded that in to become the proud owners of a Cessna 180 on floats.

For timber cruising and road locations, an aircraft was a very necessary piece of equipment. An injured logger could be flown to hospital in a hurry by landing on the Fraser River right at the back door of the Quesnel Hospital.

Al would walk over a thousand miles a year as he cruised the timber, laid out new roads, and blazed sale area boundaries. Without an aircraft he would have had to walk twice as far. There were many encounters with bears and moose. Twice he spent time up a tree to keep out of the reach of a mother bear. Al well remembers trying to chase moose off a plowed road into the deep snow. "It was not unusual for them to just turn, put their head down, and charge the vehicle. More than one grill and front fender were smashed. One big cow stood on her hind legs and pounded the hood right down onto the motor, smashing the radiator with her front feet."

Garner Bros. Cariboo logged that Narcoslie country on the big timber sale for the next 10 years. That 20-year sale T.S. 54079, granted to Westply, was the last long term timber sale issued in the Quesnel district. The logs had to be scaled in both cubic and the old B.C. board foot log scale. Later sales were scaled in cubic only.

When government weigh scales were installed later, it became mandatory to weigh all log loads being hauled over the government highways. The truckers and contractors were then paid by weight. This eliminated scaling in the woods and was also a step forward in safety.

The B.C. Forest Service, the mill owners and the loggers were happy when one load in ten was scaled at the millyards to get the weight conversion for the various areas and species. Though weigh scales were cursed in their early years, they became a blessing to the Cariboo timber industry later on. Everyone involved gradually realized that no one got gypped when weight became the basis for payment.

The next big change in the industry came when Ray Williston, B.C. Minister of Forests, declared jack pine to be merchantable timber. He also encouraged the establishment of pulp mills throughout the Prince George and Cariboo Forest districts by offering jack pine and other low grade trees at salvage prices. This was like allowing extra quota for better utilization of the poorer forest stands. Williston made it profitable to harvest the wood down to a four inch top. This created the need for more automation to handle the smaller sized logs. The mills could now sell their pulp chips to the newly-built pulp mills. These chips, at times, were the only profit keeping many of the lumber mills operating.

The Canadian Car Company began building a special small log mill they named Chip-N-Saw. Instead of sawing the log, this machine chipped the log square, then it proceeded on to the edgers to be sliced into 2x4s, 2x6s and other sizes. After first going through a barker machine, those small logs just zipped through. The pulp chips came out ready to be sold all in one single pass, eliminating wasted slabs and labour.

Ernst Forest Products of Quesnel was the first in the Cariboo to have enough courage and money to buy and start up one of these new machines, installing it southwest of Quesnel on Garner Road, just west of the Fraser River. This new way of producing chips and lumber was an instant success.

The writer now must take the reader back some 25 years to when he first met John Ernst who was then logging with horses for his small portable mill.

I had been invited to contract log for Weldwood and needed to see this Cariboo timber and what was needed for road construction. Ian MacQueen was showing me over their Narcoslie show and turned west off the government road at Slim Montgomery's cattle ranch and we headed up this steep narrow logging road in Ian's four wheel drive pickup. It was early spring and it needed a four wheel drive to get up some of those wet grades. About four miles up from the turnoff we came to this portable mill with lumber stacked everywhere. There was a shack built of slabs and rough lumber and a barn of sorts. We got out, and I was introduced to John Ernst. We had brought along John's mail.

"Bills, all bills. That's all we ever get up here until breakup is over," John said disgustedly.

He tied up his heavy logging team and invited us for coffee in his two room shack with an old wood stove, a rough board table with oilcloth covering it, a few rough benches, and some shelves. The water was in a bucket. The yard around the house and barn was six inches deep in mud.

179

The little portable mill sat about 50 yards away and up the hill. It had a 52-inch circular saw for the head rig, with wooden rollers to the trim saw. Both were driven by old car motors. There was a shed roof over the head saw and that was the sum total of John Ernst's mill.

"When do you consider breakup is over?" I asked.

"In another 10 days, if it doesn't snow, we should be able to haul lumber," John answered.

"Maybe three weeks," Ian said. "Usually starts in late March and is thawed out by May. Then the roads become dry enough to haul over".

"How's the timber cut out?" I asked John. "Looks like it makes good lumber".

"I only log the fir, and it's good."

"You fellows think a coast logger can make any money up here?" I asked.

"Everything depends on weather and roads in this country," John said seriously.

"I'll tell you one thing, John, if we do come to log here this road will be widened and ditched," I assured him.

Ian agreed and John laughed, adding "Maybe I'll be able to haul this damned lumber out if you do that."

We thanked him for the coffee and drove on out to look over the Weldwood timber. Good quality, but scattered. It had been a horse logging show up to now, and it was evident that extensive road building had to be done. Even in the four wheel drive we had to use the winch line to get over Deserter Creek where a culvert had plugged and washed out.

We went through the timber and discussed price and procedure and I told Ian we'd give it a try if they would go 50-50 on the main road costs for the first two years. That's how simple it was to get started logging in the Cariboo in 1952.

"What do you think of John and his mill?" I asked as we passed on our way out.

"He cuts good lumber, but has trouble with the logging. Spends all his money foolishly buying land and timber. I don't see how he will ever make a go of it," Ian prophesied.

John Ernst went on to make millions.

Each year Garner Bros. Cariboo negotiated a new logging price with Weldwood. It was a year-to-year contract as they never would give longer deals. Actually, I believed it was a better system than a long term contract because it was a mutual agreement for renewals. We felt there were always other contracts waiting if we should want to make a change.

In the 1960's, Weldwood's research people developed a new glue to bond jack pine and spruce. They peeled jack pine and used it as filler for either fir or spruce plywoods.

Bill Walker, an excellent logger, came in as a partner in Garner Bros. Cariboo after Bill Eastman left. Walker was the push at the 100 Mile operation. He was responsible for their first rubber tired skidder. It was rough and rocky ground at the 100 Mile show, and this new skidder really made money for them. They also had two cats, a TD-14, a D-6, and an Insley air-tong shovel loader. Walker hired a small front-end grapple loader to unload at the mill and to load the peelers on rail cars. That grapple signalled the end of the hydraulic and air-tong track loaders. With the rubber-tired loader and with the 404 Timber Jack Skidder, the outfit was more flexible and could make a good profit even on rocky ground.

The cat-mounted tree shears were the next big logging change. The power saws and fallers were practically eliminated overnight. In the smaller timber and jack pine the ground was usually flat and ideal for shears to cut and stack.

Even the larger timber was felled by shears a year later. The first shear principle for the bigger trees was a pusher with a heavy chainsaw mounted on the front of a D-6 cat. The chain was about one and a half inches thick—that's the size of the cut it took out. You could come up to an 18 inch with the D-6 and it would be cut off low and on a pile in less than a minute. The stumps were less than 10 inches high so the machine could drive right over them. The trees could be pushed sideways and piled in wind rows. There was no undercutting necessary because this big chain cut fast enough to zip through the tree without splitting it. As soon as the tree pusher started the tree falling, you could lift with the machine and throw it 10 to 15 feet while it was still in the air. The shear itself, ready to mount on the front of a new D-6, cost about $10,000, including the cat it would cost very close to $100,000 by the time the machine was fitted out for cutting trees.

"The shear cutting was much safer than hand falling," Al

remembers. "We never had an accident while using this system. I believe Garner Bros. Cariboo were the first to use the chain shear in the Cariboo.

"When we were falling the jack pine and smaller timber, the buncher would actually grip the tree to hold it firm. The shears would squeeze in, much like a huge pair of scissors and the two blades would cut downwards on an angle toward the stump so it wouldn't shatter the tree itself, but the stumps would split away. While the trees were falling they could actually be placed into piles. This worked very well for grapple skidders. The skidder operator could back up to the pile, drop the hydraulic grapple over half a dozen logs, close the grapple, and be heading for the landing with these full length trees in less than a minute. This procedure eliminated the need for chokers and the hooker. It also eliminated a chaser at the landing. When the trees were properly bunched, it saved choker setting and choker unhooking, so it was another change for safer and more profitable logging with better utilization of the trees.

"There had been a tornado that blew down several miles of spruce timber east of Quesnel. The B.C. Forest Service and Weldwood wanted it salvaged before it rotted. We moved all our 100 Mile equipment to this blowdown. It took the best part of a year to put in roads. Every load was weighed and a slip issued when the trucks drove over the government scales.

"This was the late 1950's, when the highway logging trucks started using a short log trailer which soon got named 'The Pup'. This was also when we started getting paid by weight. There would be two government-licensed scalers: one a Forest Service scaler, the other a mill scaler. It was only necessary to total their scale sheets, take the average and change pounds to cubic feet. They had the weight slip from the truck driver. This reduced the number of men on the landings and speeded up loading.

In the fall of 1968, Al phoned and said he would like to see me. I said, "Sure. What's going on around Quesnel that's so important?"

"The Minister of Forests is putting up for sale a huge area of pulp timber along the Garner main road from our shop at the highway south for over 20 miles. I'd like to buy a section and make a tree farm out of it."

"Don't know if I can help much, but I'll drive up this weekend." Al had picked up maps from the forestry office showing the available land.

"If you want two sections apply for four," I advised. We spent the entire weekend looking for survey stakes for the land he wanted. We were at the Quesnel forestry office on Monday before the doors were open. Al knew the head ranger well and he invited us into his office, then closed the door.

"Now, what brings you fellows in so early?"

Al explained what he was after and pointed out the area on the map.

"Do you have a sawmill with some quota?" the ranger asked.

"You know we are loggers, and that we built the road out there," Al answered.

"I doubt very much if you can qualify," the ranger said. "But I'll take your application if you'd like to try. There is to be a high level hearing here in Quesnel this coming Friday, and, as of right now, no one knows exactly what will come out of it. John Ernst has already applied for almost everything available in the area," the ranger advised.

I didn't stay for the hearing, but the following is the local newspaper report on November 18, 1968:

Cattlemen Singed By Timber Barons Blast

QUESNEL—Resources minister Ray Williston listened for 12 hours Friday to stories about timber barons devouring the Cariboo, ranchers that were a financial burden to the B.C. economy, and the right of every man to smell "new-mown hay".

Williston, assisted by Agriculture Minister Cyril Shelford and a group of pencil-wielding civil servants, was conducting the long-awaited hearing into land use in the area surrounding Quesnel and Williams Lake.

A total of 32 briefs, mainly from the two conflicting groups—the lumber industry and the ranchers—were presented during the session, which drew a crowd of more than 250.

The basic argument was shown to be clear cut: the ranchers said they were being squeezed economically by "timber barons", who already had 85 per cent of the Special Sales Area in question, while the lumber people maintained that ranching was uneconomic and

183

represented a few pioneers who were putting a burden on the rest of B.C.

"It is people, not resources, that make a nation strong," said Dr. France Word, a gentleman-rancher who presented the Quesnel Cattlemen's Association brief.

"Give them a place to smell the new-mown hay.

"The way it is now, with the timber barons controlling so much of the land, I feel I should run home and throw a tarp over my ornamental trees..." Dr. Word went on to say the Special Sales Area, although it was once a blueprint for successful utilization of the land, was now far from that.

"No one minded when 86 per cent of the land was controlled by the timber barons," Dr. Word said, "but now the 86 per cent wants to devour the remaining 14 per cent.

"Farmers are just about the only group left who do not demand a price for their products in relation to the cost...

"It would seem the government should make every piece of land suitable for farming, available for farming".

The Cattlemen's president said new channels of communication between the ranchers and the government were needed.

The giants of the forest, he said, "would not be impeded, they would just have to watch where they put their feet".

In direct contrast to Dr. Word's almost emotional appeal for the individual's right to have his place in the sun was a brief prepared by H.J. Goodman and H.K. Williams, two registered foresters.

The foresters presented a 21 page bombshell that stated, when the smoke had cleared, ranching was nothing but an economic disaster.

The foresters' report stated their conclusions were based on a survey of 80 ranches averaging more than 3,000 acres. The best figure they could come up with was a production value of $6.45 per ranch acre (before costs) opposed to more than $30 per acre yielded from pulp wood harvest.

Part-time ranchers, the brief stated, averaged 650 acres and operated at an annual loss of $1,300.

"Land in pasture is tied up at low economic yields", the clinical analysis concluded, after stressing the Crown received more from an acre of forest than the rancher did from an acre of his land.

The Goodwin-Williams brief prompted an avalanche of questions.

"If you can make $30 per acre on pulp, shouldn't you have higher stumpage rates?" asked Agriculture Minister Shelford to the applause of the audience.

"When you cross the Fraser River, do you use the bridge or do you walk on the water?" asked Mrs. Chuck Meyers, a rancher's wife who described the brief as "biased".

184

"I'd like to know the source of your information," said a rancher who maintained the statistics were undoubtedly related to ranches only in partial production.

The land use hearing was set after an angry confrontation between the ranchers and the lumbermen in May of this year.

Certain recommendations were made by the deputy minister of Land, Forests and Water Resources, but these failed to completely satisfy either party.

Williston said after the Friday hearing that an interim report would be available within six weeks, but could not give a date for issuance of a final decision on the problem.

Within two weeks, Williston's decision was reported in the Vancouver Sun, November 30, 1968:

Government Orders Land Use Study

VICTORIA—A team of experts in agriculture, forestry and economics will be set up by the provincial government to study land use in a disputed special sale area in the Prince George-Quesnel region, it was announced Friday.

Resources Minister Ray Williston said that he and Agriculture Minister Cyril Shelford have studied 33 briefs presented to them at a public hearing in Quesnel Nov. 15, and have been unable to resolve the land use issue.

The hearing was called to discuss establishment of a special sale area surrounding present agricultural land in which settlement would be limited and a pulp harvesting area set up. The proposal was opposed by cattlemen.

The area of the land in which there is conflict between forest and agricultural interests is about 150 by 30 miles.

Williston said that a moratorium will be declared on all agricultural and graze lease applications in the special sale area until the scientific study is completed.

After his tree farm application was turned down, Al decided to buy a section of land at the north end of the Quesnel airport. He bought some Hereford cows and a good bull, and began thinking seriously about retirement. He was nearing 60, and had spent 26 cold winters in the Cariboo before he decided to sell everything and move back to the coast.

In 1973, Al sold his company shares to the three remaining

Three slingload lifts are required to unload each truck.

partners and bought a little farm at Sooke on Vancouver Island. The climate was a nice change.

"Unless you're born and raised in that dry cold weather it really begins to get in your bones after your 50th birthday. At least that's how it seems to me," Al said.

John Ernst and Al retired the same year. The last time they met was for breakfast at the Bluebird Motel in Vancouver. A month later Al had a phone call from Quesnel to say that John had died from a massive heart attack.

"There have been a few changes since you punked whistles on that little homemade donkey at Crofton, like grapple yarders and the shears at Quesnel," I suggested to Al.

"There's probably been more changes since I quit than there was all the time I was working," he observed. "Get away from logging for six years and you don't even know the names of the machines being used. Hell," Al said, "They're using helicopters with grapples now," and he laughed.

"Gyppo loggers are still with us but they have to be rich gyppos and ready to change. It takes $3 million just to put one helicopter yarding nowadays," I said.

"You need half a million dollars just to start with a good truck and a new skidder," Al commented.

In January, 1988, I was chatting with Cliff Coulson at the Truck Loggers' Convention in Vancouver, and he said, "Joe, I've just spent over $3 million developing a grapple, and buying a reconditioned Sikorsky S-61 helicopter."

"If you have that much money, Cliff, why do you need a helicopter?"

He gave me a funny look, then a slap on the shoulder, and said, "I do believe you're showing your age, Joe."

We both laughed at that one, even if it was less funny than true.

A 30-ton slingload on the skyline crossing the Fraser River to the Western Plywood mill. Courtesy of *Northern Pictorial* Jan. 31, 1959. Photo by Funn.

Dr. Lindgren's mating trap

The above trap contains a synthetic odour similar to that produced by the female bark beetle at mating time. This irresistible attraction induces the male to fly into the trap from which there is no escape. Therefore, millions of bark beetle eggs will not be fertilized and never hatch.

These insects at their peak have destroyed more trees in the pine and spruce forests of the B.C. Interior than was used by the forest industry.

Dr. Lindgren of Pherotech, the originator of this trap, believes it has a great future in the control of the bark beetle.

Courtesy of Pest Management Protection Branch, Victoria, B.C.
Photo courtesy of The Canadian Forest Service.

Grace and Earl Laughlin with son Alvin, 1950.

CHAPTER 17
Grace Laughlin

Earl Laughlin was born and raised in a logging camp, and was
on his own as a whistle punk at 13. He worked at Port Alberni
for a while, then went to Ladysmith to work on the rigging for
Comox Logging at Nanaimo Lakes.

He really wanted a logging truck, so he went to Vancouver
and made a deal with Bill Ferguson. Bill arranged a log hauling
contract for him at Port McNeil. From there he went to Galiano where he met Grace.

Grace Bell was sitting on her doorstep getting a little sun.
Earl Laughlin was shouting over the phone at Charlie Philp,
the Mack truck dealer. All the logs were cut, cold decked, and
ready to come out of the woods, but the trucks had not arrived
as promised. Earl slammed down the phone and stomped out
the door.

"That's the day I met my lover. He smiled at me and said, 'Grace, I want you to come back to camp with me. I really need a good cook,'" Grace recalls with a twinkle in her eyes.

"I went to Vancouver, handed in my notice, then packed my belongings, caught the boat to Galiano Island and started cooking at Earl's logging camp. That cookhouse was the worst mess I'd ever seen."

She hired a flunkie and the two of them prepared the meals, cleaned the bunkhouses, and did laundry for 25 men.

"Earl handed me a double bitted axe and a seven foot bucking saw with two handles," Grace remembers. "We got the wood in tree lengths, then had to cut and split it to fit into the stove. Earl tried to get the big dry snags because they would burn well and get the stove hot enough for baking bread and cakes. There were no power saws in those days. The farmer next door had a 'Wee McGreggor' drag saw and he often cut some big blocks for us. His pay was usually a loaf of fresh bread.

"I stayed at camp from June until after Christmas, then quit. That was when Earl decided we better get married. That was when I took over the bookkeeping for him.

"After Galiano was finished we moved to Halfmoon Bay, just west of Sechelt, and bought another outfit named Logco Ltd. We started dealing with John Feigle, the owner and general manager of Bay Lumber Sawmills in Vancouver. Feigle was a tough man to deal with. He often cut log prices and never said a thing about it. We found out what was going on when our bank account was $15,000 short. We had logged over 18 million feet of logs for them and didn't know what to do."

My brother Lloyd often dropped in to see Grace and Earl. He had a float plane and would deliver their mail and any parts they might be needing for the old Mack truck. On one visit Grace was home by herself. Over a cup of coffee they got talking about Lloyd's financial troubles up at Knight Inlet. He and brother Al wanted out. They had lost over a $100,000 when log prices nose-dived in 1950. Grace asked a lot of questions about the show at Knight Inlet, and what the price would be.

"For $50,000 you can have all the camp buildings and 15 years cutting rights," Lloyd told her.

Grace recalls, "We didn't have that kind of money then. Earl

190

came home a couple of days later and I told him all about it. Lloyd was in Vancouver, so we flew down to meet with him. We asked Lloyd and Al if they would be interested in a deal that would see us pay them one buck for every thousand feet of logs we put in the water. They agreed to our terms. Evans Lumber owned the timber rights, so they had their lawyers draw up a three-way contract and we all signed. That was the best deal we ever made in all our lives!"

Charlie Philp was still in partnership with Earl, but he was losing interest and didn't want to be part of the Knight Inlet show. Philp said it was too far away from home, and offered to sell his shares to the Laughlins for $2,500 cash. They didn't have the cash, so they drew up an agreement to pay him off at a dollar a thousand. When they came out of that office, Philp was out, Earl was vice-president and Grace was president of their new company.

Grace said, "Lloyd flew us back to Halfmoon Bay. We sent three fallers ahead to Knight Inlet. The cookhouse and camp buildings were already there so they moved right in and started to work. Earl and I moved there in April, 1951 and brought all our crew and equipment with us.

"That was one of the happiest days of my life. To know that we were set for at least 15 years. That's where I learned to log. We were logging for Evans Products, the same as Al and Lloyd had been doing. We logged as if it the timber was our own— stump to dump at market price, less so much for stumpage and the cutting rights.

"We made good money there. We had a good crew that stayed with us year after year. There was one faller that worked with Earl on Texada Island in 1944. He was still with us when we left Knight Inlet in 1965."

"Earl didn't want me to do the cooking but there were times when I had to fill in. The cooks would stay a couple of months or so and when they went down the road, I would take over. We only had a crew of 12, so there wasn't very much to it. Book-keeping and the office work took up a lot of my time. I operated the radio telephone, transmitting for 10 tugboats and three airlines. Someone had to be near the radio phone most of the time, especially for the planes."

Grace wanted to know more about what the men did in the

woods. She taught the new cook to operate the radio phone so she could learn to run the grader. She liked it so much that she just had to try a little bit of everything.

"The funniest time was the day I decided to run the TD-14 bulldozer. Earl drove the gravel truck to the pit and I was supposed to take the TD-14 down so he could load gravel over the built-up log ramp at the next pit. It was a couple of miles down the road. Earl showed me which levers to pull to get the machine going. About half way there, I accidentally hit the wrong lever and the bulldozer headed for the bush. I was frantically pulling and pushing those levers, and finally got it stopped right in front of a cabin. It was a little exciting as I had knocked down a bunch of alder trees, but I had sense enough to shut the engine off. That's where Earl found me, sitting in the seat acting as if nothing had happened. He showed me what to do, so I put it in gear, backed it out onto the road and finally got the thing to the gravel pit."

During the summer months, Earl would often stay in the woods until dark. One night he put his empty lunch pail on the porch railing, went into the house and was washing up when he heard something rattling around out on the porch. He went out and there was a grizzly bear with his lunch pail in its mouth. He pulled the pail out of her mouth and put it back on the porch railing, then chased the bear off. He went back in the house, but that bear was determined to have whatever was in the pail. Earl was getting annoyed, so he went out and shouted at her "Get out!". The bear reached out and grabbed him by the arm.

"Earl came roaring into the house, holding onto his wrist and yelling, 'the bear bit me!' He had a tight hold on his arm. I finally got him to take his hand away and when I pushed up his sleeve it was like turning on a water tap. The blood just gushed out. I tied a rope around his arm to stop the bleeding and sent one of the crew to get the first-aid man. He took the rope off and told Earl to raise his arm up in the air to stop the bleeding. It was dark and we couldn't get a plane to take Earl to hospital. In the morning we flew directly to Campbell River. When I told the doctor what had happened I don't think he believed us. He asked Earl if the animal that bit him had been tied up, because it should be tested for rabies. Earl's eyes got really wide and he said, 'Well! how do you go about tying up a grizzly bear? They really don't like that'."

The wound was cleaned and bandaged and Earl was told to get the drain tube taken out of his arm in a few days. Dr. Bowers, a sportsman from Indiana who came in to Knight Inlet to hunt grizzly bears, took the tube out. Jim Stanton was the big game guide there, and he was 90 years old when he flew out with Dr Bowers.

"The last time I saw Jim Stanton he was in hospital. That would be 1983. That was two days before he died at 101 years old," Grace said.

She had her own experience with the same cantankerous bear. "That bear once took a swing at my head and gave me a love tap with its claw. I bled a bit, but was healed up the next day. That's how I have this white streak in my hair."

"In order to help control this bear, Earl and I lived away from the camp cookhouse and tried to keep the bear over near our cabin. We fed her lots of mash and about a dozen loaves of stale bread a week. She was around for 10 years, and every other year she would bring her family in. Once that bear brought her two cubs right onto the porch. She wanted to show off her babies. While she was there, our dog came around the corner. I don't know what happened to the dog but the bears sure scattered. The mother bear chased her cubs into our house then stood out in the yard. Those babies made a beeline for one of our bedrooms. They were so scared both cubs piddled all across the floor, then jumped up on the bed. One cub jumped from the bed onto the dresser and saw its reflection in the mirror. We found it cuddled up against the mirror and we had quite a time trying to get it away from its reflection without wrecking the dresser. Earl finally took it by the scruff of the neck and put it on the floor. Then both cubs walked out to the living room, jumped up on the chesterfield and snooped around. They sized the kitchen up and then walked out the back door.

"The cause of all these goings-on was Herbie, the black Labrador dog. We'd got him and the camp cat as part of the deal from Lloyd and Al. Herbie was always after the bears, but the bears usually ignored him.

"Herbie had other problems. In the winter the wolves would be forced down by the deep snow. They were often around the beach and river bottom. Our Labrador had a close call one night. Earl was over at the shop and he heard the dog fighting down by the river. When he shone the flashlight down to see what was happening, a big grey wolf took off like a shadow and Herbie ran into the shop to Earl. A later incident did not have such a happy ending. Herbie was killed by the wolves when they came into camp one night. Frank, our night watchman, opened the door and the dog just shot out and dashed around the side of the bunkhouse. The next morning all that was left of Herbie was a few bones scattered about in the yard."

As well as bears and wolves, there were cougars in the area. Earl and Grace were doing some monkey-wrenching on the donkey after dark one night and had to drive five miles back to camp. As they came around a corner the truck headlights shone on a pair of eyes. A cougar. A 100 feet further down the road the headlights picked up a deer lying on the side of the road spewing blood from its neck. The cougar's kill. They didn't have a gun with them, so they drove home and got one.

"By the time we got back the cougar was on top of the deer," Grace remembers. "I held the flashlight while Earl took aim and shot it. The bullet just grazed the top of its head and knocked it out. When we walked closer, the wounded cougar came at us, and Earl had to finish it off with a second shot at a distance of no more than 10 feet.

"There were lots of wild animals up there. When we put on snowshoes and went out after them we saw their tracks in the snow. I saw quite a few bobcats. Once we came on a wolverine eating a fawn it had killed. Earl shot it.

"We helped lots of deer and goats out of the saltchuck. The animals would go down the bare rocks onto the beach when the tide was out and the snow was deep in the woods. When they tried to get back up they would slip and in they'd go. We built a shed with troughs to hold water and hay, and we bought tons of crushed oats and hay each winter. The snow was so deep, the poor things would have starved to death. We had 27 tame deer around one winter.

"There were some shelves in the shed and we put raisins and rolled oats out for the racoons. We bought the raisins in 25-pound boxes. They loved them and could easily open the cupboard doors. Every once in awhile they would decide to come in the house.

"We also had a pet seal. The mother had either been shot or she had deserted her young one. The boommen from the other camp found the baby on a log. It was just laying there for a few days so they decided to bring her over to me. I didn't know what to do with it so we got some fish from the gillnetters and fed her. During the day we would leave her in the inlet and she fished for herself. Earl would go down at night to pick her up. When she saw the red truck driving down the dyke she knew it was time to come home. She would lay on the surface and wait for him, then swim to the beach. She'd just lay there until Earl went down to pick her up. He would put her in the truck and she'd stretch out on the seat and rest her head on his knee. I didn't have much success in trying to house-train her, so we put a little bed in the back storeroom. We named her Pansy and we had her for seven months. One day a pod of killer whales went by and we never saw her again.

Grace summarizes her life at Knight Inlet: "We lived there for 15 years and I loved every minute of it."

Earl, Grace, and son Alvin left Knight Inlet in 1965 and moved to their home in Vancouver and Alvin started school. Earl was still contract logging and he spent a couple of years in the Prince Rupert area. Alvin and Grace would visit with him every other week, or he'd come home. When Earl quit contracting Grace and her son moved to Fanny Bay while Earl took a foreman's job to run camp for a friend for another couple of years.

"We bought this great big home with 11 bedrooms and there was just me and my son rattling around in it. Alvin was going to school, so I decided to put the house to some use. I opened it up as a guest lodge and started taking in tourists. We were open all year long but summer was the best. During the winter I'd take in people who needed a place to board for a week or more. We did all right and it helped to pay the mortgage and taxes."

Earl moved back to Fanny Bay, bought a John Deere skidder and logged at Horne Lake until 1973.

"When we sold out at Fanny Bay we bought a trailer park at Sooke. It was the beginning of another adventure when we moved there," she recalled. "We opened a little store, and it worked so well we put in a laundromat. Between the trailers and the 15 houses in the trailer park, along with the store and laundromat, we were working about 16 hours seven days a week."

Earl had lived with a bad heart for a number of years, but when he had an attack in November, 1974, he went to the hospital and never came out. He was scheduled for a by-pass on Monday January 18, 1975 but he died at eight on Sunday morning. He was 70.

Grace ran the trailer park by herself until 1980. "When it finally sunk in that Earl was gone, I was glad to have something to do. He had been beside me for 28 years and I missed him very much. There is a lot involved when a husband passes on. My son was at that difficult age, 15, neither a boy nor a man. I finally sold out the trailer park and went to live near my sister in Merritt. I stayed for a couple of years and since then I've just been kicking around. I never remarried. I met a man who was very special to me, but I felt it just wouldn't work for us."

Earl was a man who did it all, and enjoyed doing it. That's what a gyppo logger was in those days.

Grace always said, "If Earl couldn't do it, then it couldn't be done."

Herbie discussing territorial rights with mother Grizzly.

Ollie in his Cat on Galiano Island, in 1947.
Hooker Gordie Marlett, standing by the arch,
claims the 12-foot log was the largest
ever taken off the island.

CHAPTER 18
Ollie Garner

Unbelievable as it may seem, my brother Ollie was kept out of school when he was six years old to be a whistle punk.

The Garners were logging the Cotsford timber at the north end of Saltspring Island. Mother made up lunches for the loggers. She would put Ollie up on our Clydesdale horse, hand him the lunch basket and he'd ride the half mile out to where the men were logging.

Ollie remembers, "I was past six, going on seven, when Tom taught me the logging signals. He was hooktending and used the Clydesdale to pull the main line out to the woods.

When 10, little Ollie had learned to fall trees by himself. He used an old bicycle inner tube tied to the other end of the falling saw, stretched out, then fastened to another tree or stump. This would hold the saw straight and help pull it back. He had been shown how to do this by an old Swede pole-cutter.

The next year he and sister Pearl fell, bucked and yarded a six section boom of good fir logs.

"I'd run the donkey and she'd be the hooktender. We yarded as far as 500 feet. We'd roll the logs down the landing with peavies onto this old White truck. After they were dumped at Burgoyne Bay, Pearl and I did the booming. Dad hired this guy with a winch to pull the swifters on. Just can't seem to remember his name," Ollie said.

The spring Ollie turned 12, he was punking whistles and chasing for Mike Lumavitch. Mike had a big steam donkey and was hooktending down at the bottom of a creek. Ollie remembers him yelling up to him, "Ollie don't you dare pull that whistle now you son of a bitch, or I'll be dead and you won't get paid!"

Loggers are rough and ready. Old Morgesson, a bachelor, was the woodcutter and fired the steam donkey. He and Mike got into a big argument so Morgesson picked up a crowbar and threw it at Mike's head. It just about tore his ear off and hit him on the shoulder. When Mike was able to get on his feet, he picked up the crowbar and chased this guy down the road yelling "Your fired!".

When the depression was at its worst in 1933, Ollie had a big row with Dad and came over to Vancouver Island to live. His first job was working up on Mount Sicker Road loading out some big fir logs from behind the Holman Farm.

They were just about finished there when Tom bought his first bulldozer. It was the first TD-14 narrow-gauge International used for logging on the coast. Built in Chicago these machines started with serial number 501—Tom's cat was serial number 756—it came with a logging winch and a hydraulic blade. It cost less than $6,000. Jack Lockhart was the service manager and the one and only repair man. Mrs. Cordiner, the secretary, did all the bookkeeping and knew every customer, those who paid their bills on time and those who didn't. These three formed, and were, B.C. Equipment Limited. The little company soon expanded to become one of the major equipment dealers, selling thousands of bulldozers and other equipment to the loggers of the north-west. The old TD-14 is now 54 years old, and is being used on Galiano Island. Fred Robson is the proud owner and, unless he can find used parts he has to turn them out on his lathe.

At first, when the machine was new, Albert May drove and Ollie was the hooker. After using this TD-14 for several years, Tom sold it to Robson. This was in 1936 when log prices were low. Tom was bossing for Empire Stevedoring on the log ships and he put Ollie to work running side for the next two years. Ollie suffered a badly-broken ankle when a big log rolled over his foot. He was in hospital for over a month, and was off work for another six months.

"One night brother Tom phoned me," Ollie recalls, "and asked if I was well enough to go hooking on an old gas 60 for Albert McNeil at Crofton. I said sure. That old 60 cat would burn 45 gallons of gas in eight hours, a full barrel. We'd just hang another barrel up a tree on the drum line, then run a hose from the barrel to the tank. 'Better than packing buckets,' Albert would say."

After they finished at Crofton, Tom gave Ollie a small patch of timber to log out on the gulf side of Valdes, the long narrow island between Galiano and Gabriola. He moved in a donkey and was using a dilapidated old house for his crew. Ollie's foot had healed enough so he could rig the spar. Robson needed work for the TD-14 so Ollie offered him the job to swing the logs from the spar tree to the beach. He said he could be there in a couple of days. Ollie recommended that Fred hire Gerald Steward who had a good boat and log raft for moving machinery.

"It shouldn't take Gerald more than six hours to make the tow," Ollie said.

To load the TD-14, they beached the raft on a falling tide and when it had gone dry Fred drove his cat on to the centre of this log raft. They waited for the tide to come in, and then watched in dismay as the raft did not rise until the water was half way up the cat tracks.

They saw Gerald's sleeping bag and suitcase come floating out of his small tent on the end of the raft where he sometimes slept. Robson grabbed the pike pole, hooked it into the suitcase, hauled the mess in, then threw it up on the roof of the cat.

"Start the cat!" Gerald yelled. "We'll pull a couple of those big drift logs off the beach and under the machine so it will float."

When the drift logs were in place, they passed the drum line around and under the end of the raft and hooked it up to the

199

blade. With the line cinched up tight they headed out into the gulf. If the raft did roll over now, the cat would remain hanging upside down under the water.

"Better than losing it," they agreed.

Out in the gulf a wind got up, and they had to slow almost to a stop to prevent the raft from diving under. It took them over two days to make what should have been a six-hour trip. Luckily it was a tail wind or they would have lost everything.

Once the cat was ashore on Valdes Island, they shook hands and had a good laugh. Robson headed for the old house to get some sleep and Stewart stayed with his boat and raft in case the wind shifted.

Ollie, his wife Jean, and their three man crew patched up an old house on Valdes so it was good enough to live in. There wasn't any glass in the windows, so they had just hung up bed sheets. Now with Fred Robson's arrival there would be six sleeping there. There were a lot of mice in this old building and Jean would scream every time one ran across her bed in the night. Fred would wake with a start and shout, "For God's sake, woman, keep it quiet! We need some sleep." This would wake the rest of the crew and there'd be cussing and grumbling from every corner.

"If you guys don't like it, get another cook," Jean would shout back.

Robson's cat, after being partly submerged in salt water, had some sort of a breakdown almost every day. Then Fred burned the clutch and had to go to Duncan to get parts. He was expected back that same night.

A week went by and still no Fred. They were out of grub and living almost entirely on clams. Young Georgie Georgeson came by in his gas boat, and Ollie asked him, "Got a rifle? We've got to get some meat."

"I've got a 25-20 but only two shells," Georgie told him and handed Ollie the gun and both shells. Ollie knew where some deer usually bedded down so he sent Jean and Georgie to drive them out towards him.

"Sure enough, here comes a nice two point buck. I got him first shot right between the eyes," Ollie remembers. "We had a good feed of liver and steaks that evening." There was one shell left, and they sure needed it before Fred returned.

No phone, nothing. Just waiting. Every day they'd listen for his speed boat. Ten days later Fred arrived with the repair parts and a few groceries, very few groceries. Jean took one look, cussed, and said, "I'm naming this rat ridden place Starvation Bay!"

Robson then lifted out a wooden box with chicken wire covering the top and handed it to Jean, grinning, "Guaranteed Mousers!"

Jean took one look at the two tabby cats, gave Fred a kiss on the cheek, then hurried into the shack. That finished the rats and mice, but the name Starvation Bay remains.

That job done, Ollie and crew moved the outfit down to Montague Harbour on Galiano Island, and Jean was back to Duncan to look after her two children. Brother Tom had been logging in Montague for several years, and Ollie, an expert at tightlining, went in to finish the logging along the steep shoreline and cliffs. They sold the house on Drinkwater Road, loaded everything into a van, and moved to Galiano.

Ollie bought a truck, a donkey, and a boat. Tom helped with the financing. It took several years of logging before Ollie was clear of debt. When he did finally get the equipment paid for, it was either worn out or out of date. In 1951, he had almost a million feet of logs in the water that couldn't be sold. Prices had fallen off by 50 per cent.

"We had the Montague Harbour beaches lined with booms so they went dry at low tide, trying to keep them away from the teredos. Those damn big worms die unless the logs float most of the time. The slump lasted six months. At the end I didn't have a cent. I finally sold the whole lot for pulp at a break even price," Ollie said. "The life of a logger ... "

Ruby and Bert Blackwood were their neighbours near Duncan, and Ollie had told Bert about his logging on Galiano, and invited them to come over if they ever ran out of something to do. Ollie was busy welding on his cat when the Blackwoods finally drove up.

Ollie shut off the welder, and the three of them drove up the island to an old farm where there was a good stand of cedar and an old house. The Blackwoods decided to move in.

Ruby was a working partner with her husband. He had bought her a pair of Paris cork boots, which the makers declared to be the smallest they'd ever made. A narrow size three.

"I wish I hadn't thrown them away after I finished logging," Ruby said. "They'd be museum pieces.

"I was helping Bert with the falling and doing some peeling. The buyer from Vancouver told us he wouldn't buy the poles unless I peeled them, because, he said, I did such a good job! From there Bert and me went up to cut at Cooks' old farm, and that's where the eagle chased me! Every day at noon, when I went for water to make the tea, this big eagle would come swooping down at me. I told Bert I wasn't going for any more water. I could feel the wind from his wings as he came right over my head. Every day he would dive-bomb and scream at me. There was a nest in a tree about a hundred yards away."

Ruby logged with her husband for three years, then he hired a young man to take the other end of the saw.

"The stumps are still there," Ruby says. "I can see where I quit because the stumps were not cut so crooked after that."

In 1947, Paul Adank bought a big two-man power saw. It was the first power saw on Galiano. The old Swede hand fallers didn't like this noisy contraption. They figured it took more energy to carry the thing around than it did to cut the tree down with a Swede-fiddle and they refused to help use it.

Ollie had built a home at the south end of the island looking out on Active Pass. Tom owned considerable land on Galiano Island, which included some 18 miles of waterfront property. By now the merchantable timber was all logged but the land was still taxable. On his way to Vancouver in April of 1951 Tom tied his airplane in the bay in front of Ollie's house, came in and put his briefcase on the kitchen table, saying, "Ollie do you want the land I own on this island? I'm on my way to town to sell it, but I thought I'd drop in to see if you were interested."

"How much do you want for it?"

"A thousand bucks."

"Tom, I haven't got a thousand bucks right now."

"Well it doesn't matter, you can pay me when you get the cash if you're interested. There's over 2,000 acres along a very narrow strip with 18 miles of pretty good waterfront," Tom said to Ollie.

"No Tom, I don't want it. Too many loggers going broke," Ollie said.

Tom went on to Vancouver and sold the land to Powell River Ltd. for $5,000 cash that same afternoon. When MacMillan Bloedel and Powell River amalgamated, this Galiano land was part of the deal. They put in a couple of contractors who have been cutting a minimum of 20 truck loads of logs a day for the last 30 years, and this same acreage through reforestation is presently producing more than they are cutting.

Ollie logged on Galiano for several more years until he finished cutting his timber. He was square with the world and had nearly $100,000 in the bank, but figured he was still too young to retire. The log market was good and Ollie had the opportunity to go up to Smith Inlet for Nayloss Logging.

The only booming area was the Likley Lagoon, but the timber was half a mile inland around Long Lake. The contractor who had been logging there before had tried to drive logs down the river and had gone broke. Ollie knew the only way was to build a swing road from the lake out to the lagoon.

The first 100 yards went fairly well. Then they hit the bog. His D-8 couldn't make it through, and sunk in until the mud came up and hit the fan. He had to winch the cat out backwards and was lucky he didn't loose it.

They cut logs 30 feet long and up to two feet through, then laid them crosswise in the mud ahead of the cat. He tried again to get the D-8 through but the timbers kept going down, down, down, and the mud hit the fan again. He put a second layer of logs on top of the first. Again it didn't hold the weight of the cat. He punched it three layers deep, and you could just see the top of the tracks as the D-8 finally made it through. The worst area was the last 500 feet up near the lake, where the punching sunk so deep the mud still came half way up the tracks. They blasted a nearby rock bluff and shoved the loose rock in on top of the punching until it settled down with rock showing above the goo.

"Down at the lake there was a gravel beach, right where those big spring salmon come in to spawn. Bing Crosby and Bob Hope used to come in there to fish," Ollie recalls. "They'd throw a big party for the loggers every time. Sometimes there'd be no work done for a couple of days."

In order to haul gravel, Ollie built a sturdy 'pig' (a sled about 12 feet square) and dragged it down to the beach using the arch.

He'd use the blade to load it, then the cat and arch would haul the awkward load and dump the gravel on the road. Two weeks and 500 loads later, Ollie had a road good enough to take a four-wheel drive pickup across. Now they were able to get fuel in for the donkey along with other supplies.

"This was the only road in all of Smith Inlet, and the only place a mother could walk with her children. One Easter Sunday, two families came in just to walk up this road to the lake and have a picnic on the sandy beach. One family had travelled over 50 miles in their speed boat to get there. The rest of Smith Inlet was nothing but muskeg, rock and Devil's Club."

"That must have been what broke you, that road?" I suggested to Ollie.

"No it wasn't just that. Before we could start logging, I had to build this huge raft and A-frame. It had a million feet of logs in it. The logs were 110 feet long and about two feet at the top end. The A-frame's sticks were both 132 feet long and topped with a steel cap. I cut and welded the caps myself, then put in the holes and anchors for the guylines. It took over a mile of heavy cable to lash and hold the A-frame float together.

"Why I needed to go logging up there I'll never know," he confessed.

As well as the expense of road and rafts at Smith Inlet, Ollie had barely got started when log prices plummeted to about $30 per thousand, delivered in Vancouver. The towing and stumpage costs amounted to $25 a thousand. That left $5 to fall, buck and yard into the lake, swing the half mile to the beach, and then boom and swifter. If he tried to log, the net loss would be a minimum of $10 a thousand. In less than two years, Ollie had to abandon the show. He'd lost his $100,000 and was another $100,000 in debt.

When Ollie described his predicament, his banker suggested that he declare bankruptcy and pay his creditors 10 cents on the dollar.

"The people that gave me credit are my friends. I'm going to pay them every cent I owe," Ollie said and walked out.

Back on Galiano, Ollie had an old D-7 cat, a $17,000 mortgage on Rawlick's house, but no cash. He made a deal with Rawlick for a $1,000 advanced prepayment on his mortgage.

Now he was able to buy diesel for the D-7 and some groceries. The next day he started taking telephone poles off his own property. They just dragged the poles to the beach with the old cat and boomed them right in front of his house. His brokers, McKay & McCallum, told him they could sell all the poles at a fairly good price. This way he made enough money to keep going. He was determined to pay off the money he owed from the Smith Inlet fiasco.

At this time, the author had a pretty good logging show going on Redonda Island, operated by Foulger Creek Logging, a subsidiary of Garner Bros. When I heard about my brother's problems, I gave Ollie a phone call, explained the Redonda show and told him I was ready to retire. Would he like to take it over?

"Don't have any money," Ollie said.

"You don't need money. Just take over the shares and pay as you go," I offered.

"Let's go up and look it over tomorrow," he suggested.

"Be at the Marina in Montague Harbour at seven in the morning and I'll pick you up in the plane," I said.

Next morning Ollie was waiting as I taxied up to the dock. We spent two full days checking the equipment and timber, and by the time we landed back at Montague, Ollie had decided to take over the logging at Redonda.

"I'm going to get a scow to go up to Smith Inlet and bring down the D-8, all the camp equipment, and one of those big donkeys," Ollie stated.

"Give me a call when you get it loaded. I'll fly up and land you back at Redonda."

In less than a week Ollie was producing logs on Redonda at Doctor Bay. His equipment from the north was already there and working.

Ollie had a reputation on the B.C. coast for putting in some very steep truck roads. Only Phil Whitaker could compete with him. On Redonda, when it was necessary, he'd go way beyond safety standards. I personally checked one short road with an Abney level after he'd finished. For over 100 feet the grade was 40 per cent. Unbelievable!

"First, we tried snubbing with the loading machine," Ollie explained. "Then we tried wrapping stumps: Finally we would choke the full load with a long strap and hook on to that with the D-8 and let the truck slide down the hill. My son-in-law, Rocky, was driving the truck and didn't feel safe with that snubbing line on the back end.

"'You guys are going to get me in trouble. Just let me go', he said. He went down that 40 per cent grade with all 18 tires sliding. The gravel was piling up over a foot high in front of every wheel.

"I can tell you, he didn't ask to try that a second time. After that we'd put about 40 tons of logs on that Kenworth, cinch her tight, choked the load and snubbed to the bottom of the hill on the drumline of the D-8," Ollie explained.

That hill was so steep the D-8 could not pull the arch up it. The cat could barely go up alone; then they'd have to winch the truck up to the landing. That Kenworth had been especially designed and built for steep grades.

"Without that truck, I'd have been broke at Redonda," Ollie believes. "It had extra heavy rear end gearing with the slowest ratio possible. I remember on the other side of the mountain we blew at least one tire every day we hauled there."

Ollie was driving a huge load down this mountain. He knew something was wrong with one of the tires on the driver's side. He opened the door and looked back! The front outside rear tire practically blew up right in his face. When he had dumped the load and was taking off the flat tire he found an empty 303 rifle shell in it. Ollie just laughs, "Talk about 'One for Ripley'. Even if there was another such rifle shell on the island, it would have to stand exactly at the perfect upright angle with the big end resting on solid rock to go through a 12-ply truck tire."

There was a mobile slackline steel spar that was purchased by Ollie when he bought Foulger Creek Logging. Because it was so fast on the skidding line, he named it "The Sputnik".

"Timed her at 700 feet in 28 seconds in high gear," Ollie would brag to other loggers. "Rig her up and be logging in 20 minutes," he'd say.

There was one very steep gully with some great big windfalls in it that had to be yarded up onto the flat on top. "The Sputnik" was much too fast and did not have enough power for this big stuff. To slow it down and increase power, Ollie had to use a block purchase on every one of those big bruisers.

Within five years, Ollie had paid for Foulger Creek in full, including all the equipment. He had also paid off his debts from the Smith Inlet fiasco. He did, however, find it necessary to sell off some of his equipment to make the final payments. He had been lucky to hit the log market on the rise while he was at Redonda.

During his logging career, Ollie had many devious ways of getting along with the forest rangers. On one occasion he had called for the rangers to come and inspect, and, hopefully, sign the clearance for one of his timber sales so he could get the deposit back. To check the timber sale, they would have to walk up the mountain about two miles. Ollie was very worried because the fallers had accidentally cut several big fir trees outside the sale boundaries. This could cause a lengthy delay in clearing the timber sale, plus triple stumpage on the trespass.

The forestry boat dropped the ranger off. Ollie invited him in to have coffee in the cookhouse. Jean put out and sliced half a good chocolate cake. She had made some fresh coffee. She knew this young man was a bachelor. Ollie brought out the papers and map and they discussed the sale.

"We ate the cake, then I brought out this bottle of whiskey and we cleaned that up," Ollie said with a grin. By now it was almost time for the forestry boat to come back. Ollie suggested, "Maybe we should go look at the timber sale."

"I've seen it already, you did a good job up there," the young ranger said and signed the release paper. They shook hands and he boarded the forestry boat. They were the best of friends from that day on.

In earlier years, the policy of the Forest Service was to let the district rangers use their own good judgment as to whether a sale area should be burned or not after it was logged. In steep rocky areas like Redonda, where slash burning is virtually impossible to control, it was usual to burn just the refuse left at the landings and leave the steep slopes. If a fire did run wild in such terrain it would kill everything and burn off 90 per cent of the topsoil. Nothing but brush could grow back for years. In the early 1960's, a blanket policy was implemented calling for clear cutting and overall slash burning. Ollie tried their new method on one of his steep sales. It made him decide to sell out. He considered the new policy much too dangerous, expensive, and stupid!

"I just didn't like knocking down good young trees and setting them on fire. If a fire did get out of control it could burn off half the island and I'd have no more timber anyway."

Richmond Plywood had advanced monies, and therefore had an interest, and first refusal, on the Redonda logs. They offered Ollie $100,000 for the Foulger Creek shares, which included the timber quota and most of the equipment. They gave him $15,000 down and the balance to be paid within two years.

Ollie and I chatted a few months later at his home on Galiano Island: "How do you like retirement, and how do you see your past logging experiences?"

"It's been a lot of fun with lots of heartaches. A lot of trouble and a lot of nothing," Ollie summed it up.

He had been home for less than a year, had $35,000 in the bank, all his bills paid, and was beginning to invest in real estate. He bought a 15-acre block with the main public road going right through the middle of it. The west half was waterfront and the east half had three good springs. The water when tested, proved to be excellent.

"I knew before we tested the water that it was good. The spring just bubbled right up out of the rocks. It was cold as ice and ran all year. We used to dip it out to mix with whiskey," Ollie explained.

Chuck Horel and Ollie had gone to the Divide School together on Saltspring Island. Chuck was now in real estate in a big way. Being good friends, Ollie called him to come over to help lay out the subdivision. There were 22 good lots—11 on each side of the government road. In less than a year, Chuck had sold every lot at an average price of $16,000. After Ollie had paid Chuck and the survey charges, there was a handsome profit. He would have payments with interest coming in every month for the next 10 years. Ollie had hit the real estate market when it was booming and it just kept on going up. Over the next 15 years Ollie located more than 500 wells on the Gulf Islands. He would never take money, but has been known to accept a good bottle of whiskey to cover travelling expenses.

Ollie is unbelievable with 'a willow wand'. He once came over to Nanaimo to witch a couple of wells for me. He'd just walk over the ground with a green forked stick shaped like a

"Y", held in both his hands, the main thick part pointing forward. When he came over water this stick would twist in his hands and point straight down. I tried, but the stick wouldn't budge. When we joined hands and held each side of the willow with our free hand, it would twist the bark off to point at the water. It's a weird feeling.

A good part of Ollie's success with real estate is due to his witching ability. He still owns several good properties on Galiano, plus the 100 acres where he lives. This he calls 'The Farm'.

Ollie's first wife, Jean, died on a hunting trip in the Cariboo shortly after their return to Galiano. His old partner Bert Blackwood took sick and died about the same time. Ollie and Ruby Blackwood met again a few years later, became engaged and married. Today, they both thoroughly enjoy their life on their island farm.

Ruby keeps a couple of very fine Arabian mares which she enjoys riding, while Ollie keeps an old D-6 to clear a bit of land with when he thinks he needs more pasture. Ollie has just had his seventieth birthday and enjoys helping his neighbours do their haying, or any other job that needs mechanical knowledge and equipment.

One of Ollie's typical tight-line shows at Montague Harbour.

Joe Morris, I.W.A. 1-80 President 1948-1952.
Courtesy Local I.W.A. 1-80 Bulletin.

CHAPTER 19
Joe Morris

Joe Morris was sorting and stacking kiln dried flooring from a highball machine in the planer mill at Chemainus in the early thirties. Belonging to a union in those days was very important to him. Joe joined the L.W.I.U. (Lumber Workers Industrial Union) when it was considering a merger with the L.S.W.U. (Lumber and Sawmill Workers Union). The L.S.W.U. was partially under the control of the powerful United Brotherhood of Carpenters and Joiners with their head- quarters in the United States.

By 1934 Joe had studied and earned his ticket as a qualified lumber grader. He and a half dozen of his union buddies from Ladysmith became active organizers at the Chemainus mill. John Humbird, General Manager and owner of the big sawmill was not receptive to unions. When he found out what was going on they were all fired.

"That was not unusual in those days," Joe snorted. "My next job was north of Campbell River as a chokerman. I worked there until the camp closed, then got a job with Lake Logging on the boom at Crofton. George Grafton was in charge of that export log barking crew of 70 men. Grafton had worked at their logging camp west of Cowichan Lake in 1934 and was partially responsible for having the L.W.I.U. recognized as the bargaining agent for their 300-man camp.

After Joe started work at Crofton, Bill Mee, a union boom man from Vancouver, visited the log barking crew and signed up all the men in one afternoon. Right out on the floating logs Joe Morris was elected acting president and he asked me to be his secretary. We were known as the Crofton Log Export Local. The Vancouver Union went out on strike the week after our being signed up and we were asked to put up picket lines at Crofton. This we did, and both Joe Morris and myself were fired and ordered to stay away from the private Crofton Export property by the police.

"Stay off private property or be jailed!" we were warned.

Joe Morris next worked on the rigging at Ladysmith for Comox Logging. He took a course in log scaling during the winter of 1937 and in the spring he was scaling their log booms. That following winter he was in hospital with pneumonia for several months, and it was the spring of 1941 before he had recovered sufficiently to volunteer for the army. He was overseas for the next four years and came out of the war as a First Lieutenant. He went back to his scaling job but during the weekends and evenings he was busy organizing and signing up many of the returned soldiers and persuading them to join the I.W.A. Morris became very active in union affairs. Comox Logging was out on strike within two months, due, in part, to Joe's agitating and pushing for a shorter work week. That was in the fall and the strike lasted six weeks. When the loggers went back to work they had an increase in pay and a decrease in hours. They had won the 44-hour week. Joe had argued that the shorter hours would give more returning service men a chance to get into the work force.

Joe Morris was nominated and elected first President of Local 1-80 of the I.W.A. in 1948. He was soon talking and pushing for a further reduction to a 40-hour work week. It was

211

his job to inform Jim Sheasgreen, the Ladysmith manager of Comox Logging, that the majority of the workers had voted for a 40-hour week. He used the same argument that a shorter week would mean more returned men on the job, and successfully negotiated the 40-hour week with no work stoppage and the same take-home pay. The rest of the coast loggers soon demanded similar working conditions.

"That's how the 40-hour week was initiated into the lumber industry of British Columbia," Joe said proudly. It was a big feather in his union cap.

The lumber industry was booming because of demand and higher prices. The I.W.A. was active and Joe was climbing further up the union ladder to the position of 2nd Vice-President of the Regional Council. Tony Poje followed Joe Morris as president of local 1-80, and held that position until he resigned to act as personnel manager for Crown Zellerback in 1956.

To keep things in balance, how was the I.W.A. faring in northern B.C.? Don McPhee and Roy Spur were both bosses in the Eagle Lake district, northwest of Prince George. They were just starting to get rid of their hayburners (horses) and using cats and trucks for logging and road building. They needed experienced operators. To get them they would have to match the higher wages being paid to the coast loggers. In 1945 they had applied to the Labor Relations Board for a higher wage rate and were turned down.

Don and Roy then invited an organizer who was active in their part of the Interior to come in and sign up their crews. Jake Holst was president for the I.W.A. in the Prince George area and Tag Morgenson was secretary. In a matter of weeks there were half a dozen of the bigger operators unionized. Now these unionized companies could ask and get a better wage rate from the labor board and would be able to hire experienced union loggers from the coast.

In early 1953 the I.W.A. coast loggers were on strike for higher wages. The Interior was negotiating but couldn't get a settlement. Employers in some interior areas were daring the unions to strike. When a strike vote was taken at 26 operations, 13 voted against, and 13 for a strike.

Joe Morris was advocating strike at a special meeting of the I.W.A. executive of local 1-424 in Prince George. Speaking later to a packed meeting of loggers and mill men, he stated,

"We have to call a strike. If we don't strike now we have no union! We might as well kiss the Interior goodbye forever."

All the Prince George planer mill crews walked off the job next morning and set up picket lines in a wildcat strike. By the end of the following day, all the organized lumber mills were behind picket lines and that strike lasted 103 days.

I was then owner-manager of Garner Bros. Cariboo Ltd., who were contract logging for Western Plywood. Most of our crew had previously belonged to the I.W.A. in Duncan. We had about 25 men working, including the fallers. The local I.W.A. informed management at the plywood plant that they were intending to put up picket lines at the mill if our group didn't join their union and sign the agreement. Ian McQueen, then manager for Western Plywood, got pretty excited and rushed out to our logging show to discuss a course of action.

"Let's go to your office and try to contact Joe Morris," I suggested.

"You know him personally?" Ian asked.

"Sure do," I assured him. "We worked together in 1935."

We contacted Morris in Prince George, and arranged to pick him up that evening at the Quesnel airport. Meanwhile, I called our crew together out in the woods to explain the situation and ask them what they wanted to do. Sarge Gibbs, the head faller, said that his crew would pay union dues, but didn't want to be lowered to the rate the union was striking for. "We want to keep our falling contract just as it is." Gordon Spears spoke for the rest of the crew. "Our yarding and landing crew is getting at least 10 cents an hour more than the union guys will get if they win the strike. I lost enough time and money in Duncan because of strikes. We're better off to pay dues and keep on working."

Our two cat operators said they wanted things to stay as they were.

"There's a meeting called for eight o'clock this evening in the lunch room at the plywood plant. I'd like to see everyone there if it's at all possible. Ian McQueen, Joe Morris and the local

President of the I.W.A. will be there. If we handle it right, we may settle the thing tonight. Be there if you can. It's important," I said.

Earl Reynolds, our bookkeeper, came with me to the Quesnel Airport to pick up Joe Morris. At 6:30 we held a short meeting in our room at the Cariboo Hotel. Earl and Morris soon found out they had played on the same baseball team in Vancouver almost 20 years earlier. By the time we had downed a couple of hot rums and chatted about the past, coffee and sandwiches arrived and we got serious.

"How's the best way to handle this one?" I asked.

Morris had done all his homework and knew exactly what the Quesnel union wanted and intended to do.

"If we can't settle tonight, the picket lines go up tomorrow morning," he stated. "I can't stop that unless we get some kind of an agreement tonight."

"We pay better wages than your union is striking for," Earl reminded him. "Our men don't mind paying dues, but they don't want their wages lowered."

"How does your outfit feel about the dues being deducted from the pay cheques?" Morris asked.

"You mean union checkoff?" Earl asked.

"Yes. That's one of our main concerns up here."

"That part's easy to handle in the office," Earl assured us.

"If we get that, I'll sign for the I.W.A. and the agreement can be completed tonight," Morris agreed. We shook hands and headed for our meeting with the crew.

There were 20 of our men present. Ian McQueen, Joe Morris, Earl Reynolds and myself were at the main table. Joe Morris spoke for about 10 minutes and explained the union's position. Then it was my turn and I asked Sarge Gibbs to report for the fallers.

"We don't mind paying dues and being members, but we don't want to vote. Neither do we want to be bothered going to meetings," Sarge said, then sat down.

Gordon Spears spoke for the rest of the crew. He was quick and to the point: "We've had our meeting. We are ready to sign up and pay dues. We are getting along just fine without the union, but we don't want a free ride either."

Earl Reynolds then explained the checkoff system to our

crew and I offered to pay half the dues. A show of hands of those in favour of joining the union and staying at work was unanimous. Every member of our crew signed for a union card.

McQueen, Morris, Reynolds and myself went into the main office, and Earl rattled off the fastest union agreement ever made in the Cariboo. I hadn't realized he could type so fast. By the time everything was signed, sealed and witnessed, the Quesnel president and union secretary had issued receipts and been paid in full for the first month's dues.

From a corner cupboard Ian produced four dozen beer and a couple of bottles of Black Label Scotch. Soon everyone was talking a mile a minute. Next morning Joe went north and our loggers went to the woods. There were no signs or pickets at the plywood mill and everyone seemed happy. It stayed that way as long as I owned the Quesnel outfit. Our logging show was never bothered again and the men never missed a day's work.

When Garner Bros. Cariboo had their Christmas party at Quesnel a couple of weeks later, Bill Eastman described the tough situation for strikers in Prince George. Bill had visited the I.W.A. office, Local 1-424: "It's a tough show. They are serving nothing but moose stew in their soup kitchens. Their kids need shoes and some warm clothing. I'd like us to take up a collection. They are in tough shape and I'll drive up and deliver whatever we get."

Our crew all put a $20 bill in the hat and promised toys and clothing to help make a better Christmas for some very needy logging families at Prince George. The I.W.A. union collected enough money to give every family an extra week's strike pay for Christmas.

"Many people said to me afterwards that it was one of the best Christmases they ever had," Joe Morris recalled.

At the beginning of December that year the government formed the first Industrial Inquiry Commission in B.C. with Judge Law as chairman. Morris and Judge Law had a little disagreement over the rules of the Inquiry.

"What actually happened," Morris said, "was that the hearing was closed immediately after the employers submitted their case. There was nothing for the union—not even a report."

But if Morris could not speak to the commission, he could talk to the union membership. In mid-December, Joe was at

Giscome speaking in the camp cookhouse. He was telling everybody what had to be done and why they couldn't accept what the Industrial Commission had offered. Then he looked down, saw the crumbs and made a big show as he brushed them off the table, into his saucer. He looked around at his audience, held the saucer high and let the crumbs spill back onto the table.

"Brothers," he said, "I'm sure you are not ready yet to take crumbs from the table, and I'm speaking of Judge Law's table!" Joe emphasized.

The crowd clapped and shouted their approval. Within two days, that story had gone through the north and seemed to be the rivet that galvanized the union machine together.

"The men would have stayed on strike for the entire winter," Morris believed.

Management realized the union would stand strong, so they called a meeting on Boxing Day. The strike was settled on New Year's Day after Joe and the union leaders had stayed up all night on New Year's Eve, shaping and completing the new contract. On the third of January, 1954, the settlement was finalized, and the members were back to work with a 10 cent hourly raise.

Joe generated a lot of respect and trust in the lumber industry. At the time of our interview in 1987, he was in his early seventies, and was chairing a committee for the federal government on Labor Relations and Management. He was also working on a program designed to provide income for people who lose their jobs due to technological changes. He is still proposing shorter hours and a work sharing scheme.

Lumber prices hit the skids in 1985 and forced many mills into bankruptcy. Sooke Forest Products was one of these, and was later taken over by the men who worked there with the advice of Joe Morris and the I.W.A.

"The mill is now making a better product at less cost because there is no debt," he explained. "Every person working in that plant owns a part of it, and they all profit by hard work and increased production. They are all working together to protect their investment and keep themselves employed.

"In the old days," Joe stressed, " most bosses came up through the ranks. Today a lot of them come from a university.

Most don't have the needed practical experience. At Sooke Lumber Products, the workers choose a man that knows his job to be their boss."

Joe had other thoughts, saying, "There's not nearly enough attention being paid to reforestation. This has always been a job creator and a sound investment. We should learn to grow trees as fast as we cut them, like they do in Norway and Sweden."

"The laws on tree farm licenses need to be changed so there'll be more inspection to ensure that the people who have been given custody of what is our birthright will properly utilize every tree of every size and provide, without delay, for a new crop."

Joe's union involvement led to international activities. He was elected to serve as vice-president at the International Labor Office near Geneva, Switzerland. He was subsequently made president of this world office, the only Canadian trade unionist to hold that high position. Though he could only serve as president for one year, he was elected to serve again as vice-president for three additional years.

"That was the greatest honor in my life," Joe told me with pride.

His Geneva appointments led the Japanese Government to invite Morris to act as advisor at their National Safety Council meetings.

"These were 12 day affairs and the delegates were treated like royalty," Joe remembers.

"I was recently on a tour with officials of the Russian Government to see firsthand their forests and related industries in operation, and advise them on safety. Though the Russians have a tremendous amount of good timber, I noticed their policy is to replant as they cut.

"They cut the trees in Siberia with regular power saws, but when the backcut is in far enough, they connect this automatic wedge to the exhaust with a piece of flexible hose. The wedge opens in the cut and the tree falls over. I had never seen this done in other countries.

"They were using tree shears in Russia with a heavy circular saw doing the cutting. The saw was mounted on a large cat. They would dump the trees in piles, then yard them to the

Joe and his family in September 1955.

landings with grapple skidders. They loaded the whole tree
onto the trucks—tops, limbs and all. Everything went to a
combination saw and pulp mill where they would dump this
mass into a great big steel trench rigged with powerful flailing
chains. The chains would pound off all the branches and bark,
and the cleaned logs would be hoisted up onto a log deck where
circular saws cut them into lengths for the gang saws. The
branches and the bark would be ground up and conveyed into
the pulp mill which screens and sorts the mixture. Some of the
ground material is used for fuel and the rest is used to make
particle board." Morris predicts that Russia will be our toughest competitor in the foreseeable future.

Their lumber products are of very high quality and could
compete anywhere in the world. Joe should know about
quality—he was a grader in the Chemainus mill. Though he
was not free to travel as he wished, the Russians arranged trips
for him to most of the places he asked to see.

218

"Their unions are very different from ours. Their chief concerns are working conditions and safety. They don't have any strikes, but they have a lot to say about grievances. A boss usually acts on the union's recommendations. If the union has serious complaints against a boss, that boss is moved."

Joe and his family lived several years in Ottawa while he was a labor consultant for the federal government.

"In 1979, we were all glad to come back to good old British Columbia," Joe's wife said.

There are four children in the Morris family. Their eldest boy, Joe junior, is director of safety for a pulp and paper mill in Ontario, and their daughter, Helen, runs a bookshop. Number two son, Ivan, works at Campbell River as a B.C. scaler, while the youngest son, Pat, is the corporate secretary for the B.C. Ferry Service.

"Union responsibilities kept me on the move for months on end. At times I had to cover the entire province. Yet, the children turned out pretty well. Their mother practically raised them single handed during the war and in their teenage years. If I had to do it all over again, I'd do it the same way," Joe Morris concluded with a laugh.

When I asked Joe how he gets along with today's big wheel for the I.W.A., Jack Munroe, he just laughed and said, "Sometimes he listens to me, sometimes he doesn't—just like my kids!"

Joe Garner in 1931.

CHAPTER 20
Joe Garner

In the spring of 1931, Bill Brown and I started to work for 'Gyppo' Joe Kerrone on Mount Sicker. He was snubbing logs down a steep incline railway to the bottom of the mountain. From there Bill Ferguson hauled the logs to Crofton to be boomed and scaled. Number one fir logs sold for $12.50 a thousand delivered in Vancouver; #2 fir was $7.50. No one wanted #3 logs, so they were just left in the woods to rot. For setting chokers the pay was 25 cents an hour. Jim Kerrone, Joe's brother, was the highest paid on the job. For hooking and doing the high rigging his pay was 55 cents an hour. Bill Brown was a chokerman. I was paid 50 cents an hour to build a cook house and some bunk houses for the Chinese fallers and rail-road crew. Allen Brodie was my helper at $2.50 a day. We also built a couple of small shacks where ladies of the night would arrive on pay days and sometimes on weekends.

Times were really tough by the end of 1932, and one had to do whatever was necessary to make a living.

When needed, I helped make up rigging and worked on the incline rail line putting in rollers and rub-blocks to keep the snubbing line up and off the rocks. In the winter of '33, Bill Brown and I worked with Bill Ryan and Magnus Colvin building a huge donkey sleigh for the big single-drum steam snubbing machine.

Kerrone went broke in 1934 and I started work at Crofton for Jack Simpson who was the boom boss there for Lake Logging. I built some new bunk houses, fixed up the cookhouse, built a new one-room office on pilings, then helped Jack put in the log dump and repair the old rail line and wharf. Bill Brown took a job in the Queen Charlottes on Lyell Island for Kelly Logging. The camp building had been there in 1917 when the Whalens logged spruce for World War One. Bill remembers the lice and bed bugs were so hungry he packed up and left after one week. From there Bill worked at several other camps as he made his way south, including Rock Bay, Jervis Inlet, Merrill Ring, and Wilson camp just north of Campbell River. Closer to home, Bill went head loading for Hillcrest Lumber Co. where Lem Traer was woods boss and George Parlee was Bill's side-push. Hillcrest closed down for lack of lumber orders and Bill moved to work on the rigging at Lake Logging's camp west of Cowichan Lake in 1935.

That same year Hunter and Round, the owners of Lake Logging, decided to put in an export plant at Crofton to ship logs to markets all over the world. Ed Mould was sent from Vancouver as office manager for the newly formed Crofton Export. Ed and I had played baseball on the same team in Vancouver in 1931, Ed at second and I was short stop. The day he arrived, the first thing I did was invite him to come out to Chemainus and take over second base for the Green Lantern Senior A team. Frank Crucil owned the Green Lantern Hotel and sponsored the ball team. We won the Vancouver Island championship in 1935 by beating out the highly-touted Longshoremen's team. In the last game of the finals Ed was the hero when he drove in the winning run by smashing a line drive double against the centre field fence.

"The beer is on the house," Frank announced when the ball

players jammed his beer parlour. Frank Crucil was a good sport and a good logger. He was killed on the side of Mount Sicker when a log rolled over him on a steep road. The media had declared him a millionaire not more than a week before his death.

Once they got going, the Crofton Export made some huge profits. Lake Logging sold logs to the new company at an average price of $30 B.C. scale and the Crofton Export sold for an average of $70 Brerereton scale. This was roughly a 400 per cent profit because 1,000 board feet B.C. scale when it was trimmed and processed cut out to approximately 1,700 board feet Brerereton. Ed Mould later described the business as "A Real Gravy Train!"

While working in Crofton harbor Jack Simpson and I, with the help of a piledriver and crew, put in three big dolphins. A dolphin is three or more pilings lashed together, and the Crofton dolphins contained 20 large fir pilings driven down some 15 feet to bedrock, then lashed around the top with three-quarter inch galvanized cables.

"Don't you think the teredos will chew that piling up pretty quick?" I asked Jack.

"Should last 10 years," Jack said with a shrug. That was in the spring of 1935. Within a month there was a lot of teredo borings drifting in the water near the dolphins. When I told Jack it was pretty serious he came out to have a look.

"Hell, I can fix that Joe," he said. "You get a box of 40 per cent dynamite and bring it Monday. I've got fuse and caps at home. We can blast those bloody little borers to hell!"

Monday morning Jack fixed up three bundles each containing 10 sticks of dynamite. He put a blasting cap on each five-foot length of fuse, then waterproofed the fuse and caps with thick black grease. After fastening the fuse and caps in the bundle, he laid the three charges on the back seat of our big flat-bottomed skiff. He wrapped each charge in some old lead sheeting so it would sink to the bottom quickly.

"Joe," he said "you do the rowing and I'll light the fuses. Go to the north dolphin first. When I light the fuse and drop it in, row like hell for the middle one. When we do the last one row like hell for shore so it don't blow the bottom out of this boat!"

As I rowed away from the middle dolphin, the first charge

went off about 100 feet away. It lifted and shook the skiff, but it didn't seem all that dangerous. As we were leaving the last one I must have slowed up on the rowing a bit because when that last blast went off the boat heaved up on end, Jack lost his balance and fell head first on top of me. After we got straightened out, I rowed back so we could have a look. There were about a dozen rock cod floating around. Otherwise everything looked okay. We divided the cod to take home! Nothing was wasted in the 30's. A couple of months later there were more borings in the water so Jack thought we should blast again. We had certainly underestimated the Crofton teredos. Another thing we had underestimated at Crofton were the winds that sometimes blew down the Chemainus River Valley. A big empty freighter was tied to the dolphins to start loading logs when a hurricane wind came offshore and struck the ship broadside. The three dolphins broke near the bottom and everything was being blown toward the reefs at the south of the harbor. The captain, with both anchors down, was barely able to hold the ship off the rocks. Jack Simpson took one look and gave the best demonstration of cussing I'd ever heard. He signalled Harry Rumley, his tug boat skipper, to the dock and gave him orders to head for Vancouver and bring back a scow load of arsenic piling.

"The scow will be loaded and ready by the time you get there," Jack said.

"Pretty rough in this wind to start across the gulf," Harry complained.

"It will be a damn sight rougher here if you don't get going!" Jack exploded.

When we examined the broken pilings in the three dolphins there was nothing left but a lot of worm holes. The remains looked much like a bunch of honey bee combs. From that day on, any pilings driven at Crofton were either creosote or arsenic-treated. The new dolphins were finished by the end of the following week and were in good condition some 10 years later. Any tools, such as axes and saws, turned a bright green color after cutting into those poisoned pilings. We all had to protect our hands with rubber gloves.

The teredos were not the only parasite problem in Crofton. In 1936, an ultimatum came from Australia stating, "Either bark all logs, or cancel all orders". When Ed Mould phoned his customers he found that the Aussies were objecting to the Ambrosia Beetles that attack and live under the bark on the fir logs. They were afraid these parasites would hatch out after the logs arrived in Australia and infest their fruit trees. About half of all logs being exported from Crofton were going to Australia, so rather than lose the business Ed Mould and Jack Simpson began barking the logs. It was necessary to hire 70 extra men with good axes to keep up with the orders. Ed soon found the extra footage gained on a shipload of barked logs more than paid for the additional labor to bark them.

There were sometimes as many as 19 ships loading logs in Crofton. Wall to wall logs and ships. There would only be enough longshoremen to put one gang on each ship to keep the captains from complaining.

The log export workers at Crofton were unionized in 1936 by the Vancouver unions. Joe Morris was barking logs along with the others, including myself, when union president Bill Mee came over and signed up 100 per cent of our crew. We were known as the Crofton Log Export Union. Morris was elected acting president of our local and he appointed me his secretary. Within 10 days the Vancouver unions were out on strike, and we were asked to put up picket lines at Crofton, which we did. This strike spread and shipping was practically halted on the B.C. coast until the following spring. It turned into a nasty situation when police protected the strike breakers and the picket lines were broken. Harry Bridges, the Longshore Union President from the States, had come up and stayed at Bob Rae's house in Crofton. Bob was president of the Chemainus Longshore Union, and Bridges was advising him on how to run the strike. After the fracas ended disastrously for the union workers, Bob Rae was blacklisted and both Morris and myself were fired. The only good that came out of that Crofton strike was a friendship that has lasted over 50 years between Joe Morris and myself, and the decision to start in business for myself.

Crofton Export continued loading logs after the strike. The last ship loaded was the *Weizer*, a German freighter.

Ed Mould recalls, "She left Crofton in late August of 1939. When war was declared on September 1, she had just cleared the Panama Canal and was captured off Mexico by a British gunboat. She was escorted in to Galveston, Texas, where both ship and cargo of 10 million board feet of peeler logs was confiscated.

"Were you paid for that cargo?" I asked.

"Before the *Weizer* left Crofton we had all our money in the bank. The beginning of the war was virtually the end of log exporting in Crofton. All freighters were needed on the east coast to haul men and supplies to England and France," Ed said.

Shortly after the war ended brother Tom and I formed a new company, Garner Bros. Construction Ltd., and proceeded to build 100 new homes at the foot of Cowichan Lake for the federal Central Mortgage and Housing. These homes were needed for the men returning from the war and taking jobs with the Hillcrest, Honeymoon Bay and Youbou sawmills. This was a major project because the land donated by Carlton Stone was an uncleared logging slash. We first had to clear the acreage, then put in streets with water and sewage systems.

In the following two years, we opened three new logging camps up the coast and formed Garner Bros. Cariboo Ltd. to do contract logging at Quesnel for Western Plywood.

Everything just seemed to keep expanding until Tom and I decided one day it was time to end our partnership. One of the main reasons was that Tom wanted to move from Duncan to Vancouver. After 30 years of successful and pleasant relations, we called in our lawyers and accountants and divided about $2 million worth of property, equipment, timber and cash. There really wasn't much cash to worry about because we had been growing at such a rate. This was in the summer of 1955, and by that fall I had, for health reasons, begun to dispose of my assets and logging camps. Foulger Creek Logging Ltd. was sold to brother Ollie, and Garner Bros. Cariboo went to brother Al. The retail store of Garner Builders Supplies was sold to the manager, Joe Gergle. Cowichan Housing went to Tom Gillespie, the accountant, and Shorty Berkey, the superintendent.

With the logging, construction, and other business pretty well sold or closed down by 1957, our family left Duncan on June 15 and moved to Victoria. We bought a big house on a couple of acres on the beach at the end of Haro Road. My wife Pat was 38 years old, and she packed up me and our five kids:

Dana age sixteen, Joanne ten, Tom eight, Ed six, and Gerry three. Of course, there were all the pets—two dogs, a couple of cats, four rabbits, a rooster, and two Bantie hens with half a dozen baby chicks each.

In August, 1957, shortly after we had moved in, we all remember Tom flying over from Vancouver and tying his plane on the beach in front of the house for a couple of days while we visited. He brought us a lovely vase as a gift for the new house and took all the kids up for a ride. It was a very personal visit and he just didn't seem to want to leave. We had arranged to meet in Duncan for the first day of grouse season on September 10. On September 6, Tom was killed instantly when his float plane crashed while making a glassy water landing on Desolation Sound. This was a terrible shock for me and I decided to dispose of all the remaining logging equipment.

In the spring of 1959, Bob Kincaid, a friend and truck logger from Prineville, Oregon, phoned to say that Steve Tremper of Vertol Aircraft had called. Steve wanted Bob and me to go down and see the start on Vertol's first 107 helicopter. We had previously asked Steve about logging with a Vertol 107. Steve picked us up at the airport in Philadelphia and we did a tour of the Vertol plant. Construction on the first of three helicopters was underway. The main frame of the first chopper was about 30 per cent completed. Several men were working on the engine mounts. On a bench, just in front of the 107 frame, were two turbine engines.

"Those engines are hand-made," Steve explained. "This one is a Lycoming, the other is a General Electric. They weigh only about one tenth as much as the present radial gas engines, but will deliver double the power. Small as they look," Steve said "each one will produce 1,500 horse power, or more."

Bob Kincaid walked over to the bench and with an arm under each end of one engine, he actually lifted it up clear of the bench, then gently set it back down.

"The weight of these new style engines should give the 107 about 2,000 pounds more payload," Bob estimated.

Steve then took us for a demonstration ride in what he called, "A Flying Banana." This twin-fan helicopter picked up a sling load of six small logs on a 200-foot cable and flew it around over the plant for about 10 minutes. Bob Kincaid and I became very excited about the possibilities of heli-logging. Our trip resulted in a hurried directors' meeting of Pacific Helicopter to arrange a further meeting with Vertol management to confirm a delivery date for a 107 Vertol, equipped for logging.

Jim Storie, Denis Hagar, Bruce Samis, Bob Kincaid, and I, all directors of Pacific Helicopter, flew from the Seattle-Tacoma airport to San Francisco. Then on one of the very first jet flights of the new Boeing 707, we travelled on to New York at an unheard of altitude of about 40,000 feet. Steve picked us up in a helicopter at New York, and flew us to Vertol's head office at Morton, Pennsylvania, for a meeting with their president Don Berlin and his board of directors.

It was agreed that we, Pacific Helicopters, should acquire from the B.C. government a substantial amount of inaccessible timber along the rugged coast. They, Vertol, would complete three 107 Vertol helicopters equipped for logging as fast as possible.

Next morning, June 26, 1957, Kincaid and I boarded a 707 that was to take us to San Francisco with a half hour stop-over at Chicago. As we were preparing to land at Chicago's Midway Airport, the captain's voice came over the intercom telling us he was going to take us on a sightseeing trip over the Great Lakes before landing. It never entered our minds that we might be in trouble and this was a way of getting rid of excess fuel.

It was a clear morning, and after about 45 minutes we were back over Chicago looking down at the Midway Airport. There were a dozen or more firetrucks and ambulances parked on either side of the main runway, which looked, from the air, like it was covered with snow. The stewardesses and co-pilot walked up the isle to make sure everyone was securely belted in their seats. We were told the 707 was going to make an experimental landing in the shortest distance possible. I can remember the captain making the final announcement before setting her down, "I'm going to reverse all engines as we touch the runway, and come to a full stop as soon as possible. There should be no danger if your seat belts are snugly fastened."

In seconds we were on the runway and stopped, with fire trucks pulling up on both sides. We had made a belly landing on the foam that looked like snow. The hydraulics had failed to lower the landing wheels. Three older passengers died of heart attacks. Several others were seriously injured. There were over 100 passengers on board, and those who could travel were taken to a nearby hotel dining room. After a couple of hefty drinks we were questioned by one of the airline's medical doctors, then asked to sign a paper saying we were not hurt.

Bob and I were on a DC-6 heading for Seattle within an hour. Though we were both home that evening, Bob's luggage somehow went via Australia and it was almost two months before it arrived at his home in Prineville, Oregon.

Three years went by.

The following is a later letter from Steve Tremper written on March 25, 1960:

Dear Joe:

After studying all aspects of logging by helicopter for over three and one half years, it is most gratifying that we now have a specific program toward actual tests of this operation in British Columbia.

We, Vertol Aircraft Corporation, will bring a Vertol 107 demonstrator helicopter to British Columbia in the summer of 1961 to conduct logging operations as per the following telegram recently sent to Mr. James Storie, President of Pacific Helicopters, Ltd., by our President:

"Vertol is very interested in the potential use of the 107 helicopter for logging. Our Economic Study (Report SR-398) indicates favorable economics. From the demonstrated performance of the 107, we are confident of its capability to perform the operation as defined in my letter 59 3069 dated August 12, 1959. Therefore, we propose a joint participation arrangement where Vertol will provide a 107 helicopter equipped with T58-6 engines plus service and technical assistance in the summer of 1961. Pacific Helicopters would participate by paying operating expenses during demonstration period and would sign a purchase agreement to become effective on satisfactory completion of the demonstration. Terms will be developed with you for early implementation of this very interesting project."

March 8, 1960   Don R. Berlin
                                                 President, Vertol

We are preparing the necessary legal documents to conclude our joint participation arrangements with you; the details of these arrangements have been discussed with Jim Storie.

I plan to be in Vancouver in the near future and would like very much to inspect the proposed logging sites. My visit will be followed by other specialists so that we can be completely acquainted with the operation.

I am personally very gratified that the program has worked out so well and I am looking forward to working with you in starting this new era of logging technique.

My sincerest personal regards.
Sincerely yours,
H. S. TREMPER
Manager, International Division

Steve came up in June, 1960 and he and I flew over the timber we had selected. The Forest Minister Ray Williston had already agreed that the timber be for heli-logging. This parcel was in the vicinity of Doctor Bay on the Redonda Islands. Steve was so impressed that he announced he would like to join us as a pilot and be part of our company.

"You should get some idea of timber weights and you can't lose," he advised us before leaving.

Acting on Tremper's advice, Pacific Helicopter hired D.W. Smith to do an interim study on the unit weights of Douglas fir and red cedar. Maurice Ayers did the study. In order to heli-log successfully, the weights of logs must be estimated so the choppers do not try to lift excessively heavy loads. Once we knew that Douglas fir weighed 45.5 pounds per cubic foot and that the cedar was 34 pounds, our fallers could buck the logs into lengths that the Vertol 107 helicopter could safely haul.

Within days, Pacific Helicopter had a meeting with Ray Williston. The following letter summarizes the highlights of that meeting:

PACIFIC HELICOPTERS LTD., VANCOUVER A.M.F. B.C
October 21, 1960
The Hon R. G. Williston,
Minister of Lands and Forests,
Victoria, B.C.
Dear Sir:

We wish to thank you for the opportunity to meet you in Victoria on October 19th and to discuss further our proposals for experimental helicopter logging.

It is our understanding that we reached agreement in principle on several points. First, it is our responsibility to select and apply for areas of timber which can properly be classed as inaccessible by any present conventional logging method. It is up to us to obtain agreement of the District Forester in Vancouver as to the inaccessibility of the timber applied for.

Secondly, we understand that the first sale might include a volume of perhaps 20,000 to 40,000 MBM, but that subsequent volumes of timber, adding up to a total of 100,000 MBM would be made available to us under the same terms and conditions applying to the initial sale.

We understand that the selection of trees to be cut is not of great importance, but that trees which are cut must be utilised to the fullest possible extent.

We further understand that you are prepared to make available the first 100,000 MBM of inaccessible timber in the form of a direct sale (or sales) without competition, as a stimulus to the development of new logging techniques. With this purpose in mind, you will have the Forest Act reviewed to determine the authority for this procedure. If necessary, consideration will be given to amending the Forest Act to provide for setting aside inaccessible timber for experimental purposes such as we propose.

If our understanding of any of the points discussed at our recent meeting are not correct, would you please let us know at your earliest convenience.

Yours truly,
Pacific Helicopters Ltd.
J. D. STORIE
President.

Within a month, Ray Williston had agreed to support the heli-logging experiment, in that he would agree to Pacific Helicopters picking out three million cubic feet of high-grade trees from land inaccessible to conventional logging. Williston was even agreeable to amending the B.C. Forest Act to allow direct sales of this quantity of timber "provided agreement can be reached on a suitable area of inaccessible timber for the first timber sale."

In spite of the B.C. Government's support, the heli-logging did not go ahead. After all the time and expense of getting the 100 million board feet of timber located, cruised, weighed, and approved by the forestry department, when we put the proposition to our board of directors of Pacific Helicopters, only the two loggers, Bob Kincaid and myself, voted to proceed. This vote resulted in Pacific Helicopters swapping shares with Okanagan Helicopters, and the merging of the two companies into one.

Our heli-logging plans were some 25 years ahead of their time. Things worked out well for Pacific shareholders who made a nice profit on their investment. However, I must state that it was a great disappointment to Steve Tremper, Bob Kincaid and myself. The three of us kept and framed a copy of Williston's concurrence regarding the timber agreement. I refer to it as my Million Dollar Letter. The price of that first 100 million was to be at 'salvage rates'. The average price was to have been approximately $1 per 1000 feet, B.C. Scale. The reason for this low stumpage rate was reasonable, because the timber would either be logged by helicopter or remain where it was to become a fire hazard and go to waste. Although we never got going on heli-logging in the 60's, today over 50 per cent of the timber we had selected has now been logged by helicopter using Boeing Vertol and Sikorsky machines. It is interesting to look back and observe that Boeing bought controlling interest in Vertol the same week we were to have signed our logging agreement with Vertol.

In the spring of 1987, I was invited to visit the Hood Canal logging operation where Columbia Helicopters were harvesting some old growth Douglas fir in the steep and rugged mountains near Olympic National Park in Washington. The show was about 30 miles northwest of Hoodsport, west of Highway 101. The crews were on early shift because of the dry weather, so Dick Shumway and I were up early to catch their work crummy at 3:45 a.m. Up the mountain, we were in fog and clouds at 3,500 feet. Around 4:40 a.m., at 4,000 feet we were in the service landing where their Boeing Vertol 107 logging chopper was waiting for the weather to clear so they could go hauling logs. This early morning bad weather gave us a chance to meet and talk to the pilots and crew. John Meadows was the man in charge of the project and he introduced us to his chief pilot Rito Schwartz and his co-pilot Dave Haynes.

"Would you like to be shown through the ship?" Schwartz asked.

Bill Brown and hunting dog—In the mid 50's Bill and Joe were partners in salvage logging at Port Alberni.

"Sure would," was my eager reply. "From the outside this 107 looks almost identical to the ones we looked at in Philadelphia some 30 years ago."

"Come on inside and we'll show you some changes," Dave Haynes invited. First we walked to the back end of the chopper on a two-foot wide light metal walkway stretched over the bare ribs of the frame. There was no inside lining over any other part of the aircraft except this perforated walkway. At about eye level the two General Electric CT-140-1 turbine engines were bolted to the ribs on either side of an aluminum transmission case.

"This is what we call our mixing box. It feeds equal power to both sets of propeller blades. If either motor should fail, this box feeds the 1,500 h.p. of the operating engine evenly. Without a load we can fly quite safely on one engine," Dave Haynes explained.

"Well, they sure as hell didn't have that 30 years ago!" I assured them, as we walked to the forward end and the pilots climbed into their seats and described the instrument panels and the dual controls.

"Either of us can fly this ship if one of us had a heart attack or passed out," the co-pilot said proudly. There were three different controls to release the log load hook in case of a serious hangup, or too heavy a load. Two were electric buttons, and the third was a sort of manual guillotine that cut the cable and dropped everything.

"Number three is what we call 'An abort', but we haven't had to use it yet." Both pilots explained and demonstrated proudly how Columbia had designed, manufactured, and installed the plastic protrusions on either side of the cockpit, so pilots could have better vision in all directions, including the ground.

"You've just shown me the cure for something I've worried about for over 30 years!" I told them. "Those lookouts were certainly not on the early 107s."

Dick Shumway had been with the service engineers and was amazed to find practically all the maintenance was computerized.

"Press a button," Dick said, "and you get a list of any and all of the parts that might fail during the next 1,000 hours."

We were shown how the big plastic water bag could be hooked up in 10 minutes to drop 1,000 gallons of water on a fire. By the time we had met the two hookers, Troy Marchan and Bob Howard, and their two chokermen, the weather was improved enough to start logging. It was better than any picture show, to watch those 10,000 pound loads sail through the air off those steep ridges and be set down on the truck landing as gently as you would lay a baby in its crib. Round trips were happening about every two minutes or less.

233

Bill Waddington at the controls of a
Martin Mars water bomber.

CHAPTER 21

Bill Waddington

THE MARS WATERBOMBERS

Bill was born in 1921, at Cumberland, B.C., then an active coal mining district some 40 miles north of Nanaimo. When the mines closed during the depression his family moved to Vancouver.

"My first job was at the Vancouver Sash and Door factory," Bill remembers. "It was usually slow during the winter and I'd have to go elsewhere to find work."

Hearing that a boomman was needed at the Homathko Shingle mill, Bill applied and was hired. One day while working there with snow and ice on the boomsticks, he was offered a job as deckhand on one of Cliff's big tugs.

"It couldn't be any worse, I thought, so I decided to try the towing business." His tug worked mostly around the North

Arm of the Fraser River, and with little more than a year's experience, he went from deckhand to skipper.

"In 1941, on my 20th birthday, I joined the R.C.A.F. The war was raging in Europe and they needed pilots. I was soon sent overseas and attached to a bomber squadron. During the next five years we bombed over France, Germany and Italy. It didn't seem to matter if the weather was good or bad, we were ordered to fly the missions."

Bill returned to Vancouver in late 1946 and his first move was to see if his old job was available. It was, but Fred Hollaway, the general manager, suggested he should get a government log scaling certificate. Working by day with the scalers, and studying at night, Bill wrote the scaling exams and had his ticket within a month.

"One of my first assignments was to scale three sections of peeler logs at Powell River. At exactly 8 a.m. a brand new Cessna 170 nosed up to Vancouver Airport's seaplane dock on the river where I was waiting. The pilot jumped out and grabbed the wing strut with his left hand, then extended his right in my direction, asking, "I'm Bill Sylvester. You the one for Powell River? Put your gear in the back and get into the front seat," and when the plane was out in the river he radioed the tower for takeoff clearance. This whole procedure took less than three minutes. Once clear of the airport traffic they chatted.

Sylvester sure perked up when he heard Bill had been a bomber pilot.

After landing at Powell River, Sylvester asked, "How long will it take you to finish scaling the boom?"

"About two and a half hours."

"I have to take a logger from Redonda Island to Campbell River. By the time I fuel up and fly back here you should be about ready to go. Swing her tail in over the boom, so she's facing out," Sylvester said, as he climbed in. Bill watched him till he was airborne.

"I'd just finished lunch and was ready to leave when the plane landed and taxied in alongside the boomstick. We were cruising toward Vancouver when Bill casually asked if I might be interested in being a pilot with his outfit. Grinning from ear to ear, I nodded yes. He immediately let me take over the

235

controls until we were ready to land in Vancouver. I was hooked. I put in my notice the next morning, and by mid-June B.C. Airlines had themselves a new bush pilot."

During the next 12 years, Bill Waddington's job took him to just about every lake, river and inlet along the west coast. He carried mail, scalers, loggers and some booze. He delivered machine parts of all sizes, and the mechanics to repair the broken-down logging equipment. There were many mercy flights. Sometimes it would be a ruptured appendix, a broken leg or maybe a logger's wife in labor. If a doctor was needed in a hurry, a float plane was called. Weather was always a factor in emergencies.

"I had some close calls during those years. Along the B.C. coast, wind, fog, rain, snow, icing, and darkness always had to be considered. As bush pilots we were told to use our own judgement. We lost some great pilots during the early years of flying. Johnny Boak and Tom Garner are a couple that come to mind."

Waddington left B.C. Airlines in 1959, but like all bush pilots, he was always aware of the hazard of forest fires and the need to improve ways of fighting them.

Forest fires have annually burned thousands of acres of good timber worth many millions of dollars. They may be started by lightning, sparks from logging operations, careless campers, or even the sun shining through a piece of broken glass. They have been fought by men using shovels, axes, bulldozers, and tank-trucks with high pressure pumps. If the wind was favourable, "backfiring" was used as a last resort.

Bush pilot Dan McIvor once used MacMillan Bloedel's Grumman-Goose, with five-gallon plastic water bags to douse a snag fire started by lightning. He also experimented with a Beaver aircraft but found it too small to have much effect on anything but the small fires. Some flying tankers with 1,300 gallon capacity were being tested for fire fighting in California, but these big land-based planes had to be refilled with water at a major airfield with special equipment and were not suitable for B.C.'s rugged coastal conditions.

Dan McIvor, who usually flew H.R. MacMillan on his inspection tours, mentioned one day that he had heard about some U.S. Navy planes called Martin Mars. He suggested to

H.R. that these Mars Flying Boats would probably be very useful in putting out forest fires, and the water bomber idea took wing. In late 1959, Forest Industries Flying Tankers Limited was formed. MacMillan Bloedel started the company inviting other forestry companies to become involved. British Columbia Forest Products, Western Forest Industries, and Tahsis Company all invested; Pacific Logging joined later.

The Mars flying boats were the brainchild of Glen L. Martin. Five of these giant seaplanes were built for the U.S. Navy during the war. They had official serial numbers, but were all given first names from military operations in the South Pacific. Their given names were: *Marshall*, *Marianas*, *Caroline*, *Philippine*, and *Hawaii*. The first flight of one of these aircraft took place on June 23, 1942.

On April 5, 1950, the *Marshall* caught fire during a routine flight near Honolulu. It landed safely, but the crew were unable to put out the fire. There was no loss of life, but the plane was totally destroyed. The remaining monstrous flying boats were in service for almost 10 years and became known as the Four Old Ladies.

The following lists but a few of their great deeds:

—flew 4,728 non-stop miles from Honolulu to Chicago.

—carried 68,327 pounds of cargo on a single flight from Maryland to Ohio.

—transported 301 sailors and their gear from San Diego to Alameda.

—carried more than 200,000 passengers with no loss of life.

In August 1956, the last four Martin Mars were retired from the U.S. Navy in mint condition. Many potential deals fell through, and in June, 1959, the planes and all the spare parts were sold for scrap.

H.R. MacMillan and Air Vice-Marshal Lee Stephenson were friends and had discussed the possibilities of the Martin Mars being converted to water bombers. When the Mars were in the scrap yard, MacMillan decided to send a team of men to San Francisco to see if the flying boats were still available and usable. They learned each plane had cost the junk dealer $23,650 and were advised that $100,000 would buy all four planes with tons of spare parts and tools. Only a couple of hours before demolition was slated to begin, they received a wire from headquarters to close the deal. They also arranged to buy 35 engines, worth about $3 million, for an extra $3,500. These 2,500 horse power radial engines were complete, brand new, and sealed in waterproof cases. This was just too great a bargain to miss, so they closed the deal before anyone realized the potential. To this day, some of these same engines are being used to keep the B.C. water bombers flying.

Everything was finally delivered to the Patricia Bay Airport near Victoria. Fairey Aviation of Canada got the contract to convert the *Marianas* Mars to a water bomber. A 6,000 gallon tank was installed in the cargo area. It had four compartments that could be emptied separately, or all at once. They finally mastered the design problem for the pickup probes, which had to withstand the terrific force of loading the water while planing at 70 nautical miles per hour on the surface of a lake or inlet. When the *Marianas* conversion was completed in 1960, Dan McIvor picked his crew. The water bomber began test flights.

The first big fire they were called to put out was on a very steep hillside above Cowichan Lake, in back of Youbou. They made seven trips, dropping 42,000 gallons of water, and the fire was doused in a matter of hours. The second test was at Ramsey Arm where there was a fire in some large windfalls and old growth cedar. This fire was out after dropping 22 loads of saltwater (132,000 gallons) on it. Everyone was impressed and satisfied that the water bombers could do the job.

A water bomber base consisting of a haul-out ramp, hangers, shop and crew quarters was built at Sproat Lake, west of Port Alberni. The lake is long enough to allow these huge seaplanes to scoop up a load of water and still have enough room to safely gain speed and altitude.

During the late summer months of 1960, the *Marianas* Mars was kept busy and dumped thousands of gallons of water on many fires of all sizes. On June 23, 1961 this plane hit the tree tops while dropping a load of water on a fire at Northwest Bay. Chief Pilot Bud Richmond, Bobby Morin, Jack Edwards and Wally Wiggins died in this crash. A thorough investigation turned up no evidence of mechanical failure or defects, but there had to be a reason for this terrible loss.

238

Conversion was begun on the *Philippine* and rushed through with only minor changes to the probes and water tanks. By the end of the 1963 fire season, the *Philippine* was credited with saving enough timber to pay for all her costs twice over. Her experienced crews had put out lightning fires in areas so rough that ground crews could never have been able to get near them. About half of the fires put out were on steep mountains where even bulldozers were of little help. By mid-September of 1963, the *Philippine* had dropped more than 500,000 gallons of water on dozens of fires, large and small.

While conversion work was being done on the *Caroline*, her engines had been removed and she was moored at the edge of Patricia Bay Airport. A hurricane-force wind snapped her lines and tossed the plane into the nearby trees. The frame was twisted and smashed beyond repair. She would never fly again.

The last of the Mars, *Hawaii*, was converted with only minor modifications. She and the *Philippine* continue their fire fighting duties to this day. These big birds are moored on Sproat Lake, and every year, from the beginning of April until the end of September, they are ready to fly at a moment's notice. Between them, they have dropped millions of gallons of water on many a raging forest, assisted in fighting fires for the government forest services and other forest companies when requested, and once even helped to control a large industrial fire in New Westminster.

Bill Waddington was promoted to general manager and chief pilot of the Forest Industries Flying Tankers Limited in 1966. The company's president, following Ernie Shorter, was John Hemmingsen who was then responsible for their timber holdings, including fire prevention, fire fighting, and slash burning.

Waddington learned the history of these impressive aircraft and outlines a typical scenario, explaining the procedures used in the bombing of fires:

The fire boss has his headquarters set up below, near the fire. He is waiting for the ground-to-air conference that will plan the attack on a forest fire raging out of control on the side of a steep and very rough mountain. Heat-created winds are sucking the fire up the slope faster than the ground crews can move in the equipment to fight it. A Mars water bomber has been called to bomb the fire so the ground crews can work up the sides and pinch it off.

The first plane to appear is *Bird Dog*, the call name for the spotter plane which will act as eyes for the fire boss, and also be his communication link with the water bomber itself. Only a few minutes behind *Bird Dog* is the big Mars *Philippine* with her first 6,000 gallon load of chemically thickened water.

The fire boss and the spotting plane keep in constant communication:

"*Bird Dog* from fire boss. *Bird Dog* from fire boss. You're in sight. Do you read me?"

The fast approaching Grumman Goose, will reply in seconds:

"Fire boss from *Bird Dog*. I read you, what is your location. Over."

"*Bird Dog* from fire boss. I'm at the bridge on the main road north of the fire. Use the river as your north south line. We've got crews working up the east and west flanks but we can't reach the fire's head. What do you see? Over."

"Fire boss from *Bird Dog*. I have you located. River north and south affirmative. The fire is flaring up in three draws in the south corner. You have a spot fire about a quarter of a mile due west of your headquarters. Over."

The ground crew check map co-ordinates and pin-point the spot fire. It was probably ignited by sparks that leap-frogged ahead of the ragged edge of the main fire. The fire boss radios this information to the fire-line boss. There is a crew standing by and ready to go in.

"*Bird Dog* from fire boss. Make the first drop on the spot fire. Men are on their way in. Knock down those draw fires, then cool the head of the fire. Over and out."

The big Martin Mars arrives on the scene. The size comparison between the two aircraft is similar to an eagle and a sparrow. The crew of the water bomber has heard the exchange between *Bird Dog* and 'fire boss', but there must be no mistakes. *Bird Dog* relays his information and the orders directly to the water bomber. All radios are silenced except those between pilot and engineer as the big plane lines up for the bombing run.

The ground-crew is already in sight of the spot fire. They were told there would be a water drop, so they keep looking upward while going forward. Suddenly the bomber appears, 200 feet wide and about 200 feet up. She is an awesome sight as she sweeps across the tree tops.

The plane lifts away, and the water-drop fans down towards the target. The dense and wet blanket of gelled water is 250 feet wide and nearly 800 feet long. It covers the spot fire with about an inch of

240

water. The men on the ground are close enough to hear the hiss and see the steam rising in clouds. There is a loud cheer as they move forward with their backpack cans, axes, shovels and other hand tools to put out any smouldering remains.

The Mars is already on her way to the nearest place to refill her water tanks. In a matter of minutes the huge flying boat is skimming the surface at 80 mph. The co-pilot takes the controls, and the chief pilot lowers the two intake probes. The crew feels the check and drag as 30 tons of water are sucked into the tanks in 22 seconds. Gelgard, a water thickner which acts as a fire suppressant, is injected into the tanks at the same time. The probes are retracted, and the first engineer returns the controls to the chief pilot for lift-off.

The loading is no problem to the skillful pilot and flight engineer who are practised in this sort of team work. As you watch the big water bombers gracefully sweep down and pick up tons of water, then fly through the smoke and air turbulence for a low level drop of pin-point accuracy on a blazing mountain side, you believe they had been designed specifically for this type of work. The big Mars will continue to make this round trip again and again until her part of the job is done. She can carry on ceaselessly until dark, and then resume work at dawn if still needed.

It is policy for the flying crews to rotate from bomber to *Bird Dog*, so they better understand each other's problems. This makes for total team work and coordination. Barring accidents or sickness the same crews stay together on the job all year.

"We found the best pilots were those with not less than 7,000 hours of bush time along the coast. Without good men at the controls, nothing is worth a tinker's damn," concludes Waddington.

During the winter months the two big bombers are completely checked over. Every control and all connecting parts are taken off, cleaned, and inspected. The rivets and all the sheet metal forming the wings and hull are examined. Replacements are made if there is wear or corrosion creating any weakness. Everything must be perfect by spring. The crews' lives depend on the job done through the winter.

241

MARS WATER BOMBERS

SIZES OF THE MARS WATER BOMBERS

OVERALL LENGTH	120 ft
HEIGHT	48 ft
HULL BEAM	13.5 ft
HULL DRAFT	5.5 ft
WING SPAN	200 ft
GROSS WEIGHT	162,000 lbs
WATER LOAD	60,000 lbs

POWER PLANT

Four 18-cylinder Wright Cyclone engines each with a takeoff power of 2,500 H.P.
Curtis Electric propellers with a diameter of fifteen feet two inches.

OPERATING DATA

CRUISING SPEED TO FIRE	175 mph
DROP SPEED	140 mph
LANDING APPROACH SPEED	110 mph
TOUCH DOWN SPEED	80 mph
FUEL CONSUMPTION Cruise	350 gal
Operations	650 gal
FUEL CAPACITY	11,000 gal
OPERATIONAL DURATION (Normal)	5.5 hrs
AREA COVERED Single drop	3-4 acres
DIMENSION OF DROP PATTERN	
Average width	250 ft
Average Length	800 ft
DROP HEIGHT (Desirable)	150-250 ft
WATER TANK LOAD	6,000 gal

Martin Mars water bomber being readied for another fire season. Photo courtesy of Alberni Valley Times, May 8, 1974.

Waddington sums it up: "*Hawaii* and *Philippine* will be 41 years in service next spring. There is nothing on the market as yet that can do the job as well as the big Mars. After hundreds of flights and thousands of hours I think they are great. They can go on for a while, but not indefinitely. Maybe big helicopters will be able to take their place.

Like my wife, the Big Birds are not getting older, they're just getting better," Bill believes.

Monty Mosher, General Manager of Forestland
Industries, Chemainus, B.C. 1988.

CHAPTER 22
Monty Mosher

Monty's maternal grandfather started logging with oxen in
Vancouver about 1885, the year before the city was incorporated. On his father's side, the Mosher family was logging and
sawmilling in Nova Scotia in the 18th century. His paternal
grandfather and one of his great uncles came west in 1902, and
did their first logging on the Sechelt Peninsula. From there,
they moved to the Fraser Valley across from New Westminster.
   They built a sizable sawmill just south of the present Pattullo
Bridge. The Great Northern Railway was being built to connect New Westminster with Washington and the U.S. When
lumber markets turned bad in 1912, construction on the promised spur line to their mill was halted. Monty's great-uncle,
Cliff, and his grandfather had over a million board feet of
timber and ties stacked in the yard ready to be shipped via the
spur line that never arrived. In the depression of 1912 when the

American government cut off the funds for that rail line, it was the end of sawmilling for the Mosher family in B.C.

Monty's father went overseas with the army in the first world war. When he came back in 1919, his brothers were logging up coast on both Minstrel and Hardwick Islands. There's a Mosher Bay named after them on Hardwick Island where they logged.

"Another great-uncle had a camp in the Sechelt area. There's an old one-drum steam donkey in the Sechelt Museum that he bought new in 1906. It has the 'Mosher Logging' name on it."

There were 13 children in his Dad's family, five girls and eight boys. In 1932, when Merrill, Ring and Wilson re-opened their logging camp at Rock Bay, Monty's Dad moved into the married quarters and went hooktending on a cold deck machine. The bush camp was located on a tributary of the Salmon River, about 15 miles up the track from the Rock Bay beach camp and log dump. Jobs and money were scarce, and only the best loggers were able to find work.

"Shortly after the start of the Second World War, Dad took a job in the shipyards so his family could be near better schooling. They gave him a foreman's job right off the bat, and because of his rigging knowledge, he was put in charge of all the cranes and derricks at the South Burrard shipyards in Vancouver. He wasn't there six months before he wanted to get back out in the woods, but he was frozen in the yards until the war was over.

"All the cousins, brother Frank, and myself went up to Toba Inlet during our school holidays in 1943 and '44 to work for our uncles. They had a double swing A-frame show on a steep sidehill. It was a float camp and they were A-framing from cold decks into the bay. There were two machines strung out in tandem 2,000 feet above the A-frame.

"I was 13 years old and helping set chokers and whistle punking for the A-frame on the hot pile. It was a jerkwire show, and the whistle wire ran all the way down the mountain to the A-frame."

Monty well remembers finding out when to give a signal and when not to give a signal. He and his Uncle Bill were chasing and setting chokers at this hot deck. Monty figured the turn was ready so he ran over, grabbed the whistle wire, and gave it a big yank. Sometimes you could hear the whistle at the A-frame,

245

and sometimes you couldn't. Anyway, he gave it another big pull to make sure, then turned to see his uncle walking back towards the butt rigging and chokers.

"It was one yank for go ahead, and one for stop in those days. So I thought, if the signal went in, that turn is going to go ahead and probably kill my uncle. But if it didn't go in and I blew again, then the A-frame engineer will go ahead anyway. I was trying to figure out what to do next, when Uncle Bill turned and started to walk toward me. He was right in the middle of his "go ahead" shout when the turn exploded out of the pile and sailed out just over his head. He fell forward to avoid a limb and I thought he was dead," Monty remembers.

When Uncle Bill got to his feet and walked over, Monty learned in a hurry who was to decide when to give signals and who wasn't.

"You don't do your own thinking when you're a kid. You do what you're told!" his uncle snarled, yanking him to his feet while shaking his big fist in his face.

"I knew when he sent me back to school early that year, he wanted that lesson to be remembered. That's over 40 years ago and it's as clear in my mind as yesterday," Monty admits.

When B.C. Forest Products started a new camp up the coast at Vancouver Bay in 1946, Monty's father was hired as woods foreman. He stayed up there until things were going smoothly, then was transferred to Port Renfrew as superintendent of their Harris Creek camp. Young Frank and Monty worked there through their 1947 summer holidays and helped their father set up and rig their first land-based A-frame to transfer the loads from the trucks onto the rail cars. The jumbo rigging could transfer a full load with ease. When about 20 cars were loaded, a steam locie would haul them away and switch in the empty log cars.

"In 1948, Dad was killed in a car accident while in town for the Christmas holidays."

After that, the Mosher brothers worked mostly for Tom Coates at Copper Canyon until they graduated from U.B.C. There wasn't a lot of money around, so they had to take their university schooling year and year about. The first year they flipped a coin. Monty lost and had to work so Frank graduated a year ahead. They both came out of U.B.C. with an engineering degree in forestry, his brother in 1953 and Monty in 1954.

Shortly after Monty finished university, B.C. Forest Products at Caycuse had started a trainee logging program for promising university graduates, so Monty began working there at the union hourly rate with a guaranteed salary of not less than $275 a month. A logger with experience could earn well over this minimum guarantee. Bob Robertson was the woods foreman at Caycuse and he put Monty rigging back spars for the slack-line under Lorne Atchison. Lorne was getting a bit old to do much climbing so Monty did most of the rigging under his experienced eye. Monty has always contended that young engineers should spend time on the rigging.

"The only way to learn what deflection means is to start untangling those chokers after the butt rigging has been dragged out through the brush." Monty stayed at Caycuse for about 10 years, hooking and rigging on the slack skyline machines, and at times rigging on the back end for the skidder. On the skidder they always used two cables (two skylines), which made changing from one logging road to the next much faster. The connecting shackle had to be spotted in exactly the right position for the tailholt, otherwise the carriage couldn't get in close enough to the spar for landing the logs. Monty never wanted to be responsible for spotting the cable, so he just let the old timers take care of that. Hank Mowiki and Lorne Atchison were the two men he learned from.

Shortly after graduation Monty married Verna in Vancouver. She was teaching, and stayed with her class until the end of the school year, then they lived in one of the Olson's fishing cabins on the Cowichan River while they were waiting for a house at the Caycuse camp. They lived in camp for almost 10 years.

From Caycuse they moved to Tofino where Monty was promoted to logging manager. It was while they were at the west coast their four children were born—Douglas, Lorraine, Russell, and Christopher.

Doug is the only one to follow logging, and like his father had also started working in the woods during summer and other school holidays at 13. He graduated in forestry at U.B.C., then went on to the University of Alaska to get his Masters in Science and Business Administration.

"After graduating, young Doug stayed in the north country

247

setting chokers for Silver Grizzly Helicopters, under a big Sikorsky (S-64), and stayed on to become a hooker. By the time he came south a couple of years later, he was one of the more experienced aerial loggers in British Columbia, and had written his thesis on the Cyclo-Crane. He was studying for his R.P.F. (Registered Professional Foresters) certificate in 1985. I did not go for my R.P.F. when graduating in 1954, but now to submit plans or documents to the B.C. Forest Service it was necessary to have an R.P.F ticket. After 30 years, I decided in 1984 to study and go through with my son.

"This studying is kind of hard for an old man," Monty admitted. "Whether they thought I knew enough or whether they just felt sorry for me is a good question. In any event, it was the first time a father and son had ever received their R.P.F. ticket on the same day."

Father and son share the same hopeful vision for the future of helicopter logging. There is definitely a future for any type of aerial logging system that can harvest the inaccessible timber on the steep sidehills and mountains along our coast.

Monty, as a director of the Aero Lift Company, was closely involved with the Cyclo-Crane from its inception. He was then logging manager for Pacific Forest Products, and took care of the arrangements with MacMillan Bloedel, B.C. Forest Products, Silver Grizzly Helicopters, and the Tahsis Lumber Company. These companies had all decided to financially assist, and be involved in, this aerial logging experiment.

The following are some excerpts from a verbal presentation given to the B.C. Truck Loggers Convention in early 1983 by Monty Mosher:

"My topic today is Balloon Logging, but perhaps a more apt description would be Aerial Logging. Loggers on the coast have always dreamed of that Big Hook coming down from the sky, picking up their logs, and ballooning them into the landings. So—the concept is not new. The desire for that sky-hook was the reason somebody originally climbed up a tree and hung a block to get at least a little lift—the first high lead logging system, and we have been trying to improve on that ever since.

"As some learned individual once said, 'If you are doing things the same way tomorrow that you were doing them yesterday, then you'll probably be doing them wrong'.

"One of the main reasons loggers want that elusive sky-hook is ROADS AND BRIDGES. Any self-respecting, red-blooded, natural born B.C. coast logger HATES building roads. Roads destroy loggers. There has never been an air hammer built that doesn't aggravate your ear drums, when it's working, which is seldom. Compressors and air are like generators and electricity. Loggers don't understand them and don't want to. There has never been any piece of road equipment yet that wasn't specifically designed to self-destruct, just when you needed it most. Loggers love cherry-picking, but they hate building roads. Powder gives everybody, with even the slightest intelligence, a headache.

"Roads or bridges have probably been the reason for more bankruptcies, or near bankruptcies, in the logging industry than everything else combined, including the government with its associated bureaucracies.

"Roads will drive you nuts, and no matter how much care and attention you take, or what you do, someone will come along and tell you it's in the wrong place, not up to standard, and just not good enough.

"On top of all that everybody HATES us for doing it. We are HATED for doing something we HATE DOING.

"However, we are basically all road builders, like it or not, and just do a little logging on the side if there is any time left after arguing with the various unions, governmental agencies, bankers, suppliers and head office, and then defending ourselves against the attacks of yet another self-interested group. And it's getting worse every day as the accessible timber stands peter out. The name of this gathering we have here should be changed from the 'Truck Loggers Convention' to the TRUCK-ROAD-BUILDERS-AND-DEBATING SOCIETY Convention.

"But don't despair, Road-Builders, there is a glimmer of light on the horizon. I have some slides to show you that will probably explain things a lot better.

"Slide 1. Here are some of the roads I was talking about. Steep but no real problems other than cost and the fact that the trucks have to grind all the way up and then grind all the way down again.

"Slide 2. Here are some other roads, also steep, but with lots of problems. I'm not sure whose claim it's on, but I'll bet there are some people in this room who would sure as hell like to forget it, and I believe one of them is a lady. Did you fellows ever hear a lady swear? I mean really swear! Could drive a person into selling out.

"Slide 3. Here we have a nice bridge 210 feet long over a nice river, or so it seems here. This was the fifth bridge in that same spot. Since then the spruce stringers have been replaced by steel, at great expense I might add, so now we have the sixth, or did have, last I heard.

"Now if we had an AFFORDABLE aerial logging system with sky-hook, be it balloon, helicopter or whatever, one that could reach out a mile and not worry about deflection, rock bluffs, rivers, minuscule landings, and so on, we'd have it made. I'll show you the difference as far as roads are concerned.

"Slide 4. This is a standard road system for a conventional Hi-lead grapple yarding operation, and most of these roads have already been built. You may have seen some of them recently.

"Slide 5. This is the road plan required for an aerial logging system on the same claim for the same volume:

—24 miles instead of 85 miles.

—58 landings instead of 203.

—Most of those 24 miles are the easy ones to build, maintain, and drive on.

"Think about it. Twenty-four easy miles as opposed to 24 easy miles, and then 61 more real tough ones. Then there's that environmental pressure I alluded to earlier. In the interest of dignity and good taste I'll not express my views on that subject in mixed company. Instead, I'll quote from a thesis one of my sons wrote when he graduated from U.B.C.:

"'A fanaticism for the retention of the pristine forest within certain powerful segments of the population has resulted in many compromising constraints and regulations being imposed upon forest managers. This public pressure has required the forester to develop expensive modifications in road construction, and yarding procedures, in order to minimize erosion, water siltation, land slides, and wherever reasonable, road density. Consequently, a greater need for aerial logging systems has developed since most of the detrimental impacts of logging practices on the natural environment are due to road building.'

"Slide 6. In the meantime we are still going with some version of the standard Hi-lead system which really hasn't changed that much since the beginning. We have gone through the skylining and cold decking, and double swings with hot decks, big skidders and pre-setting chokers, etc., etc., but in most cases we are back either to grapple yarding, or this.

"Slide 7. Balloons, for instance, of all shapes and sizes have been used for over 20 years. This slide shows four balloons, used in Oregon by Bohemia Lumber, tied to conventional rigging to assist lift.

"Slide 8. There are helicopters—lots of speed, lots of flexibility,

250

and lots of problems. An expensive free flying vehicle. This one is a Sikorsky (S-61).

"Slide 9. This is a Boeing Vertol which has about the same capacity, five tons.

"Slide 10. This is the biggest Sikorsky (S-64) and can produce 160 to 170 cubic meters per flight hour, and usually flies about 1,200 hours/year. At $5,000 per hour the cost is about $30 a cubic meter. THAT IS for the helicopter alone. Throw in falling and bucking, chasers, support helicopter, materials and supplies, camp costs, loading, hauling, water handling, scaling, forestry costs and all the rest I've missed, and pretty soon you are looking at $65 to $75 per cubic meter. You don't want to make too many mistakes and fly out too much pulp.

"So WHAT IS THE ALTERNATIVE? Obviously a combination of the former two.

"Slide 11. A free-flying lighter-than-air vehicle. Lots of people are trying to build these:

"Piaseki, the guy that invented the Vertol is tieing four helicopters together under a Blimp, at Lakehurst. It's called a "Helistat".

"Goodyear are also talking about something the same.

"Van Deusen is trying to make a rotating ball hold up a flying wing back east somewhere.

"The French have their Dinosaur and the English their R500. However, all of those are negatively buoyant like the helicopters, so we are putting our money on the CYCLO-CRANE. 'VOILA!'

"Slide 12. (Picture of the Cyclo-Crane) Now, isn't that magnificent? Right! But what the hell is it? Well, it's a free flying lighter-than-air vehicle which we hope will do all those things previously listed. This happens to be a baby one—a two-ton model to prove up the concept.

"How did we ever get tangled up with such a contraption? Well, I'll tell you. Several years ago a guy who talked and looked like a used car salesman came around to see several people in the logging industry about a balloon with wings in the horizontal plane, called the Aero-Crane. I happened to be one of the fortunate few, so I listened to him for a while, or at least long enough to conclude he was completely nuts. 'I'll fix you', I said to myself. So to get rid of him I sent him to see the two crankiest guys I could think of, Percy and McKercher, but that didn't work. He was back a year later with another idea, and saw Vern Wellburn. Through Vern's efforts, a syndicate of B.C. Forest Products, MacMillan Bloedel, Tahsis and Pacific was formed to look at this new Aero-Crane turned on its side called the Cyclo-Crane.

"Crown Zellerbach was involved temporarily at the outset, but in a move that may well prove to be the smartest one they ever made, they backed out prior to selling out. Some time later Silver Grizzly got into the act, thank goodness. Their contribution was not only money, but some badly needed expertise on our side. Anyway, what is it? and I quote from an engineering study:

'The Cyclo-Crane is a hybrid aircraft intended for ultra heavy vertical lift with a goal of extending helicopter type services to areas of higher lift and lower cost.' The center body of the Cyclo-Crane contains sufficient nonflammable helium to lift all of the structural weight, fuel, crew, plus 50 per cent of the intended slingload. This vehicle is a two-ton slingload device, 184 feet long. The bag diameter is 65 feet by 135 feet long and the distance between engines is 140 feet. There are four engine and wing assemblies.'

"Slide 13. The Cyclo-Crane again. How is it supposed to work? Probably pretty hard for most of you to understand, but hang in there. Nod your head once in a while so the guy sitting next to you thinks you are smart, and don't for KEERIST sake ask any questions. I speak from experience.

"In hover, the Cyclo-Crane rotates at roughly 13 rpm, and cyclic command on the wing system (the wing airfoils in this illustration are red) is used to generate the amount of lift required for 50 per cent of the slingload that is not supported by the net aerostatic lift of the system. As the center body rotates, the upper wing generates lift by virtue of a position angle of attack, the wings that are passing the neutral on either side of the vehicle are in trial, and the lower wing also provides a lift force by virtue of a negative angle of attack established in this position. The airfoil sections are symmetrical and allow the wings to generate lift under the influence of the cyclic commands of the system. When the pilot commands lateral movement, the wings in neutral position on either side of the vehicle are instantly actuated to provide the thrust desired by the pilot.

"As the vehicle moves forward, the angle of the wing is adjusted relative to the center body, and the path of flight of each wing is now defined by a helix. The inner airfoils, which are grey in these slides, are called blades. They act in the manner of large propeller blades and provide the motive force for moving the vehicle through the air in the transitional phase when the pilot commands a forward motion of the vehicle. These inner airfoils (blades) are supplied with a collective command. That is, all blades move to an equal angle of attack, and

252

the action is quite similar to 'a controllable pitch prop' on a normal aircraft. As the vehicle moves through the air, from the hover position, the rotational velocity of the entire system is reduced while holding the airspeed.

"The velocity of the air over the wings in hover is 70 miles per hour when the entire vehicle is rotating at 13 revolutions per minute. As the vehicle begins to move forward, the inflow through the rotor system would tend to raise the airspeed over the wings if a constant rate of revolution were maintained. The Cyclo-Crane reduces its rate of rotation from 13 revolutions per minute toward zero in this transitional phase, and thereby maintains a constant airspeed over the wings. In this manner, once the wings have been completely reoriented to the forward flight position, that is, 90 degrees from their position in hover, the vehicle is no longer rotating and the entire vehicle is moving through the air at 70 miles per hour. This maintains the same airspeed over the wings as was experienced in hover.

"Now doesn't that make sense? Why didn't I think of it! But, do we really care? As long as it flies and moves logs who cares why it goes, as long as it goes. Princeton University has studied the Cyclo-Crane and has concluded that it is as controllable as a helicopter of equal capacity.

"In addition it should be a lot safer. You don't have to worry about red-living, because if the turn is too heavy it just won't pick it up, or if it does pick up a heavier load it just wont fly quite so fast. And again, you can't fall DOWN and crash, you can only fall UP.

"If all the systems fail with a turn, you just go down until the weight is supported by the ground and you hang there like a kid's balloon. If all systems fail when you are empty, then you start taking off until you reach 6,000 or 7,000 feet or more and stay there until the support helicopter comes and tows you home, or you vent helium until you float back to earth or water or whatever. Anyway it sure as hell beats crashing.

"Vern Wellburn has designed a grapple for this already. I'll show you that later.

"Slide 14. This slide shows the 30-foot model floating in a big blimp hangar in Lakehurst, New Jersey. Having accepted the Cyclo-Crane principle the syndicate agreed to finance 'Phase I' which included a series of studies and research by some smart people at Princeton University, and the construction of a one-third scale model of a two-ton Cyclo-Crane to verify the size and shape of the bag and to determine fabrication techniques. The model was made by I.L.C. Dover of Delaware, a balloon manufacturing company. They also build space suits that go to the moon and are used by the space shuttle people. They also have lots of smarts. That was successful, so the next step or 'Phase II' was to construct the actual flying model or the two-ton Cyclo-Crane.

"I.L.C. made the bag while other people like Switzer Aircraft and our inventors put together other bits and pieces. The whole works was shipped out to the Blimp hangars in Tillamook, Oregon, for assembly and testing. It was all going to cost about $1 per thousand.

"Slide 15. This slide shows the bag partially inflated with helium (in Tillamook) so it could be worked on. All the rigging had to be stuffed into the partially-inflated bag through this hole in the front, then hooked together inside the bag. And you think you've got rigging problems.

"While all this was going on, the partially-inflated bag was held down with sand bags. The jovial looking chap on the left is our inventor, Art Crimmons, previously referred to as the 'Used Car Salesman'.

"Slide 16. This slide shows the Cyclo-Crane as it approached the mooring mast. That long rope from the nose will be threaded through the fairleads on the mast and the machine pulled in and locked to the mast by the nose cone.

"Slide 17. There she is attached to the mast and ready to go through all kinds of tests and adjustments prior to testing in free-flight. We are rapidly approaching the end of 'Phase II' and we have only overrun the original $1 per thousand budget by a little over 300 per cent. Sounds about normal.

"Here you are seeing the vehicle in free-flight. It wasn't planned that way. However, it happened and it's what you call 'testing the experimental machine to destruction'. Here you see the bag after the aforementioned test which was completely successful.

"Slide 18. This is a used wings and blade. Now, what happened? Well . . . On October 22, 1982 at about 10 a.m. the vehicle was blown from the mast and severely damaged. Wind predictions at that time were from 20 to 40 mph. A decision was made to leave the vehicle at the mast to test the structure under these modest wind conditions. The actual wind conditions are unknown, but were estimated to be in excess of 80 mph. As destructive energies on the vehicle were several hundred times more than expected, the mounting bolts securing the vehicle to the mast were simply sheared off, the vehicle was blown downwind into a neighbouring field among some grazing cows and literally destroyed itself. Anyway, we'll start again because we need this machine.

"According to the latest and most reliable estimates we are talking about 800 to 900 million cubic meters of timber. For the sake of you

254

middle-age guys that is 300 million cunits, and for you old guys that is 150 billion board feet of timber. That would keep 100 16-ton Cyclo-Cranes working steady for over 40 years.

"Like I said before, 150 billion board feet and then some, just on the B.C. coast. Gawd knows there are probably other places in the world that have even more. We haven't even mentioned power-line construction, arctic and off-shore oil and gas, search and rescue, Coast Guard surveillance, the military, let alone moving people. Like I said, 'there is a light on the horizon'.

"A lot of you are probably still wondering 'Why?' Well, maybe some of you remember 'Panicky Bob Robertson', Woods Boss extraordinaire. He came screaming into the landing one day many years ago when we were swinging the slackline around the tree and it just so happened that at that moment a few of us young greenhorns were standing there, grouped together, figuring out what to do next. He leaped out of his pickup and before even attempting, if you can believe this, before even attempting to ascertain the state of our health, or even to say 'Hi there'! he suggested that it would probably be better if we weren't standing around like a bunch of loving sheep waiting for the lovable gate to open, and that perhaps we should be doing something, even if it was wrong, he thought we should be doing something. I haven't quoted him verbatim of course—but I wish he was here so that I could finally tell him 'We are doing something, Bob—even if it's wrong—we are doing something'.

"Thank you for your attention, 'ROAD BUILDERS'".

Monty received a standing ovation.

After the convention, Monty added: "There are only two places in the States with hangers big enough to hold these Cyclo-Cranes. One's in Lakehurst, New Jersey, and the other is at Tillimook, or Tillimuch as the Americans call it, in Oregon. If they agree with all the test results that have been done with our model, and it can be scaled up to a 25-tonner, they will finance a new prototype which will cost about $30 million.

"In a helicopter you either make the right decision or you're dead. With a Cyclo-Crane if something goes wrong, you've got three or four hours to figure out what to do next.

"I have little knowledge of helicopter technology, and don't attempt to even speculate on solving aeronautical engineering problems. If you have something up there like the machine we have in mind, which at its maximum speed is turning over at 13 revolutions per minute and is being driven by standard engines, you're not going to instantly die if an engine should fail. It makes a lot more sense than using these sophisticated machines and trying to step down from 50,000 to 600 revolutions per minute, which is the present maximum wingtip velocity," Monty explained.

He is very sure someone is going to develop the right ship. He's even put his money where his mouth is.

"It had better bloody well happen", he says. "It's going to be a great revolution one of these days, as soon as one of those things are properly equipped. There's lots of interest and lots of money being spent on the lighter-than-air concept so it's going to come fairly soon.

"If Russia and the U.S. quit making war missiles, they'll have plenty of money to spend on such things as helicopter logging.

"If we run out of fossil fuel (petroleum), you might be surprised what will be used for power to haul logs."

Changing the subject, I asked Monty, "What do you think of Tree Farm Licenses?"

"Looking back to 1945, when the Sloan Commission made its first recommendations, sustained yield was a good concept. At the time, something was needed to encourage some long-term investment in the industry. From that point of view, the Tree Farm Licenses with the Public Working Circles (large timbered areas set aside, where the smaller operators can buy their timber) left sufficient timber available for the smaller operators. Now 40 years later, I believe that the TFL's have served a purpose, but now it's neither necessary nor advisable to have the larger companies continue to tie up the forest lands in British Columbia. I believe they should increase the opportunity for acquiring timber and make it fair for all.

"There are some other changes that should be made. The small independent contractors or loggers have to be given a reasonable chance. As it is now, if you improve your efficiency under a contract system the companies want it all. If you can reduce your price by two bucks, they want to reduce your contract by $2.50. They seem to figure that if you can cut it by $2, then you can probably survive a $2.50 cut. They want all the benefits and a bit more. It's pretty discouraging for a contrac-

Martin Mars water bomber dropping tons of water on the blazing Rayonier
and Scott paper mill on the Fraser River at New Westminster, August 1966.
This fire was brought under control by the water bombers and made the
lumber industry realize the value of these huge flying boats as fire fighting
machines.

Forest Industries Flying Tankers' Staff at Sproat Lake, Spring 1979.
Left to right.

Back row Hal Newman, Flight Engineer
Gary Borgford, Mars Captain
Richard Jones, Accountant
Bill Waddington, Chief Pilot and Manager
Len Bateman, Chief Engineer
Walt Champness, Co-pilot/Engineer
Vic Demers, Flight Engineer
Tom Kellough, Mars Captain
Paul Verreault, Co-pilot/Engineer.

Front row Eric Sorensen, Engineer
Barry Simpson, Co-pilot/Engineer
Jim McInroy, Sheet Metal Mechanic/Flight Engineer
Mel Melson, Flight Engineer
George Stewart, Avionics
Peter Lauren, Mars Captain
Bob Sideen, Flight Engineer
Mickey Markewick, Store Keeper
Dennis Holt, Sheet Metal Mechanic
Alf Bull, Flight Engineer.

Forest Industries Flying Tankers' Staff at Sproat Lake, 1988
Left to right.

  Back row Al Jack, Engineer
       George Broughton, Caretaker
       Gord Gray, Engineer
       Vic Demers, Engineer
       Jerry Linning, Office Manager/Accountant
  Third row Cliff Schwindt, Helicopter Pilot
       Roy Copeland, Engineer
       Reg Young, Pilot
       Ian Thomas, Engineer
       Jim McInroy, Metal Worker
       Eric Sorenson, Metal Worker
  Second row Ron Kromrey, Engineer
       Mary White, Storekeeper
       Barry Simpson, Maintenance Manager.
  Front row Walter Champness, Engineer
       Jack Waddington, Chief Pilot
       Tom Irving, General Manager
       Steve Belanger, Engineer
       Dave Porter, Engineer
       Hugh Fraser, Pilot
       Paul Verreault, Deputy Maintenance Manager

Hawaiian Mars alongside the float at Sproat Lake showing it's tremendous size.

Old Hilcrest Lumber mill at Shatlam, 1934. Filers and filing room. Left to right: Ed Portelance, John Gellette and Lee Portelance. Courtesy I.W.A. 1-80 from Wilmer Gold Collection.

Victoria Lumber, Camp 10, west of Cowichan Lake, 1937. Typical filing room for the old hands. Courtesy I.W.A. 1-80 from Wilmer Gold Collection.

Cyril Dawkin, with his Wee Mac-Gregor drag saw, at his wood yard in South Wellington, just south of Nanaimo, 1930.

Earl Laughlin and Charlie Phelp in 1949. They were partners at Half-moon Bay.

The Mosher Family — 1926

Left to right.
    Back row   Cliff, Luke, Frank (Monty Mosher's father) and Fred.
    Third row   Foss, Heggie, Bill and Slats.
  Second row   Alice, Lill, Carrie, Stella and Pearl.
    Front row   Grandfather Harry and Grandmother Margaret.

Monty Mosher, working for B.C. Forest Products, preparing to climb and top a back spar for the skyline on a Washington skidder at Cayacuse Creek, September 24, 1959. Cowichan Lake is in the background.

Laurette and Jim Stanton at their cabin. Jim was the world famous guide for big grizzly. Friends and neighbours of Earl and Grace Laughlin at Knight Inlet for 15 years. Jim lived to be 101 years old.

Commodore Hotel, Vancouver, 1943.
1. Stan Bloomfield
2. Frank Mosher
3. George (Panicky) Bell
4. Tom Coates
5. Phil Wilson, (Merrill, Wing and Wilson)

Neil Thompson co-pilot, Joe Garner author and Bob Hawthorne chief pilot standing beside Coulson's S-61 Sikorsky, the morning of July 27, 1988 at North West Bay, MacMillan Bloedel operation near Parksville, Vancouver Island.

Jim Vox, MacMillan Bloedel Regional Supervisor, and Brian Dunn, pilot of Coulson's new Gazell SA-341. This is a French built turbo powered small chopper capable of doing 150 m.p.h. It has a bambi bucket for fire fighting and can be used as an air ambulance.

Chief pilot, Bob Hawthorne, inspecting the S-61, after landing for refueling. Note fuel tanker truck and crew bus at the service area.

Left: Another turn being lowered to the landing with Bob Hawthorne, and Neil Thompson as co-pilot. Great co-operation and skill is a must.

Right: Hydraulic grapple dropping the logs at the landing. They are averaging a 7000 lb. load every 80 seconds.

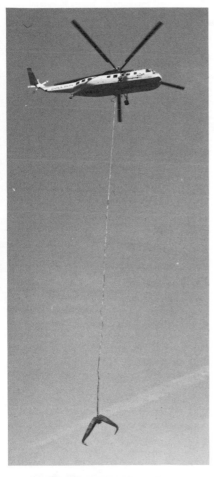

Coulson Forest Products Ltd.
using their new hydraulic
grapple July 27, 1988, at
the North West Bay Camp for
MacMillan Bloedel.

Below: Ground crew mechanic
adjusting the new 7 ft. wide
hydraulic grapple as Wayne
Coulson and "yours truly" give
some unneeded advice.

A 107 in the Fraser Canyon in 1986. This machine logged for Whonnock Lumber all summer with satisfactory results. They used the choker system and ground crews. Photo by Ted Veal.

Boeing Vertol 107 logging helicopter in Columbia's refueling and service area, where the chopper is checked three times each working day by field engineers, pilot and co-pilot. Minor repairs are carried out while refueling, but major repairs are done in their main shop where they can completely rebuild a 107. This machine can handle a 10,000 lb. load (5 tons) at sea level. It can also fly safely on either of the two 1500 h.p. turbine motors when empty. Columbia keeps a 500 gal. bucket at the service site. Should a forest fire occur the chopper can hook up in less than 10 minutes to douse a blaze. Photo by Ted Veal.

Another Columbia 107 landing a load for the log trucks. Photo by Ted Veal.

Clearing up logs on some rough side-hills in the Wallowa area, Oregon in
1985. Photo by Ted Veal.

Columbia Helicopters Inc. log landing at Wallowa, Oregon, showing a Boeing Vertol 107 delivering logs using a ground crew and chokers. Photo by Ted Veal.

Wes Lematta, President,
Columbia Helicopters Inc.

A 25 year old Vertol 107 still looking good. Photos courtesy Columbia
Helicopters Inter-company Bulletin.

An artist's concept of the Cyclo-crane. Monty Mosher, a director of Airolift Inc., says it cost millions.

tor to go out and buy this expensive new equipment to reduce logging costs, and then give it all to the company that happens to have the right to harvest the trees. There has to be a little give and take, and some further incentive to invest. The industry shouldn't have to build any more pulp mills since there probably won't be enough timber to support them. The companies have had a good run at it for 40 years. There's a renewable clause in the TFL contracts now. At the end of the 10th or 15th year, they must apply for renewal."

Monty believes a certain amount of timber should be reallocated to the independent loggers. They should have a crack at 50 per cent of the TFL volumes on a market price deal, and let the company have first refusal on the logs. But if they don't want to buy the logs at market price then the logger could sell elsewhere.

"When times are bad the crews should take a cut, and when times are good they should get a raise, and in this way they can get their share. The big companies don't seem to be able to do this, while the smaller independents can," Monty concluded.

Monty Mosher is currently running three sizable logging camps. Two are on Vancouver Island, contracting for B.C. Forest Products, and one is at Sechelt for Industrial Forest. With his head office at Chemainus, Monty operates the most up-to-date equipment such as portable grapple yarding towers and the best of trucks and loading machines. But more important than all his practical experience is his daring vision of Cyclo-Crane logging that he has been trying to implement. His courage and some cold cash could bring about unbelievable changes to the forest industry. Anything lighter than air can defy the laws of gravity and there is no telling where things might end up.

Bob Hawthorne, born 1951. Bob, as chief pilot,
demonstrates the visibility of the
plexiglas bubble installed on each side
of the Sikorsky S-61 chopper.

CHAPTER 23

Bob Hawthorne

Bob Hawthorne trained, put in the necessary air time, then received his commercial licence to fly light fixed-wing aircraft in 1971. In 1975, he borrowed enough money to sign up with the Vancouver Island Helicopter Training School and earned his commercial pilot's licence for choppers. His instructors were Bill Teag, now the Ministry of Transport Inspector, Clifford Schwint, senior pilot with the forest industry's Flying Tankers at Sproat Lake, and Ken Norrie. Bob was one of Norrie's first students.

After receiving his helicopter licence, Bob drove his car half way across Canada looking for a flying job.

"I arrived back home six months later to find a message from Don McGilvray offering me a flying job based out of the Cassidy Airport, not 20 miles from where I lived. The following spring, Bill Teag phoned to let me know that Okanagan was hiring chopper pilots. I applied, and was hired as a 'line pilot' in the spring of 1977, and had flying assignments all over Canada for the next two years."

"What do you mean by a line pilot?" I asked.

"Well, there's two systems with most helicopter companies. If you are a base pilot you can expect to be home most nights. If you're just a line pilot they will send you where the work is. I worked as far north as Fort Simpson, and east all the way to Ontario."

It was 1979 before Bob had the seniority to qualify as the base pilot for Okanagan Helicopters at Campbell River.

"Most of my flights were for the logging companies, the majors being MacMillan Bloedel, B.C.Forest Products and the B.C. Forest Service. There was a lot of timber cruising. I'd move their men to various places in the morning, then pick them up at the end of the day. Setting radio towers on mountain tops, and other such jobs became routine."

It was from the Campbell River base that Bob was first exposed to heli-logging. Okanagan Helicopters had their Sikorsky S-61 in Toba Inlet using chokers and the long line system. Bob flew support with a Jet Ranger. He would take the hooker and crew up the mountain to the felled and bucked timber first thing in the morning. There would be six or seven men that worked under the S-61. The rest of the day the Jet Ranger would pick up the empty chokers, fly them back up to the guys on the hill, and do other light work that was needed. As long as that big Sikorsky was hauling logs every one, including the Jet Ranger, was busy.

"Logging must be in my blood because I loved every minute at Toba Inlet."

It was while Bob was at Toba Inlet that he got the chance to learn to handle the big Sikorsky. At the end of the logging season he left the Campbell River base for more training in Vancouver. The following spring he was co-pilot for Okanagan, lifting log loads up to 10,000 pounds.

"We have a weight indicator on the belly of the machine, and the S-61 must fly with a pilot and co-pilot at all times when logging. The pilot's job is to fly the aircraft. The co-pilot is the fellow who looks after the engines, records the load weights and usually helps handle the throttles. The thing about a logging pilot is that after considerable experience he begins to read those logs. You know the approximate weight just by looking at them. After you've picked up hundreds and hundreds of tons, you know that some cedar is lighter than other types of wood."

Bob had been chief pilot of the S-61 with Okanagan Helicopters for almost two years when Cliff Coulson came over to watch them log. He and his son Wayne were intending to try chopper logging near Port Alberni. They asked Bob to come over and take a look at the show. The result was that he accepted their proposal and in July of 1987, he was put on their payroll and hasn't looked back since. When he started with Coulsons, they had just bought a reconditioned S-61 and were using the long line and chokers.

"In the meantime, the Coulsons had been developing a grapple system. They started flying the first hydraulic grapple ever used in air lift logging later that same year," Bob said proudly. "It took us a couple of weeks to get the bugs out. It's a whole different ball game. There are no men under the machine to get hurt when the grapple is being used.

"Where this hydraulic grapple really shines is on the short turn-around trips. When you go in and set the grapple you can immediately start putting the power to it. I find myself becoming a more aggressive pilot, for the simple reason that I don't have to worry about a damn thing on the ground except the log. The fact that there's not the constant chatter on the two-way radio from hooker to pilot makes concentration a lot easier. When I'm up there using the grapple there is nothing but the machine, myself, and the co-pilot. Believe me, it certainly is easier on the nerves. There are few good logging pilots in Canada because of the great risks and responsibilities that go with the job. A good mental attitude towards logging is important."

The Coulsons are already getting 30 per cent more production on the short hauls. Without the ground crew, the saving is roughly $2,000 a day, plus another $2,500 saving by eliminating the support chopper to return the chokers. They are now working on a lighter grapple weighing in at around 700 to 800 pounds which will increase their pay load.

"What about your hydraulic line? Is there any major problem to releasing your load if you should get in trouble?" I asked.

"What we have is an 'accumulator' inside the grapple, which actually stores up its own pressure. As long as there is electric power to the grapple, even if your hydraulic hose has been cut off, you can still jettison your load. It's only one second from full close to full open. It doesn't have to open more than a few inches to release the logs."

"What do you think it costs per hour to fly that machine, not including the ground crew and pilots?"

"The expenses run at around $2,500 an hour," Bob estimated.

"Can the co-pilot take that ship over and fly it if something should happen to the chief pilot?"

"Yes, he has his own controls. On a Sikorsky 61 the throttles are manual. Most turbine engines have governors, but these engines govern only to a certain percent, and the rest is all manual throttle. When you're coming off the hill, and using tremendous power changes, the co-pilot is working as hard as you are. He's responsible for throttles and power to handle the load."

"What if you had a heart attack, or passed out?"

"No problem. Either one of us could fly it. We both have an identical set of controls. If you should get into a real panic situation you can always jettison the whole grapple system from the belly hook with just one touch of a button. The S-61 can fly safely on either engine if one should fail."

"That's a major, major safety factor," I suggested.

"Yes, and by bucking and color-coding the logs, when we come up with the grapple we know very closely what poundage we're going to pull. It's a neat system. The logs are color-coded with yellow, blue and red to designate the weight. A log not bucked right through we call a 'Russian', and it can cause an 'abort' (to drop the load). Fallers on a heli-show are taught to grade and assess weights. Good falling and bucking is a big part of good heli-logging.

"What we are trying to do now is maximize everything right from the time the saw bites into the tree to when that log hits the salt chuck. Heli-logging is a race against time. Therefore, every pickup you make with that grapple has to be a winner," Bob explained.

"What about wind velocity?" I asked.

"Anything up to 20 or 25 knots is comfortable for the S-61."

"What does the Department of Transport tell you about flying time?"

"They tell us 120 hours is maximum flying time per month, with no extensions if you're doing logging. Fighting forest fires a pilot can go to 150 hours with permission."

"How long would it take to change from logging to fire fighting equipment on the Sikorsky?"

"We can be down, disconnect the grapple lines, and hook on the Bambic Bucket (an 800 gallon bucket for dropping water on fires) in about 10 minutes. And if the bucket is already filled and at the landing, it takes only about three or four minutes to drop the grapple, hook up the bucket, and go. When the woods are shut down because of heat and humidity, the forestry service will usually ask us to keep on logging. That way we can be immediately available should lightning strike or a careless hiker start a fire.

"At 700 to 800 gallons a drop there's a hell of a lot of water coming down. Say you have a small fire just starting. You can usually put it out with the S-61 with one single drop. With the monsoon buckets we can usually put out a blaze much quicker than with big fixed-winged water bombers. The helicopter is so versatile. It's not necessary to fly miles to a lake or the salt chuck to scoop up water. Any stream, or small lake, that's big enough to hover the helicopter over will do."

"How do the crews take to helicopter logging—what's their attitude?"

"The most important part of this system is pride and prestige, and if anybody tells you that it isn't, they're lying. It's exciting. It's challenging. It's fast, and in this particular case it's innovative. Everyone in our team is really proud of their achievements. It's a very close knit unit, almost like one big family. Besides the pilots, we have the greatest support men who are all specialists in their respective fields. Nothing is left to chance. Safety is king.

"There's also a maintenance system on our IBM computer,

called Airborn Data. At the end of each day, the maintenance crew punch the number of hours that the ship has flown into the computer. The computer will totally update every component on that ship, give a warning, for instance, like an engine's coming due for an overhaul in another 100 hours. It will show what needs looking at now, print it out on a sheet of paper, and the engineers go ahead and do it. The computer has the capability to tell you in advance of the part you'll need and print out the part numbers, and when to order so it arrives on the job about the day you'll need it. We have worked very closely with the Workmen's Compensation Board on this whole program, and they think our system is great.

"That's part of the game," Bob beams. "The working conditions are excellent and very professional. When the S-61 goes from setting to setting it moves as a whole unit. Each setting we go to, whether it's 50 miles away or two miles down the road, a cat has levelled out a large enough area where we can set the machine down and park the support equipment. We have FM radios and B.C. Tel equipment in the crew trailer at all times which keeps in contact with head office. If we need a part in a hurry, we can have it flown out to us. We have a Jet Ranger in the company to do such chores."

It was Grant Hawthorne, Bob's Dad, who was my partner when we selected and cruised the helicopter timber we intended to log with the Boeing Vertol 107 back in the summer and fall of 1961. Grant did the cruising while I kept the Piper float plane in the air where he could have a good look at the timber on those rough sidehills around the Redonda Islands.

Grant was a high rigger and in his sixties he didn't mind going up on the passline to swing the blocks around the spar tree. The year Grant retired from logging he was pulling logs out of the bush with a big diesel yarder. He started his career on steam donkeys back in 1918. Now Bob is doing basically the same job, but using a much different type of equipment. The Hawthornes have logging in their blood. If Grant were still alive I'm sure he'd be mighty proud of his son.

"How long do you think you'll be able to fly?" I asked Bob. "You're 36 now. At 50 the human body is not as flexible, nor as coordinated."

"Right. Having a pilot's licence and being proficient is based on health. Lots of logging pilots get burned out in a hurry because of working long hours." Bob hopes to be able to carry on for 20 or 25 more years. When age does become a problem he's quite sure his experience will qualify him for a management position in aerial logging.

Bob Hawthorne personifies a positive logging attitude: "Pride has a lot to do with it. The more you do, the more the pride shows up. Just like the old high riggers. They didn't have to dance a jig on top of a 180-foot tree after cutting the top off, but they did, just to show the other loggers how great they were. My Dad did it. That's Ego'!"

August 1988 at Northwest Bay. L to R — Wayne Coulson, Neil Thompson, Jim Vaux, Bob Hawthorne, Joe Garner and Brian Dunn discussing the first hydraulic grapple ever used under a helicopter for logging.
Photos by Ken Flett.

Glossary

A-FRAME: Giant A-frame structure on a big log float, which supports blocks and running lines in high-lead logging, used to swing logs from the back spar to the water or yard directly into the water.

ANCHOR STUMP: Ground anchor for guy lines, skyline or tail holds.

ARCH: Steel arch used behind a cat to raise the front end of logs up off the ground for easier yarding.

ASPARAGUS: Smaller logs bundled and strapped together for better loading and transportation.

BACKCUT: Cut put in the tree opposite the undercut.

BACKFIRE: A fire purposely set to burn a fire break. Also, gas or diesel engines firing too soon backfire.

BACKLINE: That portion of the haulback between spar and the tail blocks.

BACKRIGGER: The man that rigs the back spars.

BACK SPAR: Spar tree at the back end of skyline.

BAG BOOM: Boom sticks coupled together to encircle and contain loose logs.

BARBER CHAIR: When a tree splits leaving a slab attached to the stump resembling a chair back.

BARGE: A type of scow for transporting logs or machinery.

BEADS: Chokers, knobs etc.

BEAN BURNER: A poor camp cook.

BELL: Closed choker hook.

BICYCLE: Carriage that travels on a skyline to prevent hangups.

BIGHT: A dangerous place—inside the angle or loop of a fouled line.

BINDLE: The roll of blankets carried by a transient logger.

266

BIRD DOG: A small plane used to guide the bombers over forest fires to where water is most needed.

BLOCK: Steel sheaves to prevent line wear. Added pulling power.

BOARD HOLE: The notch cut in a tree for a spring-board.

BOOM: Logs stowed and swiftered.

BOOMERANG: Spark arrester to reverse sparks down into a screen so they don't drift out to start fires.

BOOMMAN OR BOOMCAT: A man handy with a pike pole, catty on his feet and knows how to sort and stow logs.

BOOMSTICK: A 66-foot log bored at each end, usually with a four inch auger. Uniform in size with a minimum top size of 10 inches.

BROADAXE: A heavy axe with a very wide blade and short offset handle.

BROW LOG: Log used to protect log cars or trucks while loading at a landing. Also used at logdumps to protect piling and hold rail cars or trucks in place.

BUCKER: A skilled worker who saws felled trees into lengths.

BUCKLE GUYS: Cables fastened tight part way up the spar to keep it steady.

BUCKSKIN: Log with no bark.

BULL BLOCK: The big block near the top of a spar tree that carries the main line.

BULL BUCKER: The boss of the falling and bucking crews.

BULL CAR: Big flat rail car used to move heavy equipment.

BULLCHOKER: Extra strong and long choker used on heavy pulls.

BULLCOOK: Usually a broken-down old logger who takes little or no nonsense from the crew. Keeps the camp clean, and gets in the wood.

BULLDOZER: A track machine used to build roads, yard logs and do any one of a hundred other jobs.

BULL HOOK: Large hook on the end of the drum line of a cat or bulldozer.

BULL OF THE WOODS: Superintendent or woods boss. This term sometimes related to high riggers or other toughies.

BULL PEN: Where logs are dumped and held in the water for sorting.

BULL SKINNER: Today a legend-of-yore. A man that knew how to cuss well and handle oxen from a single yoke up to a dozen. Sometimes known as bull whackers or bull punchers.

BULL TEAM: Used in early logging before horses came into use on the skid roads.

BUNCH IT: Quit.

BUNDLE-BOOM: A boom of bundled logs. Bundles are held together with wire cables or steel bundling straps.

BUNK: That part of a logging car or truck where logs rest when being hauled. A bed of sorts where loggers slept.

BUNK-BOUND: The condition that exists when logs loaded on a rail car extend far enough to interfere with logs on the next car and bind up on curves. Logging trucks became bunk-bound on sharp curves before compensating bars, or sliding reaches were used.

BUNK LOAD: The first layer of logs loaded onto a railway car or a logging truck.

BUNK SCALES: Scale came into use about 1950 to weigh logs on the truck. Public highways were limited to load weights with heavy fines for overloads.

BUTT RIGGING: Hooks and swivelled connections to the main line haulback and chokers.

CAMP TENDER: A boat that brought in the crews and cookhouse supplies. Also did odd jobs around a booming ground, or took an injured logger to hospital.

CATERPILLAR/CAT: A track machine used for logging.

CAT DOCTOR: A mechanic who specializes in track equipment and capable of swinging a 10 pound sledge.

CAT SKINNER: Tractor operator.

CAT SIDE: Good ground where cats are used to bring logs to the landing or into the water.

CAULK: Steel nails driven into the soles of logging boots.

CHASER: Man who unhooks chokers at the spar.

CAYUSE: A maverick, a captured wild horse that doesn't like work, or being ridden.

CHEESE BLOCK: Wedge shaped steel block to hold the logs in place on the bunks of the skeleton cars or logging trucks.

CHERRY PICKER: A machine for picking up lost logs or loading along a right-of-way where short yarding is feasible.

CHOKER: A closed hook (bell) and two knobs on a short length of wire rope to go around a log, and the other end attaches to the butt rigging and main line.

CHOKERHOLE: It is sometimes necessary to dig or poke a hole under a log in order to get a choker around it.

CHOKERMAN: One who hooks chokers around the logs to be yarded.

CHUCK/SALT CHUCK: The sea or ocean.

CHUNK: In high-lead operations using a wooden spar and a McLean boom—the short log hanging from a block fixed to a buckle guy which acts as a counter-weight when the boom is swung. See slack puller.

CLAIM: Timbered country staked for logging.

CLEAR: Knot free log or lumber. In the clear—out of danger.

CLEARCUT: To cut and use all marketable timber on any claim.

COLD DECK: A pile of logs left for future loading or yarding. Usually taken in on a skyline.

COLDSHUT: An unwelded link joint, like a shackle with no screw pin but with a riveted closure (can be riveted without heat).

CONKY: Unsound timber infested with a parasite fungus growth.

CORD: 128 cubic feet of loose wood that equals a stack eight feet long, four feet high and four feet wide, split or round. Such a pile is usually calculated to contain 100 cubic feet of solid wood.

CORE: Centre of a cable. Can be a steel or hemp rope. The centre of a log that is left after being peeled for plywood.

CRIB: Stack of telephone poles that floats in the water ready for transport. Some pole cribs were 50 feet long, 30 wide and up to 20 deep and lashed at the corners. Logs, timbers or boulders used as a retaining wall.

CROSS-HAUL: Now a legend, it was an intersection of two skid roads going in different directions when oxen or horses pulled logs.

CROWN FIRE: Forest fire that spreads through the tree tops and travels like the wind.

CRUISER: A skilled woodsman who can estimate the quantity and quality of standing timber.

CRUMMY: A vehicle for transporting logging crews to work.

CULL: Logs or lumber of no merchantable value.

CUNIT: 100 cubic feet of wood.

DEADHEAD: Partly submerged log.

DOLPHIN: Three or more pilings lashed together for a stronger tieup.

DONKEY ENGINE: Named because of its noisy puffing, snorting and loud whistles. A steam pot, gasoline or diesel engine with drums and cables that yards the logs from woods.

DONKEY PUNCHER: A man who operates a donkey.

DOZER BOAT: A powerful little boom boat with unique steering.

DUPLEX: A large skidder that both yards and loads logs.

EYESPLICE: A loop spliced into the end of a cable or rope.

FAIRLEAD: An arrangement of rollers or sheaves on the front end of the donkey sleighs to guide the lines so they spooled properly on the drums. Also used on the heel boom of the shovel loaders or on top of the steel spars or towers.

FAKE: Usually a gas donkey that was a bit haywire.

FALL: To cut down or fell trees.

FALL BLOCK: A long block used on skyline shows to give better lift for the turn as it heads for the landing.

FALLER: A worker who cuts down trees.

FARMER: One who logs part time and lives on a stump ranch. Sometimes called a homeguard.

FINGERLINK: A steel link that can be released under strain.

FIREBREAK: Any road or clearing that can help stop a fire.

FLAT BOOM: Usually eight sections, 66 feet wide and 540 long, of logs stowed and swiftered ready for towing.

FLOWERY HOLT: Something unusual being tried to clear a hangup.

FLUME: Used extensively to carry shingle bolts down from the sidehills into a lake or river. Rarely used for logs in Western Canada.

FLUNKEY/FLUNKY: One who helps in the cookhouse. A waitress, dish washer, or both, depending on the number of loggers.

FLYING-CHOKER: A choker with the open hook cut down so that it will free itself from the log when tension is released.

FORE-AND-AFT: Road of logs laid end to end so the old roading donkeys could slide bigger loads down to the saltchuck.

GANDY-DANCER: Railroad section worker.

GILCREST JACK: Extensively used by hand-loggers to roll or push logs toward the chuck.

GIN POLE: Short leaning spar used for loading or unloading logs.

GOAT: Small donkey usually used by the bull gang for rigging spars.

GRADE SHOVEL: A large mechanical scoop shovel usually mounted on tracks and used in road building.

GRAPPLE: Large powerful mechanical tongs used to pick up or yard logs.

GRAPPLE CARRIAGE: A carriage designed to carry a grapple out from a landing.

GRAPPLE YARDER: Machine which yards logs using a grapple. Now being used by helicopters.

GRAPPLE YARDING: New concept of removing logs by the use of a grapple, eliminating the need for chokermen.

GROUND LEAD: Old style of logging before there were spar trees. The logs were dragged on the ground.

GUTHAMMER: Triangular piece of metal hung on a wire outside the cookhouse door. The cook would bang this with an iron bar to announce mealtimes.

GUY LINE: A cable stretched between a stump and the top of a spar tree or tower to keep them in a solid upright position.

GYPPO: To log on contract. Term for any small logging show.

GYPSY: Upright steam yarding spool. One of the first steam yarding units to go into the British Columbia woods used this near Chemainus.

HAND FALLER/HAND FELLER: Logger who cuts trees down using an axe and crosscut saw.

271

HAND-LOGGER: A man working by himself. Gilcrest jacks, axe, peavey, Swede fiddles and a good rowboat were standard equipment.

HANGUP: A log fouled up in a root, snag or stump.

HAULBACK: Line attached to the main line which returns the butt rigging and chokers back to woods.

HAY BURNER: An ox or horse used for logging.

HAYWIRE SHOW: Logging operation with poor equipment and rough ground, sometimes has no money for pay days.

HEADLOADER: Almost a legend. Man who picks out the logs to be loaded and directs the loading of railway cars or trucks.

HEEL BOOM: A slanting, tapered boom (sometimes on a converted power shovel) attached directly to a machine used for loading logs. One end of the log rests against the boom while in the grip of a grapple or tongs suspended from the end of the boom, giving the engineer leverage and control to swing logs onto truck or rail car.

HIGHBALL: Descriptive of any logging operation where speed is king.

HIGH LEAD: To yard logs to the landing using a spar tree to lift the log ends so that they don't hangup so often.

HIGH LEAD BLOCK: See Bull block.

HIGH RIGGER/RIGGER: The man who tops and prepares a spar tree for logging and is usually in charge of the side.

HINDU: The cable coupling or link between the strawline and the haulback.

HOGAN'S ALLEY: Walkway between bunkhouses and washhouse. A tough and dangerous street in Vancouver.

HOG: Locomotive pulling logging cars.

HOGGER: Locomotive engineer.

HOMEGUARD: A logger who is content to remain working for one company instead of moving about from camp to camp. Can also mean a farmer logger.

HOOKTENDER: The boss of the yarding crew.

HOLT: The application of a special hitch.

HOT DECK: Is when the logs are taken away as soon as they land at the spar.

HOT LOGGING: When most turns are loaded immediately or logs are taken from a yarder as they come in. No pile is allowed to accumulate.

INKSLINGER: A timekeeper or office man.

JACKPOT: A hell of a mess. A jumble of crisscrossed logs in a bullpen, usually where the logs are dumped into the water. A log jam on a river drive.

JAGGER: A steel strand from a worn or damaged cable.

JAM: Logs or debris blocking a river.

JEWELRY: The rigging designed for attaching logs to the mainline. Includes butt rigging, shackles, hooks and chokers etc.

JILL POKE: A strong pole or timber rigged to push logs off a rail car or log truck.

LANDING: An area where logs are assembled for loading or dumped into the water.

LEVERMAN: Loading engineer—especially the engineer who operates a donkey used in loading.

LINE-HORSE: A big horse used to haul the line back into the timber before haulback cables and two-drum yarders were invented.

LOADING BOOM: Any one of variously shaped extensions jutting out from a loading machine or a spar tree to provide a means for lifting logs on to trucks or railway cars.

LOADING JACK: A block suspended on a guyline for loading.

LOCIE/LOCI/LOKEY: A steam locomotive used on railroads.

LONG-BUTT: A defective portion of a felled tree usually cut off and left at the stump.

LONG SPLICE: Two cables of the same size unstranded then wrapped (or woven) together and neatly tucked to form a continuous cable of close to the original size.

LOOKOUT: Tower on high ground used in the summer to watch for fires.

MAN-CATCHER: An employment agent whose job it was to induce holidaying loggers to get back on the job.

MARLIN SPIKES: A sharp ended, tapered steel tool for splicing cable.

MFBM: A much used abbreviation for 1000 board foot measure of lumber or logs.

MOBILE SPAR/PORTABLE SPAR: These portable steel spars are mounted on sleighs, wheels or tracks. This was the beginning of the end of the need for the high riggers and the conventional wooden spars.

MOLLY HOGAN: A link made of a single cable strand to connect cables or keep shackle and block pins in place.

MUG-UP: Coffee and a sandwich, or either, usually between meals.

MULLIGAN MIXER: Camp cook.

MUZZLE LOADER: Bunks side-by-side where men crawled in over the end. A gun loaded with a ramrod before breach loaders were invented.

NOSE BAG SHOW: A setting where a lunch bucket is necessary.

NOSE-GUY: The line that holds outer end of a heel boom suspended from the spar tree.

NUT SPLITTER: Mechanic.

OUTRIGGER: The hydraulic legs which support the corners of a mobile spar, grapple loader, or other machines.

PARBUCKLE: A way to roll or load logs on ships or trucks using two lines. Very heavy or extra long logs can be put aboard safely.

PASSLINE: The line by which a high rigger moves up and down the tree once the tree is topped. Also moves heavy block and cables into position. Usually three eighths to half inch cable.

PATCH LOGGING: A system of leaving trees for a seed source or firebreak and clear-cutting the areas in between.

PEAK LOG: The top log on any load, also known as a peaker.

PEAVEY: Cant-hook with spike on the end. Used to roll logs. Sometimes called a log wrench.

PEELER: A high-grade log suitable for making plywood or veneer.

PIG: A narrow sled formerly used on the old skidroads to carry tools and buckets of skid grease.

PILE OR PILING: A small log driven vertically into lake or ocean bottom, usually to support a wharf. Piling is also used to form boom packets and other log or ship tieups such as dolphins.

POWDER MONKEY: A person trained to use dynamite and having a valid blasting certificate.

PRE-LOAD: To make ready a complete load of logs for trucks by using a spare trailer or log cradle to save loading time.

PRE-LOG: To take out the windfalls and smaller trees before logging the main crop of big trees.

PULL THE PIN: To quit your job, get your pay and leave camp.

PUNK/WHISTLE PUNK: A person who gives the signals from the rigging crew to the machine operator.

PUSH: A woods boss or superintendent.

RADIO TALKIE-TOOTER: Takes the place of a whistle punk. (See punk.)

RANCHERS: Greenhorns or unskilled workers.

REACH: The steel tubing that connects the logging trailer to the truck. In earlier years a square timber or a stout peeled pole was used.

RECEDING LINE: A line which takes the carriage back into the woods on a skyline.

RIDER: A swifter or boomstick pulled across to keep logs from jumping over the head or tail stick of a flat boom. Usually about 14 feet in from both ends of the boom.

RIGGING SLINGER: The man who picks out the logs for the next turn, gives the signals and helps fight hangups. Second in command to the hooker.

ROLL: To rob a man while he is drunk or under the influence of narcotics.

RUB-TREE: A tree left standing in a high-lead setting and used to guide the rigging around some obstacle.

SALVAGE LOGGING: Logging done to clean up the small logs, chunks and miscellaneous pieces that remain after high-lead yarding. Originally this timber was left to rot or be burned.

SAWBONES: A doctor or first aid man.

SAW LOG: Larger logs suitable for lumber manufacturing.

SCABLINE: The haulback line between the tail block and the spar which has a block hung on it to give additional lift to the logs being yarded.

275

SCHOOLMARM: A log or tree which forks into two tops. Loggers describe it as a log that won't roll over.

SECOND GROWTH: Trees that are planted or naturally reseeded and come up after an area is logged and/or burned.

SECOND LOADER: A tongman who worked with and under the headloader.

SECTION: A portion of a flat boom equal to the length of one boomstick (66 feet). Also section of road or rail line.

SETTING: A logging side with timber within reach for yarding by one spar tree and yarding donkey.

SHAY: Gear-driven locomotive.

SHEAR LOG/SHEAR TIMBER: Timber or log used to unload logs into the water or onto the landing by pushing them sideways.

SHOVEL LOADER: A grade shovel converted to a log loader.

SHOVEL OPERATOR: A man who operates any grade shovel, grapple loader or heel boom system attached to shovel.

SHOW: A logging operation of any size.

SIDE PUSH: A strawboss, or one who bosses one complete side.

SIDE-STICK: The boomsticks on each side of the flat booms.

SIDEWINDER: A sapling knocked sideways by another tree or bulldozer or a yarded log. Very dangerous.

SKELETON CAR: A railroad log car with just the two bunks and timbers connecting the two sets of wheels together.

SKIDDER: Machine for pulling logs on a skyline at high speeds or a cat and arch hauling logs to the water or landing. A rubber tired yarder with built-in arch.

SKIDROAD: A legend. Roadway with cross logs half buried in the ground over which logs were dragged from the bush using horses or oxen. This type of logging ended around the turn of the century.

SKY-HOOK: A logger's dream for tough yarding. A helicopter.

SKYLINE: A heavy cable stretching between two spars for aerial yarding.

SLACK SKYLINE: A logging method using a skyline that can be mechanically slackened off by the engineer then tightened up again to make easier yarding. Such a system enables the skyline

276

to be pulled to the side and thus cover a considerable amount of the setting without changing roads.

SLACK-PULLER: A chunk of log hung on a line heavy enough to pull slack.

SLASH: Any logged-off area. To cut down trees. To slash a line through bush for surveying or slash a road allowance.

SLASH FIRE: A fire or fires that are set to burn the residue of a logged over area. Usually lighted by ground crews or with a helicopter using fire balls.

SNAG: A standing dead tree. A fire hazard that should be felled.

SNATCH BLOCK: Block which can be opened on one side only.

SNIPING: Bevelling of log ends to aid in hauling over skid roads.

SNIPER: The man who does the sniping, usually with a sharp axe and/or powersaw.

SNOOSE: Copenhagen snuff, used by loggers instead of tobacco.

SNOOSER: A Scandinavian logger.

SNORKEL: Wooden extension to a logging boom. Used for both loading and short yarding.

SNUBBING MACHINE: Usually a big single-drum machine with a heavy line used to hold any load from running away on steep downhill grades. Usually has water-cooled brakes.

SPAR TREE: Tree topped and limbed for use in high lead or skyline logging.

SPEEDER: A vehicle used to carry men by rail out to and from the woods. Same as a crummy, but only on a railroad show.

SPOTTING LINE: A cable used to spot and hold rail cars for loading.

SPRINGBOARD: A board shod with iron on one end so it can hold in a tree. The old timers stood on these boards to cut down the big trees.

SQUARE LEAD: Yarding at right angles to the spar tree. Not recommended.

STAG: To cut off logger pants somewhere between knee and ankle.

STAKE: The amount of money a logger takes to town for his holiday. Upright steel posts at each end of the log bunks to hold the load in a correct and safe position.

STANDING BOOM: Double boomsticks fastened and floating at the entrance to the different sorting pockets. Boomsticks that surround the bull pen or other permanent holding enclosure.

STEMWINDER: A geared locomotive; a Shay.

STOW: To put logs end to end in a flat boom before swiftering. Also stow logs or cargo on a ship.

STRAWLINE: A light wire cable used to pull the haulback out through the tail blocks, also to change roads and rigging.

STUMPAGE: The price paid as a tax to the government for standing timber.

STUMPER: A tree that slides directly into the water when it is cut down and leaves its stump. A hand-logger's term.

SUICIDE SHOW: A steep sidehill operation that's dangerous.

SUSTAINED YIELD: Harvesting only as much timber as the land can reproduce in say 50 to 70 years.

SWAMP HOOK: A hook used to roll a log up out of the mud so it can be properly choked and yarded. An L-shaped hook.

SWEDE FIDDLE: A falling or bucking saw pulled by hand.

SWIFTER: A smaller boomstick pulled across a stowed flat boom and chained at both ends, connecting it to the side sticks. This holds the boom straight and tight.

TAIL BLOCK: A haulback block strapped to a stump, so the haulback cable can pull the mainline, butt rigging and chokers back for the next turn.

TAIL-HOLT: The back fastening for the haulback or skyline. Usually a large stump.

TAIL-STICK: The boomstick across the back end of a flat boom.

TALKIE-TOOTER: A small transistorized transmitter which can blow whistle signals at the yarder or allow voice contact between the hooker and the yarding engineer.

TAME-APE: A husky individual who calls himself a logger and usually works on the rigging crews.

TIGHT-LINE: To pick logs up in the air and lower them down over rock bluffs into the saltchuck or to a lower landing where they can be loaded. It also means to hold the haulback and main line tight enough to pick the butt rigging up out of the brush.

278

TOMMY MOORE BLOCK: A very wide sheaved block used when it is necessary to pull shackles or other small rigging through and over.

TONGS: Used to load logs.

TOP GUY: Guyline uppermost on the spar tree.

TRACK LOADER: Any log loader mounted on track undercarriage.

TURN: A number of logs being yarded in one trip.

UNDERCUT: A large V cut in the front side of any tree to control the direction in which it should fall.

UNDERBUCK: To cut a log from the bottom side up to prevent it from slabbing or splitting. When the old hand saws were used for bucking it was sometimes the only way to cut a log through.

WHISTLE PUNK: See punk.

WIDOW-MAKER: A loose chunk or limb hung up in another tree which can come down without warning and kill a logger.

WIRE AXE: Usually an old axe used to cut cables when splicing has to be done out in the woods. Just lay the cable over the blade and a few blows with a sledge hammer will cut it cleanly.

*Artist's Conception of
Logging Operations*